Daniel –
Fulfilled Prophecy

Daniel –
Fulfilled Prophecy

By Jessie E. Mills, Jr., Ph.D.

Other books by Jessie E. Mills, Jr.

Results of Fulfilled Prophecy
Revelation - Survey and Research
First Corinthians Fulfilled
Ezekiel - Punishment of a Sinful Nation
Zechariah - Questions and Answers
Gnosticism in the First Century

Published By
International Preterist Association, Inc.
122 Seaward Avenue
Bradford, Pennsylvania 16701-1515 USA

TABLE OF CONTENTS

About the Author

Jessie E. Mills, Jr. was born in Florida in 1928. Entered military service in 1949, and was a participant in the Korean War (1950-1951) where he was wounded and honorably discharged as a disabled veteran. While recovering, he started reading the New Testament and noticed differences between what it said and what he had been taught.

In 1952, one of his first college courses was ancient world history, where he learned of Nero, Vespasian, and the destruction of Jerusalem in AD 70. He saw the connection with Matthew 24, and began thinking Matt. 24 and 2 Pet. 3 were fulfilled in AD 70. No one taught him this, nor was he aware of others who took this view.

By 1958 he was absolutely convinced that Matthew 24 and 2 Peter 3 were fulfilled in AD 70. About 1966 he obtained *The Book of Revelation* by Foy E. Wallace, which helped significantly. His college instructors connected Deuteronomy 28 with AD 70, and he began thinking Pompey was the first horn of the fourth beast in Daniel 7.

By 1973 he understood the full implications of AD 70 for Bible prophecy. Soon afterwards he learned about Max King. This was the first time (Fall of 1974) he knew of others who believed the Second Coming was in AD 70. A friend obtained a copy of King's book for him, but Jessie did not read it until several years later. It was very encouraging to know of others. Jessie then began to write about "fulfilled prophecy" (1973-1975).

He has written seven books, all of which IPA hopes to publish for him. Two already have been. His writings have gone into Europe, the Far East, South America, and all over the United States.

For a much fuller autobiographical summary, the reader is referred to the opening pages of Jessie's excellent book, Results of Fulfilled Prophecy, *available from the same source where you obtained this one.*

FOREWORD BY PUBLISHER

There are many reasons why I count it a pleasure to bring this volume into print. I have researched many different commentaries on the prophet Daniel, but none have a more reverent respect for the inspiration, inerrancy, and authority of God's Holy Word than this one. That alone makes it valuable, since the Bible repeatedly reminds us that a correct understanding of God's Word is impossible without both a proper reverence for the Divine Author and the intention to fully obey what His Word teaches.

Jessie Mills is an independent scholar. He truly thinks "outside the box." He has not bowed the knee to any human authorities in his attempt to understand and explain the book of Daniel. While many have been content to parrot the findings of previous generations, Jessie has attempted to dig the answers out of the original sources as much as he was able. This provides a tremendous benefit to the reader. Insights that might never have surfaced otherwise are laid open for the reader to be challenged and enriched by.

Proofreaders and copy editors are not in the habit of singing the praises of an author, since they are paid to be critical and look for problems. But the person who performed that service for this book had these good comments:

> *His major contribution is his research into contemporary history. Few take the time to do this, but it does wonders for understanding the prophetic writings. ...He shows great acumen and spiritual insight.* (Patricia Forseth)

While I may not share all of his opinions and interpretations of some texts, I still feel that use of this volume in one's study of Daniel will be extremely beneficial. Solutions to knotty historical problems that I have not seen anywhere else are common herein. And his overall emphasis on the past fulfillment of all the events predicted in Daniel makes this volume extremely valuable to those interested in the preterist approach to the Old Testament prophet of Daniel. I heartily recommend this volume for your consideration.

Many who have had the opportunity to make use of Jessie's writings over the years have told me how much they appreciate his careful historical research and closely reasoned analysis of the text. There is something here for the scholar, as well as the average Bible student. Both will be challenged to consider different ways of interpreting Daniel's amazing prophecies.

Edward J. Young, in his excellent commentary on Daniel notes in his introduction that there is very little known about Daniel himself. We know he was probably a descendant of King David's family and that he was taken into Babylonian captivity by Nebuchadnezzar at the first deportation (c. 606 BC) while still a youth. Daniel, along with other young captives from Israel, were given three years of special training for service in Nebuchadnezzar's palace. Their names were changed. Daniel (Belteshazzar) and his three friends, Hananiah, Mishael, and Azariah (Shadrach, Meshach, and Abed-nego) were the brightest of the lot. They were also the most committed to the worship of the God of Israel. It would be hard to find any young men who were more willing to sacrifice their lives to remain faithful.

Daniel remained alive throughout the rest of the Babylonian empire and for some time after the Medo-Persian conquest of Babylon. We don't know when he died, but it seems fairly clear that he did not return to Judea when Cyrus freed the Israelites and decreed that they go back and rebuild Jerusalem. Daniel evidently remained in Babylon until the end of his life.

Daniel read the scrolls and knew Jeremiah had predicted the Babylonian captivity to last 70 years. Daniel's vision of 70 heptads was given to him at the very time he was contemplating the near completion of that 70 years.

Children remember his escape from the lion's den, but Daniel conversed with angels, especially Gabriel, who said three times that Daniel was a man whom God "highly esteemed." At the end of the book, Daniel records that the "man dressed in linen" who was above the waters of the river told him that he would rise again at the end of the age to inherit his allotted portion in the age to come.

Edward E. Stevens
June 5, 2003

PREFACE

The world is flooded with millennial literature supposedly based on the prophecy of Daniel, but containing
conflicting views of the "end time." Most of it is fiction,
presented in sensational style, with little or no real Biblical substance. To find an "end of time" in the future, some
change "the end time for theocratic Israel" to read "the
end of the material universe." But Daniel's visions were
about his people and *their* end time, not "the end of planet
earth." Daniel's people had an appointed time when the
national religion of Israel would pass away, and that end
came in AD 70 when Jerusalem was destroyed.

The goal of this survey is to set forth the true meaning of Daniel. This work makes no pretension to being a
full survey on, or an exposition, of the book of Daniel. Yet
I can make no apology for it. My goal has been to lay before you a survey without fear or favor. If in any place I
have crossed over the guidelines that govern such a survey, it was not done through prejudice or for injury. I belong to no particular school and I call no man master.
What I believe, and what I present here, is found in the
pages of scripture, augmented by extensive study of the
history of the times of which Daniel wrote. Some may feel
I have overloaded the work with ancient history, but this
history throws much light on the prophecies of Daniel.

I have tried not to violate the opinions of others, and
to present an acceptable study. I have used modern
speech, stripped of millennial theories and personal positions.

My own desire to know and understand the book of
Daniel has increased over the years. Many are discour-
aged by the figures and forms of symbols, such as "beast,
eleven horns, stars cast down to earth, time, times, and a
half time, seventy weeks." Most people do not have the
time or the methods to unravel their symbolic meanings,
so they give up the task. I have given much labor, travel,
and study to overcome these difficulties. Between chapters six and seven I have given an appendage of imagery,
figures, and symbols with their biblical interpretation, to
help make this wonderful book clear to the reader.

Since completing the first printing of my survey of

Daniel, I have written other surveys, including Ezekiel and Revelation. The survey of Revelation was submitted for a Doctorate of Ministry Degree with the American Christian College, Monroe, LA. These surveys uncovered more material and thoughts relevant to Daniel, so we included them in this first published edition.

My hope is to encourage further teaching of Daniel in the church.

Jessie E, Mills, Jr.
1729 Highway 79 N
Bonifay, Florida 32425-6422 USA

ACKNOWLEDGMENTS

I feel a deep sense of responsibility for the charge entrusted to me by Alabama Christian School of Religion, Montgomery, Alabama, and much appreciation for the Church of Christ at Daleville, Alabama, without whose help, and continued support, I could not have produced this survey of the book of Daniel. I have tried to express my firm convictions here, without fear or favor, and without violating the opinions of others.

I acknowledge that each church has its own autonomy, and its leaders are at liberty to choose whatever material would best edify their congregation. This book is careful not to violate that autonomy. I respect other writers and their opinions, and wish the same for mine. None of us should castigate or prejudge another over differences of opinions. Such is detestable in God's sight.

The sparse references to literature used only expresses a very small amount of my indebtedness to many great and ancient minds. I belong to no particular school and I call no man master. I merely hope to contribute toward a better understanding of Daniel.

This book may not strictly follow the guidelines for a survey, so I ask your indulgence. It was written with nothing but the best of intentions.

Lastly, I believe the Old Testament veiled in dark language all the God-given-gospel unveiled in the New Testament, including predictions of the destructive forces which would befall the world in "that day." The New Testament cannot be understood without a knowledge of the Old. I believe in the inspiration and absolute authority of all sixty-six books of Holy Scripture. Therefore, in agreement with Jesus' statements (Lk. 21:20-22; 22:37; 24:44), I contend that all things predicted in the Old and New Testaments were fulfilled by the time Jerusalem and the Temple were destroyed in AD 70. We simply must honor the time restrictions which all the prophets included with their predictions.

INTRODUCTION TO DANIEL

Of Daniel little is known personally other than what is recorded in his book. Daniel of the captivity is commonly assumed to be the author of the book of Daniel.

Daniel is twice mentioned by Ezekiel. Once Ezekiel places Daniel as ranking with Noah and Job. "Though these three men, Noah, Daniel, and Job, were in its midst, they could only deliver themselves." Ezek. 14:14. And again, "behold you are wiser than Daniel." Ezek. 28:3.

Josephus mentions Daniel as a man with great knowledge and wisdom, and because of that, God and the kings bestowed many favors upon him. *Josephus Complete Works,* Antiquities of the Jews, bk. 10, ch. 10, sect. 1-6, pp. 222-224. The author of the Tareekh Muntekheb (Ceresh) says that Daniel was famous among the Orientals, and that he taught Lohorasp, King of Persia, and Cyrus who gave him the government of Syria, teaching these two princes the knowledge of the true God.

Josephus reports that after Persia overran Babylon, the king carried Daniel to Persia, praising him and his God. Daniel became popular with the people. He says Daniel built a tower of great beauty at Ecbatune in Susa, which stood till his day. *Josephus Complete Works,* "Antiquities Of the Jews," bk. 10, ch. 11, sect. 7, p. 227.

Daniel was descended from one of the highest families, that of the seed royal (Davidic line). His birthplace was probably Jerusalem, where he grew up in the strict sect of the law. Of his early years there is no record. However, while Daniel was still very young, we learn that King Nebuchadnezzar of Babylon was directed by God to go to Israel (in the year 605 B.C.) and carry away the king of Judah and all the seed royal. Also taken was the more prized gold dishes of the temple. Among this first carrying away of Judah was Daniel, Hananiah, Mishael, and Azariah. All four were chosen as palace servants and made eunuchs. This castration would allow them to move about the kings palace and work among the many wives of the king, as they would not have the natural passion of men.

In Dan. 1:4 (KJV) they are called "children," and in other versions "youths." It is impossible to know the exact age of Daniel, but from this inference it could be said that he was perhaps 14 to 16 years of age. Daniel had good looks, and the king desired Daniel in his palace. The Hebrew word used here for "children" in the KJV was typically used for youths between the ages of 12-25.

The custom of the Chaldeans was to select young boys about 15 years of age to begin training for work in the palace. It is not mentioned why Daniel was chosen. It could have been assumed by the king that the exiles were restless, and having one of their kindred in the palace would quell any uprising. And it could have been in the plan of God, for Daniel was to rise in power within the empire, thus placing him in a position to be of great aid to his people and to intervene for them in times of stress. Daniel was educated in the affairs of the Chaldeans, and being in authority would afford the exiles an envoy.

Daniel had been carefully trained in Hebrew learning and the customs of Israel. He understood the Law of Moses. His faith was soon tested, and he proved true to those principles given by God at Jerusalem. Daniel observed the sternest rules of temperance in eating and drinking. Daniel feared the luxurious habits of the Chaldeans, and refused to eat the king's meat.

Daniel obtained permission to abstain from the food provided him, and to test a more temperate way of living. Dan. 1:8-14. His stern principles of religion and his refusal to comply with foreign customs were rewarded with divine blessings and glorious results. After three years in the Chaldean school, Daniel passed the examination for admission to the palace and to royal favor.

One of his first acts was to interpret a dream for King Nebuchadnezzar, after all the wise men of Babylon had failed. The king was impressed, and raised Daniel at once to governor over the province of Babylon. This important office would give the king a means of communication with the exiles, and they would have an envoy in the palace.

Some time later we find Daniel interpreting another dream for the king of Babylon. In this interpretation, we are to notice especially that God's angels were the ones who were passing judgment upon the king. He would be stripped of his pride, and for seven periods of time would be deprived of the kingship of Babylon. In the absence of evidence which would show that a son or grandson had taken the reigns of government, it is only fair to assume that Daniel as the number-one man in the government took the reigns of government while Nebuchadnezzar was away. Evil Merodach, the young son of Nebuchadnezzar, came into power after the death of his father, but there is no inference showing that any son of Nebuchadnezzar took the government during the king's absence.

We find Daniel, while interpreting the king's dream, displaying the most touching anxiety, love, and loyalty for Nebuchadnezzar. It seems that Daniel over the years had come to have great respect for Nebuchadnezzar, and here begs Nebuchadnezzar to humble himself before God, that perhaps God would change His mind. Dan. 4:19-27.

After the return of Nebuchadnezzar, he sought out and praised the God of heaven. Daniel 4:34-37 is written in the first person as if Nebuchadnezzar himself had written a portion of this chapter. There is no reason to doubt that Nebuchadnezzar did not recognize that God had directed him against Judah and other nations. Further, that God had given him the kingdom for a period, and that the angels had full authority, by God, over mankind. Now the kingdom must be finally taken from Nebuchadnezzar, but not before he had confessed that God was his Savior.

Now the young son of Nebuchadnezzar was to take upon himself the control of government. Daniel's powerful position would be taken from him. It was the custom in the East, when a king died and another moved up to the throne, that all the old king's servants were dismissed.

During this period Daniel perhaps retired to his summer home. After all, by this time he must have become a very wealthy man, or he could have gone among the exiles. We find no mention of Daniel during the reign of Evil Merodach or in the short reign of his successor, Neriglissar. Nor of Laborosoarchad, who reigned for only one year. Then came Nabonidus, who reigned for sixteen years and who, after selecting his son Belshazzar to reign in his place, went out into the country conquered by Babylon and gathered up all the gold and silver idols out of the land.

With Belshazzar we again find mention of Daniel, and then only because of the Queen mother (Nebuchadnezzar's wife). Dan. 5:9-11. No more than twenty hours after becoming the new king, Belshazzar began his orgy against all that was good and holy. And while this was in progress the united arms of the Medes and Persians took the kingdom of Babylon, almost without fight. God had foretold Babylon's destruction through the prophet Isaiah (Isa. 13:1-16) and then foretells which nation would receive the kingdom. Isa. 13:17-22.

Isaiah further develops what God spoke in the beginning of Israel. Deut. 28:1-14 shows the blessings that can be Israel's. Verses 15-48 show the extent of calamity brought upon Israel because of rebellion, and deals with the captivity and destruction of Jerusalem which encompasses Babylon and the book of Daniel. Verses 49-68 deal with Israel's last destruction by Rome in AD 70.

In *Chapter 5* of Daniel, we find Belshazzar and all his nobles busy in the palace drinking wine from the sacred vessels taken from the temple in Jerusalem by Nebuchadnezzar. And suddenly there appeared a handwriting on the wall. After Daniel had been called to interpret the handwriting, and even while he was speaking, the Medes and Persians were changing the course of the river which ran through the city. With the help of a priest who had no good feelings for Belshazzar, the Medes and Persians entered the city through the dry river bed and by the priest opening the gates of the city. In a very short time the city was taken captive, as God had foreordained.

After the conquest and during the reign of Darius, or Cyaxares, Daniel once again was raised to an exalted position in the government. There can be no doubt that the Persians were not aware of Daniel during his reign with Nebuchadnezzar. It is also reasonable to assume that the Persians knew that Daniel would be the best man to run the government in Babylon. After all, Daniel possessed superior knowledge of government and was proven to be a trusted man of great character. He knew perhaps better than anyone else those things which would continue to bring tranquillity to that portion of the empire.

The human element involved in raising Daniel to an exalted position in the government may never be fully known. But we do know that God's providence was at work. Soon Daniel was tried again. His appointment was envied. Those who wanted this high position for themselves would strike what they thought to be the death blow to Daniel. They determined to take advantage of a principle in the government of the Medes and Persians, a law that said a decree that had received royal sanction could not be changed. By securing the passage of a decree from the king saying no subject could worship any god other than the king for thirty days, they would trap Daniel, and they could have him put away. They themselves would receive the highest positions in the Persian government. Little did they know that God's providence had already set the course for Daniel and would protect him. The decree was presented to the king and he sanctioned it. The spies began to watch Daniel until they caught him worshiping the God of heaven. They reported the matter to the king. The decree had to be honored. After learning that the offender was Daniel, the king was very disturbed.

The mere fact that the king grieved all night and would not eat his food indicates that he had much respect for Daniel. Early the next morning the king came to the cave where Daniel had been placed among the lions and called out, "Daniel, Daniel." And Daniel answered him and assured him that no harm had come to him. The angels had come and closed the mouth of the lions. Again we are shown that the angels watch over the righteous.

After finding Daniel safe, the king ordered those guilty of the plot, along with their families, to be thrown into the pit, where they met sudden and gruesome death.

The advantages given to Daniel by the king would enable him to promote the interest of his people, the Hebrews. Beginning here, Daniel employs himself seriously in securing the return of his people to their land. Daniel knew from reading the books of Jeremiah the prophet that the time for his people to return was near. It is nowhere intimated that Daniel himself desired to return to Jerusalem. It could be that he knew he would be of greater service to his people serving in the king's palace. It is not improbable that Daniel, in his position within the court, influenced the decree granted by Cyrus to allow the Hebrews to return to Palestine. The prayer of *Chapter 9* affirms Daniel's concern. It could also be supposed that Daniel, now nearly 80, felt himself too old to make the long journey back to Jerusalem.

Chapter 6 ends the first division. *Chapter 7* moves us back into the reign of Belshazzar, and gives a summary of Daniel's vision of the four beasts. These represented four world empires, beginning with Babylon. Dan. 2:37-38. The proper understanding of these 4 beasts, and the last beast which comes up, and the 11 horns (rulers) which rule this fourth empire, is of utmost importance. This vision is parallel with the dream of Nebuchadnezzar of *Chapter 2*, and is a fuller development of Deut. 28.

Daniel is told by the angel that during the period of the fourth beast and of the eleven horns, his people must undergo another great calamity: The Son of God is seen during the time of the eleven horns, there was a judgment decreed, and the Ancient of Days would come to earth to fight against Daniel's people. Zech. 14:1-5. The eleventh horn would make war with the saints for a time, times, and a half time (three and one-half years). During the reign of the eleventh horn the saints would receive the kingdom. Now, if the time, times, and a half time means 350 years, as some claim, then the saints did not receive the kingdom until AD 350 or later.

All the visions and messages described in the book of Daniel pertained to his people, and to their end time, as God had predestined and ordained in Deut. 28:15-68. Therefore, all that should occur in these predictions was directed toward Israel. It would occur during the prescribed eleven horns, which began with Pompey and ended with Vespasian. No other horns are mentioned in this vision. We have no authority to move any event described by the angel to another period outside the time of the eleven horns. Any other reasoning is unattainable and dangerous.

Chapter 8 is a fuller development of *Chapter 7*. It reveals the second world power as that of Medo-Persia, and the third world power as that of Greece, Alexander the Great. Out of his empire would arise one who would think himself very great and wonderful. He would cause the righteous of Jerusalem to fall; he would pull them down and trample them. Antiochus Epiphanes accomplished just this when he came into Jerusalem and laid waste to the country. He offered a sow as sacrifice upon the altar of God, burned the holy books, and forbade the Jews to worship the God of heaven upon penalty of death.

Chapter 9 begins with the prayer of Daniel expressing his concern for the Hebrew people. His prayer was not offered in respect to Gentiles, and the forthcoming answer was not given to the Gentiles, but to the Jews alone. Dan. 9:24-27 draws a very clear line between Jews and Gentiles. Notice verse 24: "Seventy weeks have been decreed for your people and the holy city." Nothing is said here about the Gentile nations. During this seventy prophetic weeks, or 490 years, the vision of *Chapter 7* would see its fulfillment. At the end of the last week would come one who would make Jerusalem desolate. The angel says: "On the wings of abomination." The eleventh horn of Dan. 7:25 made Jerusalem desolate, completely destroying the city.

In chronological order *Chapter 11* should follow *Chapter 9*, as it was given under the King Darius who came up during Cyrus' time. The book of Daniel is best understood when *Chapter 11* is read following *Chapter 9*, then *Chapters 10* and *12* are to be read together, as a part of the same vision. Again the message and vision of *Chapter 10* pertains to Jews alone. Dan. 10:14. Now one can read the interpretation of the message of *Chapter 10* by turning to *Chapter 12*. Again, *Chapter 12* is directed toward the nation of Israel: "Now at that time Michael the great prince who stands guard over the sons of your people." Dan. 12:1. Jesus quoted from this writing in Matt. 24:15. The very fact that Jesus in most of his teaching in the book of Matthew quotes from the prophets of the Old Covenant is proof that Matthew was written exclusively to the Hebrew nation, and was but an extension of the Old Covenant, further relating the calamities that should befall Israel.

Daniel is further told in *Chapter 12* to seal up the book until the end time (not the end of time). The fair meaning is that Daniel was instructed to write no more and no further interpretation would be given until the end time, the end of the Jewish age. At that time a full interpretation, or revelation, would be made regarding these visions. Such was fully accomplished when Christ informed John while on the isle of Patmos to write the commentary on Daniel. That commentary begins with Revelation *Chapter 5* and ends with *Chapter 22*.

Beyond this, nothing is known of Daniel with any certainty. From the Itinerary of Benjamin, we are told that in Khuzestan, Elam of the scriptures, there rests the corpse of Daniel enclosed in clear material, laid to rest by the kings of Persia, and that to this date his glass coffin hangs suspended under the bridge which crosses the river Ulai. We are further told by Benjamin that such action was taken to satisfy both Jews and Persians. *Itinerary of Benjamin of Tudela.* pp. 117-120.

The Old Testament concealed in dark language the gospel that was unveiled in the New Testament. The Old Testament describes the destructive forces that would befall the world in "that day." The New Testament cannot be understood without a knowledge of the Old. I believe in the inspiration of all Holy Scripture. Therefore, I believe all things written in both Old and New Testaments about Jerusalem before its destruction in AD 70 were fulfilled when Jerusalem and the temple were destroyed. Lk. 21:20-22; 22:37; 24:44. The book of Daniel closes with the angel assuring Daniel that all the events predicted in his visions would be fulfilled by the time the Holy People were completely shattered. (Dan. 12:7) An understanding of all the history surrounding Israel in the intertestamental period becomes essential for one who wants to understand what Daniel predicted. Hopefully the sketch we have provided here will stimulate the reader to a much fuller examination of that historical background as he reads through the book of Daniel and this survey of it.

DANIEL CHAPTER 1

Verse 1. This passage names the time Nebuchadnezzar came against Judah, in the reign of King Jehoiakim. The exact time of the siege is not mentioned, as some claim. The truth is that history recalls the king of Babylon laying siege for eighteen months, rather than one year during the third year of Jehoiakim (see v. 2).

Verse 2. We are told Nebuchadnezzar only had victory over Judah because God gave Judah into his hands. The time arrived for Deut. 28:15-48 to be fulfilled. Isaiah adds to the fateful words of Moses, Isa. 10:5-11, and Jeremiah further develops the pronouncement of destruction, Jer. 5:6-11 and 6:1-8. The evil from the north would be Babylon; Judah would be given into their hands. Jer. 22:23, 25-30. Judah would even be overrun a third time because God had so planned it. Thus the phrase "The Lord gave King Jehoiakim and Judah into the hands of Nebuchadnezzar" sets the tone for the whole book. Each scene shows God's pattern of judgment and the fulfillment of his plan during the reign of each empire.

On the day the captives of Judah were deported to Babylon, King Jehoiakim was not among them. He died before the deportation. He was dragged outside the city gates and left unburied. Jer. 22:19. Nebuchadnezzar took the finest gold vessels from the temple and carried them back to Babylon. Later on, the gold vessels are involved in the final fall of the Babylonian Empire.

Verse 3. Israel, the Northern Kingdom, had already been in captivity 135 years. Thus, when King Nebuchadnezzar orders the sons of Israel to be brought into his palace, he refers to the sons of Judah, namely Daniel and his three friends. Daniel and his friends were of royal seed. The providence of God is at work in the life of Daniel.

God directs Nebuchadnezzar against Judah twice more, in 596 B.C., and in complete destruction in 586 B.C. The first deportation brought the royal family to Babylon and placed Daniel in the palace of the king. The second deportation brought the prophet Ezekiel among the exiles, near the river Chebar. God's providence put Daniel in a position to give material aid to the exiles, while Ezekiel was instructed to give spiritual aid.

Verse 4. Daniel and his friends have been brought before the king for his inspection. He found no defect, but good looking young men who possessed great knowledge and good understanding of their language and their system of government. Daniel will later need this knowledge, for he is to have a great influence in the affairs of the Chaldeans. Through the providence of God, Daniel will soon rise to great power in Babylon.

Verse 5. Daniel and others are now in the king's school, and here they must remain for three years. Daniel would be about 19 years of age when he finishes school in Chaldea. On-the-job training was a custom in the East for anyone who worked in the kings court. They were paid wages from the king's income. For Daniel, the selection and pay scale would perhaps ease the grief of captivity.

Verse 6. Others sons of Judah were chosen for the king's service; however, only Daniel, Hananiah, Mishael, and Azariah are named. Perhaps God had a reason for introducing these four at the first of the book; these four were chosen to test the strength and faith of the kings. The three Hebrew children would forever be recognized as those who would not bow to the king's idol and were therefore cast into a burning furnace. Thus was Nebuchadnezzar's power set against the power of God.

Verses 7-8. Those chosen from Judah were given Chaldean names. It is quite remarkable that Daniel, at such an early age, determined to serve God and do nothing to defile his body or bring reproach upon God. Most young men, especially when they are away from their parents, are in the midst of mischief and sin, but Daniel was planning his life to walk with God. Perhaps Daniel was not fully aware of the benefits his decision would bring in his life, but he learned them, and we can learn from him. We notice several things about Daniel.

    1. In a most honorable way, he sought relief from what would defile him.

    2. He used the proper channels to seek relief.

    3. He showed constancy in his religious beliefs.

    4. He worked hard preparing himself to serve, not only the king, but God.

    5. It is also remarkable that Daniel never questioned God, became bitter or sought to quit.

    6. At an early age, Daniel knew he was his broth-

ers' keeper, being concerned for his people. No wonder God had angels watch over him.

Verse 9. God is well pleased with Daniel and grants him favor in the sight of the commander. Daniel's decision to serve the God of heaven has won for him God's public approval. This kind of approval comes only through prayer, good works, righteous living, and constancy.

Notice how matters began to fit together to accomplish God's plan. (1) The sons of Israel/Judah were given to the chief of the eunuchs to prepare them for service. (2) Those who worked in the king's house were made eunuchs. Daniel was a eunuch. Isaiah said that those who were eunuchs would be rewarded by God. Isa. 56:4. (3) Jesus said some men made themselves eunuchs for the sake of religion. Mt. 19:12.

Verse 10-12. The chief of the eunuchs was afraid because Daniel and his friends would not eat the food appointed by the king. Daniel reassured him by proposing a test. Allow them to eat vegetables and water for ten days, and if at the end they looked haggard, they would eat the king's food. He agreed, and after ten days, the chief was pleased, so Daniel retained his diet.

Verse 13-16. It is evident from v. 13 that some of the chosen sons of Israel had agreed to eat the king's food, but Daniel's test showed the ones who ate only vegetables to be in better condition, both fatter and brighter in knowledge than those who had eaten the food ordered by the king. So the chief official withheld the wine and food of the king, and continued to give them vegetables and water. Prisoners of war, captive in a land of evil and vice, separated from loved ones, no chance of married life, no family, no children to love, no wife to come home to, no one to mend their clothes, and yet Daniel and his friends maintained determination and faith which surpasses all understanding of our modern age. But no less is expected of a child of God in 1975 than was expected of Daniel in 605 B.C. Daniel determined to be a child of God because he wanted to, not because he had to.

Verses 17-21. The four are especially remembered by God and he gives them special gifts of knowledge and intelligence. But Daniel receives a gift that no one else receives, the understanding of dreams and visions. At the end of the school period, the king called all the sons of

Israel to be presented before him, and he found Daniel, Hananiah, Mishael, and Azariah to be above all the rest in knowledge, understanding, and wisdom.

Nebuchadnezzar placed the four in his personal service. They would serve the king while he was in the palace and while he was away for some thirteen years laying siege against Tyre. The four would serve in his harem, among his wives. There had to be much trust on the part of Nebuchadnezzar for him to leave the empire and his harem in the hands of the four for over thirteen years.

While Nebuchadnezzar was away pursuing the war, Daniel became governor of Babylon. He actually ran the empire while Nebuchadnezzar was at war with other countries. That is, he and God ran the empire. After being made eunuchs, the four could move about the palace, in the absence of the king, without having the natural passions and desires of a male who had not been made a eunuch.

It was a comfort for Nebuchadnezzar to find the four ten times wiser than all other wise men. Notice again the providence of God, and how it works. Daniel is being set up to run the empire in the absence of the king, and his faithfulness was rewarded when the Medes and Persians took over the empire. Daniel helped relieve the distress of the Hebrews in exile, while under the rule of Persia. So long as Jews are faithful, God will fight for them. When they rebel, He will fight against them. Daniel exhibited much wisdom during his visions, which set forth the consummation of the Jewish nation.

DANIEL CHAPTER 2

Verse 1. There appears to be a difficulty in the chronology between chapters one and two. In chapter one we notice that Nebuchadnezzar ordered the children selected for his service to remain in school for three years, and then brought before him. Now, in the beginning of chapter two, we notice this phrase, "Now in the second year of the reign of King Nebuchadnezzar." We must note that Nebuchadnezzar reigned as co-regent with his ill father for one year, then at the death of his father, he became sole ruler, so chapter two begins with the second year reign of his reign after the death of his father.

"And Nebuchadnezzar had a dream, and his spirit was troubled, and sleep left him." Before we proceed into particulars of the dream, a brief overview is warranted. The image described in vv. 38-44 was intended to point out the rise and fall of four different empires. The fifth empire, the one that shall never end, shall commence in the "last days." This phrase is commonly used in the prophets to signify the advent of the Messiah to judge the world. Zech. 14:1-5; Isa. 66:18; Dan. 7:22; James 5:6-9.

Yet there was a special providence of God on behalf of the Jews at that time. For, although suffering grievously because of their sins, and being deprived of both their political and personal liberty, God shows them that he has not abandoned them. The existence of a prophet among them is proof of His care. The direct inspiration of God teaches his servants things which could only be known to God himself, showing the Babylonians that his prophet had spoken by an unerring spirit, that the Jews were the depositories of the true religion, that He was the only true God, and that the things which his wisdom had predicted his power could and would accomplish.

This image is a political representation of as many governments as it was composed of materials. As these materials are successively inferior to each other, so are the governments presented in a descending ratio.

Verses 2-13. Nebuchadnezzar calls for the wise men of Babylon to reveal his dream. However, the wise men were not as wise as they thought; they were not able to tell the king his dream, nor could they interpret it. Because of this the king decreed that all the wise men of Babylon should die. This puts Daniel in a bad position, for he was one of those appointed to the king's court. There is no doubt that the king had made Daniel chief of all the wise men (see chapter one), for 2:13 informs us that they were looking for Daniel and his friends to kill them also.

Verses 14-16. Daniel now meets with the king's commander Arioch to make the arrangements, going through proper channels to receive an audience before the king that he might reveal the dream and its interpretation.

Verses 17-18. Daniel was granted an audience before the king, and also time to pray. Daniel shared the good news with his friends; their lives were spared. Daniel asks their prayers regarding the dream and its interpretation. God endued Daniel with His Spirit, so that Daniel clearly predicted some of the most astonishing political occurrences and changes that would ever take place.

Verses 19-20. The events recorded here are not nearly as important as the spiritual salvation of a person seeking forgiveness from God. What circumstance brought forth this revelation of the mystery to Daniel? (1) When Daniel heard about the death decree, and how it would affect his fellow wise men, he went to his Israelite brothers and asked them to request compassion from God on his behalf. (2) Daniel, although very young, knew that the only way of reaching God was through prayer. (3) Daniel was aware that this problem was beyond human abilities to solve, and that God might not intervene if he did not pray for it. (4) Daniel prepares himself to seek God's aid, which included asking the prayers of those dear to him. He prepared spiritually to seek help from God.

Verses 21-23. It is not unreasonable to assume that God not only revealed the dream and its interpretation to Daniel, but other matters as well. Daniel informs us that God is the One who changes times, gives wisdom to wise men, removes and establishes kings. It is God who reveals hidden things; he knows what is in the darkness. That is, God may know the entire future of man. And now Daniel takes time out to praise God and give him thanks for revealing the complete matter to him. Do you see people today who, after seeking God's help while lying in dire sickness and receiving a blessing, not taking time to give God the glory? Is it because we have so little time? Or, after being healed, we forget what God has done for us?

Verses 24-25. Daniel is now prepared to go before the king to inform him of his dream and to give the interpretation. Daniel seeks out the king's commander and makes a plea for the lives of those condemned. He asks him to take Daniel before the king to relate the dream and make known the interpretation. Arioch advises the king that he has found one among the exiles who can make known his dream and its interpretation. "He has found one" is no doubt a phrase selected to void the kings edict which was, "Destroy them." In view of the spiritual implications contained in vs. 20-25, the following observations are warranted:

1. The rule is that "the secret of the Lord is with them that fear Him."
2. Daniel and his three friends stood the first real spiritual test in a most marked way. The apostles in a latter day would say, "We ought to obey God rather than man."
3. Daniel and the three Hebrew children maintained a separation from the unclean, even from other Israelites who served in the palace. They were in the home of idolatry, and kept separate from it.
4. Notice: When God speaks, it stirs his people, and leads them to worship and praise Him. Many today very seldom worship God, even though we have freedom to do so as much as we please. Daniel provides an excellent example of private prayer and worship in spite of his hardship.

Verses 26-30. Daniel is brought before the king and informs him that he is able to reveal the secret. Daniel tells him it is not through any superior wisdom of his own that he is able to do this. He tells him, "There is a God in heaven that revealeth secrets, and maketh known to King Nebuchadnezzar what shall be in the latter days."

It was of God that this great king was brought to the end of all human resources. If he had been able to remember his dream, he never would have realized that he had to deal with God. He had first to be brought to the end of all human wisdom; he had to learn of his own nothingness and ignorance, and the nothingness and ignorance of all his wise men, in order that the matchless wisdom of God might be revealed to him. If we are ever to have anything from God, we too must learn the poverty of our own resources. Now Nebuchadnezzar had to be brought to the place where he learned that "Man's extremity is God's opportunity." God thus used Daniel as his instrument to reveal to the king the dream and its interpretation.

Verses 31-35. Daniel begins with great detail to relate the dream to the king. The king recognized that it was indeed the dream he had forgotten. Daniel had already informed the king it was not he, but God who would reveal the dream. After hearing the dream, the king awaits the interpretation, but while Daniel is waiting, the king's mind is being prepared to receive the interpretation which will come forth from God through Daniel.

Verses 36-43. Daniel proceeds with the interpretation: "You O king are the king of kings, the God of heaven has given to you (not one before you) the kingdom, the power, the strength, and the glory."

Here properly begins the times of the Gentiles; it is begun with King Nebuchadnezzar, not some king or kingdom before him. Nebuchadnezzar is declared to be the head of gold, Dan. 2:35, this "man of the earth," Ps. 10:18. The carnage against the Jews began here with the Gentile nation of Babylon; it was to end with the Gentile nation of Rome, when Jerusalem was destroyed in AD 70. Luke 21:20-24.

It is remarkable that Daniel declares (v. 35) that God has given to Nebuchadnezzar all power to rule, that he is the king of kings. Further, Nebuchadnezzar is the head of gold represented by this image. I make a point of this because liberal interpreters adopt the idea that the reign of the four kingdoms began one kingdom before Babylon, thus resulting in the messianic kingdom coming during the empire of Greece. Such an interpretation is absurd! The scripture is very clear who is the head of gold, or who the first kingdom should be. Daniel said:" It is you O King Nebuchadnezzar." Thus the head of gold is King Nebuchadnezzar of Babylon, the first Gentile Empire. He would be ruler over all mankind.

Since there are mixed theories respecting the correct interpretation of the image of chapter 2, I offer the following points which perhaps will act as guidelines in arriving at the proper interpretation. With the closing observations, we shall see whether or not the liberal views are fact or fiction!

    A. The image represents four kingdoms: Babylon, Medo-Persia, Greece, and Rome.

        1. Ancient history says Babylon is the first kingdom of Daniel's vision. *Guizot's Ancient History*, pp. 173-180. Babylon was succeeded by Medo-Persia, Medo-Persia by Greece, and Greece by Rome. To this, history testifies.

        2. The establishment of the kingdom of God was to appear during the fourth kingdom, or the fourth phase of the image. To this Paul the Apostle testifies, Col. 1:13; see also Mark 1:14-15 and Rev. 1:9. Since the New Testament testifies of the establishment of the kingdom during the Roman period, I conclude that the Roman kingdom was the fourth kingdom.

    B. There are at least two objections leveled against the above by liberals.

        1. "A stone was cut out without hands, and it struck the image and crushed it." The stone that was cut out was the kingdom of God, and the objection of liberal interpreters is that the kingdom of God did not suddenly destroy Rome, thus Rome could not have been the fourth kingdom. But, notice the scriptures. There is no mention that the stone will suddenly destroy the fourth kingdom, only that it will strike and crush it. Further discussion of the liberal view of the stone is not warranted.

        2. The ten toes are part of the Roman Empire, so that Rome as ten kingdoms yet lives, so the image is standing today. To this we notice:

            a. Chapter 2 mentions absolutely nothing about the ten toes representing ten kingdoms, only four kingdoms are mentioned.

            b. In every verse where the toes are mentioned it is a part of the fourth kingdom, not that of ten rulers.

            c. There is no mention of the stone smiting the ten toes, only that it will smite the feet.

Premillennialists and Dispensationalists are hard

pressed here for proper evidence. Only by adding to what Daniel has spoken can they survive. Having put aside the objections by liberals, we now look back to Daniel.

After Daniel declares to Nebuchadnezzar, "thou art the head of gold," he further declares, "After thee shall arise another kingdom inferior to thee, and yet another, a third which shall rule over the earth."

We need not go outside the scriptures to find the names of these empires. In chapter 5:31 we read "Darius the Median took the kingdom." From the book of Esther we learn that the Persian rulers bore rule over all the earth. Darius is generally supposed to be Cyaxares II, the last king of Media, or as some think Gobryas, the General who led the assault on Babylon under instructions from Cyaxares and Cyrus the Persian, who united Media and Persia in one great empire. Daniel shows us later in his book that this Medo-Persian dominion, after existing for several hundred years, would be overthrown by a mighty Grecian warrior. This was fulfilled, as we know, by Alexander the Great.

The fourth kingdom was to follow, which should be strong as iron. This can be none other than that great world power which was in existence at the birth of Christ. This was the fourth and last kingdom mentioned during this time. The Judaistic kingdom would be crushed and broken to pieces. This was the nation Moses had in mind when he said, "The Lord will bring a nation against you from the end of the earth," Deut. 28:49. Moses' concern was the last nation to make war with the Hebrews, the fourth kingdom of Daniel in chapter 2.

At the time of Nebuchadnezzar's dream, Persia was but a Babylonian satrapy. The Grecian Empire might have seemed an utter impossibility. The Hellenic states were a lot of warring tribes and kingdoms, giving little promise of their future greatness. The city of Rome at the far ends of the earth was just being founded, an insignificant little village on the banks of the Tiber.

How could Daniel portray with such accuracy the future history of all these powers unless aided by the Holy Spirit of God?

Verses 44-49. "In the days of these kings [the fourth kingdom] the God of heaven will establish a kingdom which will never be destroyed." Notice here that the inference is to a spiritual kingdom, not an earthly one. Jesus said, "My kingdom is not of this earth." Daniel says, "This kingdom will break to pieces all other kingdoms." The spiritual kingdom would destroy Judaism and the Hebrew kingdom. This is the rock cut out by unseen hands, the rock of offense, Isa. 8:14, a tried stone, Isa. 28:16, a stone engraved, Zech. 3:9. Thus we read of the stone in singular form, there was to be one stone, Eph. 4:4, one kingdom, Mt. 16:18. We are to know this kingdom will destroy all other kingdoms, Gal. 4:22-31; Mt. 15:13-14.

Observations on Chapter 2

I would remark in closing this chapter that while Nebuchadnezzar fell upon his face and worshiped Daniel, and acknowledged that his God was the God of gods, the Lord of lords, and a revealer of secrets, yet there is no evidence that his conscience had been reached by the revelation made to him of God's wisdom and power. It is likely that he understood the four earthly empires; but like many today, he did not understand the fifth kingdom, nor the stone cut out of the mountain.

We give evil its greatest powers when we believe in it. Nebuchadnezzar believed in evil, he could not, therefore, understand the spiritual kingdom spoken of by Daniel. Neither could he understand "A stone cut out of the mountain without hands." He could not understand the implications of the interpretation. In scripture, mountains express mighty empires, kingdoms and states. The stone signified Jesus Christ, Gen. 49:24: "From thence is the shepherd, the stone of Israel." That is our blessed Savior, "the good shepherd," Jn. 10:11-17. Christ is here intended as the stone, as will appear from the following passages: Isa. 8:14, "And He shall be for a sanctuary, but for a stone of stumbling and for a rock of offense, to both houses of Israel." Isa. 28:16, "Behold I lay in Zion for a foundation a stone, a tried stone, a precious corner stone, a sure foundation." (See 1 Pet. 2:4, 6, 8). Jesus Christ is here represented by a stone, but this stone refers chiefly to his kingdom which is called a mountain. Isa. 2:2, "The mountain of the Lord's house shall be established in the top of the mountains." Thus we have the church represented as a spiritual building, which He supports as a foundation stone, connects and strengthens as a corner stone, and finishes and adorns as a top stone. The stone is cut out without hands, v. 34. Without hands means it is spiritual. So 2 Cor. 5:1-4, a house which awaits us in heaven, not made with hands, means a spiritual house (spiritual body).

Now we observe that by this stroke of the stone, the clay, the brass, the silver, and the gold were broken in pieces and became like chaff, which the wind carried away. We have seen that the fourth kingdom represented the Roman Empire, which had absorbed the kingdoms of the world, and was represented by the legs of iron, with feet and toes of iron and clay. Now we find that not only the iron and clay, but also the brass, silver, and gold were confounded and destroyed by that stroke of the stone which was cut out of the mountain without hands!

Combined into the Roman Empire were some of the characteristics of the preceding three kingdoms, not only in territorial possessions, but also their political and military policies. The splendor of the Chaldeans, the riches of the Persians, the discipline of the Greeks, the strength of the Egyptians and Syrians, are mingled with the instability of those kingdoms which the Romans had subdued. Along with the strengths of the previous kingdoms, the Romans incorporated the weaknesses as well, which became the seed of its own destruction. With its pagan heritage, its persecution of the Church of Christ was the means by which it was struck and began to crumble.

In the beginning of the world, God is said to be the governing influence in his kingdom of angels. This is called a kingdom, that is, a state of prevailing rule and government. In Dan. 2:44, it is said that in the days of the last kingdom (Rome) that the God of heaven will establish another kingdom, another spiritual state of prevailing rule and government. This was literally true, for the rise of the fifth kingdom (the kingdom of Christ) took place when the Roman government, partaking of all the characteristics of the preceding empires in its grand period of imperial splendor and military glory, a few years after the battle of Actium. Rome was at peace with the world in 4 B.C. The stone, the new government, was cut out of the mountain under the Roman government, the fourth kingdom.

DANIEL CHAPTER 3

Introductory Remarks

We will now see how little Nebuchadnezzar had profited by the revelation God had made to him. We have already noticed that when Daniel explained the meaning of the dream, Nebuchadnezzar fell down before the prophet to pay homage. He had many nice things to say to him, and he gave him great rewards, but he was not brought to repentance or humbled in self-judgment before the God who had thus manifested his omniscient power. The king could appreciate the wisdom of Daniel, but he had no heart for the God who had inspired his servant.

I am inclined to believe this chapter shows Nebuchadnezzar being lifted up with pride, and he determines to make a great image (perhaps a replica of the one he saw in his dream) and call upon all men to bow to it. It was really to set forth the power and glory of man, for it pictured Gentile dominion in independence of God. Regarding the image, I would remark that liberals who love to find fault with Scripture are opposed to the idea of a 90-foot-high statue made of solid gold because of the incredible expense and unmanageable weight. But we only need to point out that Scripture does not say the image was solid gold, but rather that its exterior appearance was of gold. It was probably gold plated.

Liberals also raise a question about the absence of Daniel when his friends were cast into the furnace. We recall in chapter two that the king had promoted Daniel and made him ruler over the province of Babylon, as well as chief over all the wise men of Babylon. The scripture is not clear about the absence of Daniel; however, with his added authority, Daniel could have been out of town at the time. By this time Daniel was a very important man. There are many ways to explain his absence, so there is no sufficient grounds to question Daniel's authenticity.

Verses 1-7. The king's conduct here against the God of heaven justifies what I have said in the introductory remarks. The threat of the furnace would affect but few, since all the Chaldeans for ages had worshiped images. It was part of their life style. The decree would be of little consequence to them!

Verses 8-12. The three Hebrews determined they would not worship the image. From birth their life style had been to serve the God of heaven. As part of the royal seed, they had been taught from childhood the Law. They knew God did not dwell in images, they also knew that God had foretold the consequence of such worship. They were determined to serve God rather than man.

The special place given to the orchestra is very noticeable, much as in large worldly religious gatherings at the present time. It excites the emotions, and, thus working upon the feelings, gives people a sense of devotion and religiosity, which after all may be very unreal. In the Old Testament dispensation musical instruments were used in the ornate services, but there is certainly no warrant for it in the New Testament. People may call it worship to listen to a trained, and possibly unconverted, choir and orchestra rendering sweet and touching refrains. But the music simply acts upon the sensuous part of our nature and has nothing to do with true adoration of the Father and the Son, which must be in spirit and in truth to be acceptable to God. Those who plead for its use because of the place it had in Old Testament times should remember that time was a "typical" dispensation. The instruments used then typified the melody now made in the hearts of God's redeemed ones.

Verses 13-18. There were three in that great company who openly refused to get excited with the music of the king: Shadrach, Meshach and Abed-nego. Malignant spies soon carried the news to the haughty monarch. In a rage, the king sent for the three devoted men. He offered them another opportunity to carry out his bidding. Here began the real test for these children of God. In spite of the threat of sudden death, the three told the king that the God they served would deliver them, and if not, then they were ready to be burned. Here we see a principle: there are no circumstances in which it is too difficult to be faithful to God.

Verses 19-23. Nebuchadnezzar is now very angry. His offer of a second chance has been brushed aside by the three Hebrews. He orders them cast into the furnace now heated to a higher degree than ever before. The Hebrews, young as they were, gave no sign of doubt that God would care for them. In the hour of darkness, their thoughts no doubt were in prayer to the God of heaven. They could have recanted to spare their physical lives, but they would have lost their souls instead.

The fire was so hot that even the men who threw them into it were killed. The excessive heat serves to demonstrate the remarkable delivery of the three Hebrews.

Verses 24-27. The furnace was constructed so as to allow the king to see inside. When he did, he was astounded to see not only the three Hebrews walking around, but a fourth figure! The scripture does not tell us who this being was, but to Nebuchadnezzar it was like a "son of gods." To the three Hebrews it was the Son of God. Isaiah had spoken earlier, "When you walk through the fire you will not be scorched" (or burned). Isa. 43:2. As the three came forth, there was no smell of smoke upon them, nor a hair scorched. God's Word had been fulfilled as spoken by Isaiah.

Nebuchadnezzar again praises the God of the Hebrews. It seems that it is from the teeth only, as we see in the next verses that he does not wish to antagonize the Hebrew's God.

Verses 28-30. Nebuchadnezzar knew more than we sometimes give him credit for, we tend to miss the value of Nebuchadnezzar seeing the Son of God. We see him giving praise to the God of heaven, and admitting to angels sent by God. This no doubt has reference to the fourth being seen in the furnace.

There is no mention that the image was destroyed. Perhaps its value in gold prohibited it from being destroyed, or perhaps the excitement of the crowd when this event occurred caused the king to forget the image. The true reason we may never know, but this we do know, from this event came the decree that all Babylon should bow down to the God of the Hebrews. The three Hebrews were promoted to a high state. Again, the prophecy of God through Moses is here being fulfilled (Deut. 28:10-13).

Nebuchadnezzar made a royal decree declaring that anyone who should speak against the Hebrew God should be put to death. Yet, as before, when his dream was interpreted, he does not bow in repentance at the feet of the Lord and own him as his God. He simply speaks of Him as being their God, and while he admires His greatness and power, he does not worship and serve the Jehovah.

Some may ask what this has to do with prophecy. Why did God cause this particular bit of history to be recorded in the book of Daniel? It would have been something suitable in a history book or a devotional book, but why do we have it here in a prophetic book? For a very good reason indeed.

This event, although actual history, is a typical scene of the trial and deliverance of a faithful remnant of Daniel's people after the 70-year captivity. There is also that picture of the "Abomination of Desolation" spoken of by Daniel late in the book. There is the typical Antichrist that will arise in Jerusalem at the end of the Hebrew nation (Mt. 24:15, 2 Thess. 2:1-8). At this time, many of the faithful shall escape and be saved out of it, just as these three young Hebrew men were preserved by God in the midst of, and eventually delivered from, the furnace of fire.

Seeing Nebuchadnezzar's dream interpreted and observing his actions, we can better understand the statement of Job 33:16-17.

DANIEL CHAPTER 4

Introductory Remarks:

Again we find liberal interpreters question the authenticity of this particular chapter. Their reasons are:

1. Historical books do not record the events of King Nebuchadnezzar having been driven from his throne. Although acknowledged by *Origen* and *Jerome*, no histories mention the event.
2. Josephus makes no mention of these events.
3. If the events described in this chapter truly happened, they would have been recorded by the king himself, but there is no such record. [I deny such, and will show the king's statement.–jem]

When such arguments are made by unbelievers, it is almost inevitable that Christians engage in debate to prove the inspiration of scripture. I would remind the child of God who knows and believes the truth: we have nothing to prove. We know, and our faith is grounded on the inspiration of all scripture. Therefore let the unbeliever find evidence to prove that the Word of God is not inspired. The burden of proof has always been on the unbeliever.

Here is the king's record, which destroys flimsy objections. "But at the end of that period, I Nebuchadnezzar raised my eyes toward heaven, and my reason returned to me, and I blessed the Most High and praised and honored Him who lives forever." Dan. 4:34.

How does this disprove the liberal view? First, the statement was made by Nebuchadnezzar himself, and it was written by him, not Daniel. If you have a problem with Nebuchadnezzar writing this particular verse, look at the beginning of the chapter. Who wrote it, Nebuchadnezzar or Daniel? Notice in vs. 1-7 Nebuchadnezzar is the first person. In v. 8 Nebuchadnezzar says Daniel "came before me." In vs. 9-18 Nebuchadnezzar relates his dream to Daniel, then Daniel begins the interpretation of it. Then the king returns as first person in v. 34 and confirms that such events indeed happened. Their occurrence proved beyond doubt that God is in control, and King Nebuchadnezzar attested to this fact.

Verse 1. "[The] king to all the peoples, nations, and men of all languages." Many nations were under the control of Babylon, including Israel. Yet they had sinned, and God must judge. Jer. 22:24-30. At this point Babylon and King Nebuchadnezzar were the instruments in God's hand to punish both Israel and the known world at that time.

Verses 2-3. "It seems good to me to declare the signs of the Most High. How great are his signs, how mighty are his wonders, His kingdom is an everlasting kingdom."

Perhaps this is the proper place to make several pertinent statements respecting the matters King Nebuchadnezzar proclaimed to the whole world.

1. First, we observed that King Nebuchadnezzar is speaking. Daniel is neither speaking nor writing for him. The king makes a legal decree, one that is binding to all peoples within his empire.

2. Second, the king states that God has shown great signs and wonders before him, and Nebuchadnezzar praises God for allowing him to proclaim the great powers of God. He says, "It seemed good to me to declare the signs of God." Here Nebuchadnezzar gave credit where it was due, to God. Such statements imply that the seven periods of time were already past, since he mentions both its beginning and its end, when he believed. Before his death he became a child of God.

3. Third, "How great are His signs. How mighty are His wonders." If we attempted, like Nebuchadnezzar, to list all the great things God has done, we would never finish the writing. So Nebuchadnezzar simply says, "How great are His signs." Signs are plural, so Nebuchadnezzar had seen many. There were many "wonders," again plural, more than the king could tell. The thought the king was to convey to the world was that he now believes and attests to God's great powers, and to his system of heavenly government. If God would save a Gentile like Nebuchadnezzar, he would save anyone who turned from his sin to obey Him. Then there would be a place prepared for the redeemed sinner.

4. Fourth, Nebuchadnezzar's words, "It has seemed good to me to declare," are controversial. Look at the king's statement, "His kingdom is an everlasting kingdom." The phrase itself indicates a kingdom which will never come to an end, a thing first

decreed by God which exists forever and ever.

What constitutes a nation? What does it take before any given land becomes a nation (a people)? It takes people to constitute any kingdom; therefore it takes people to constitute God's kingdom on earth. Nebuchadnezzar became a part of that kingdom, the kingdom he himself decreed to the whole world as being everlasting, without end, which would endure forever and ever. Rev. 1:6. Controversial? Yes. Why?

On the one hand you have King Nebuchadnezzar, having been taught and punished by the angelic watchers, who declares that the kingdom was one which was everlasting, without end, a kingdom made up of sinners like himself. Therefore, King Nebuchadnezzar made a decree that the human race would never be destroyed completely from the face of the earth by saying that the kingdom would be everlasting. The king is also saying that the subjects of the kingdom would be everlasting. Right?

Today we have perhaps seventy-five percent of all people on earth looking for the quick return of Jesus Christ (the "second coming") to destroy the human race, and burn the earth with fire, that is, annihilate the earth. My Lord, what inconsistency. Can you see our problem? No wonder liberal thinkers attack our belief! We are not consistent with what we teach.

Yes, it can be said that Nebuchadnezzar was not inspired. That's true. However, the statements he makes about the kingdom can be supported by inspired men. Note Dan. 2:36-44, especially v. 44, "In the days of these kings, the God of heaven will set up a kingdom which will never be destroyed, it will itself endure forever." Now compare, "And one like the Son of man was coming up to the Ancient of Days, and to him was given dominion, and a kingdom, and his dominion is everlasting, and his kingdom is one which will never be destroyed." Dan. 7:13-14. If any of the Bible is inspired, then all it takes is one scripture to prove the inspiration of all. But, there are many more which prove the kingdom to be everlasting, without end.

In the face of inspired evidence, why do we teach that the kingdom will come to an end? Could it be tradition which started with the Roman Catholic Church?

By this time, the reader must be saying, "Mills, you have gone overboard, don't you know what 2 Peter 3 teaches? Do you not know that Peter said the world would burn up at the 'Second Coming' of Christ?"

Do we really know what 2 Peter 3 teaches? Notice the first two verses of the book. This second letter was written to the same folks to whom Peter's first letter was written. We are told in 1 Peter 1:1 that Peter wrote to the Jews who were outside the land of Israel. His second letter was addressed to the same folks who received his first letter. In 2 Pet. 3, Peter says that he desired to stir up their sincere minds respecting the things spoken to them by the holy prophets, by the apostles, and by the Savior Jesus Christ. Whatever Peter refers to in this chapter was told to their forefathers by the holy prophets. This is what Peter claims here. What did our Lord say about the fulfillment of scripture? Look at Luke 21:20-22. He says that, when Jerusalem and the temple would be destroyed by Rome (which took place in AD 70), then all things which were written would be fulfilled. The only collection of inspired writings they had at the time Jesus spoke, was the Old Testament. Jesus said it would all be fulfilled by the time Jerusalem was destroyed. Do we believe this?

Verse 4. "Nebuchadnezzar was at rest." It appears that Nebuchadnezzar wrote this chapter. It appears also that his wars were over. As God's chosen instrument he had completed the siege of Tyre, destroyed Egypt, brought all the other nations around Israel under his control, accomplished the third carrying away of Judah, leaving Judah and Jerusalem in ashes. Nebuchadnezzar now seems to design this chapter to describe a time of peace, a state of tranquillity. He had subdued the world and created the greatest empire known to man. Yet he has failed! No admission of God in his life is seen. He has gathered the world's wealth, and now he could say, "Soul, you have much goods, take your ease, drink and be merry." Lk. 12:19. But, God has other plans!

Verses 5-18. "I saw a dream." And, "I gave orders to bring all the wise men into my presence." Again the wise men of Babylon are brought before the king, but as before they fail. In his right mind, Nebuchadnezzar would not have preferred the ignorant astrologer, or fortune teller, palm-reader, or crystal-gazer! All these are rubbish compared to the divine knowledge of Daniel. But, we must remember, this was God's plan, not Nebuchadnezzar's.

Daniel, as before, was last to be called before the king. "O Belteshazzar, I know that a spirit of the holy gods is in you." It appears that Nebuchadnezzar had not yet recognized the difference between the gods of the land and the God of heaven. Nebuchadnezzar relates his dream to Daniel, even informing him that this dream and its sentence is authorized by the angelic host and is done to bring mankind in subjection to God. Then he asks, "Belteshazzar, tell me the interpretation."

Verses 19-26. Daniel delays for a little time the interpretation of the dream before the king. He is aware that this dream reveals something which God has decreed to bring upon the king. Daniel might have wished the dream was against the king's enemies, but he knew the tree in the dream that was about to be cut down represented the king. God is acting in the king's life to bring him to repentance by His divine intervention.

The greatness of Nebuchadnezzar is noted in v. 23, a tree reaching into the heavens. Isaiah spoke of this event, and how the king would react. Isa. 14:11-13. But no man can become so great in power and riches that God cannot cut him down. Such is seen in v. 24 as Daniel directs the attention of the monarch to the one living God and shows him that He presides over all mankind and their governments. (See also Rom. 13:1-3). The vision was given in a most impressive way, seemingly to convince the king of the existence and sovereignty of Almighty God. The existence of power is seen in v. 25 when the king is to be driven from his throne by divine agency.

The implications of v. 26 are far reaching. It was decreed by divine agency: "Leave the stump with the roots." The tree was taken away, it no longer reigned in the forest. Such likeness was understood in this land where most of the forest consisted of species of cypress and cedars, where, after the tree was cut down, the stump would sprout new young trees. Thus Nebuchadnezzar would be cut down, his power and reign would be removed from him, he would not be king for seven periods. But afterward, when "you have recognized that it is heaven that rules, will your kingship be restored," v. 26.

A natural question follows, "Who reigned in Babylon while the king was away from the throne?" Daniel was selected and appointed as the governor of Babylon, which included the palace; he was vice king. Could Daniel have reigned for these seven years? Recall the phrase, "You are to recognize it is heaven that rules." It is understood here that the kingdom of Nebuchadnezzar had been placed under the administration of the divine watchers. The purpose is to show that God rules in the kingdom of men, whether good or bad.

It cannot be denied in itself that the affairs of the lower world are in some respect placed under the administration of beings superior to man. Nor that events such as death, wars, earthquakes, famines, removal of national rulers, either by death or vote, are but divine deliberations of the heavenly agency. There is every reason to suppose that there would be divine harmony in the council of the superior beings. But, like King Nebuchadnezzar, we cannot see into the spiritual world until we ourselves have become spiritual. Because of this we question many events of life, and ask why did this happen? Or, Why me, Lord? If this verse holds in store any thing for us today, it teaches the divine interposition of God's agency into the government of every nation, and into the life of every person. Looking back at v. 25, notice: "The Most High is ruler over the realm of mankind, and bestows governments on whomever He wishes." To this the king draws the attention of all who would ever read his words throughout history.

Verse 27. Daniel pleads with the king to accept his counsel and repent of his sins. Nebuchadnezzar seems only to harden his heart, and Daniel can easily see that the king is destined to suffer the consequence of rebellion. Since Daniel knew that the sentence placed upon the king was a result of sin and rebellion, he pleaded with the king to repent that perhaps the judgment would be averted. God's purpose has always been to forgive man, when man sought with a contrite heart forgiveness; however, it has never been the purpose of God to remove the consequence of sin (the harm done while one is in sin).

Verse 28. "All this happened to Nebuchadnezzar the king." It is here affirmed that the sentence passed upon Nebuchadnezzar was fulfilled. This verse seems to be an interjection by Daniel. In v. 30 the king begins to speak again, and finishes the chapter. The full implications of this chapter, and that of Dan. 9:1-23, seems to be related to the exiles named by the prophet Zechariah. Notice Zech.

1:4-6: the fathers had been warned, they rebelled; the leaders warned, and they rebelled; those things purposed by God were fulfilled. Zech. 1:11: The earth was at peace; but it lasted only during the period after the third carrying away of Israel, until Babylon fell. Israel is yet in captivity, the seventy years have not expired, the people have not yet returned to Israel (Zech 1:12, 16). "Flee from the land of the North" (Zech 2:6), "escape [from] Babylon" (Zech. 2:7). So, Israel had not left captivity at this writing. Not only was the king warned by Daniel, but the exiles were warned by Zechariah.

Verse 29. "The king was walking on the roof of his palace." Ancient buildings were so constructed as to leave a flat roof; this enabled the owner to remove himself to the roof, where the breeze would strike him; many slept on the roof during summer months.

Verse 30. Twelve months have passed. Daniel gave the interpretation of the king's dream, and another year has passed without repentance on the part of the king.

The king gives himself credit for the magnitude of his kingdom. He alone takes credit, although millions of slaves were used to build the kingdom. The canal that was dug through the city was done with slave labor. Many were buried with the soil removed from the canal, and their families never heard of them again. Many perished in this great work, not only Jews but men from every nation where the king had been. He had no regard for life or suffering. From such history we can better understand why Daniel called upon the king to turn from this way, and turn to God. See *Guizot's Ancient History*. pp. 79-82.

Verse 31. There came a voice from heaven; perhaps like a thunderbolt. It was uttered from above him, and appeared to come from heaven. The voice of God was saying, "What is spoken is for thee; thou art about to cease to reign as king." Babylon was to be taken from Nebuchadnezzar and given to another. Another man would be placed over the kingdom and given the king's power and riches. The purpose was to show that the God of heaven establishes kingdoms and removes kingdoms.

Verse 32. "And they shall drive thee away" indicates this was sudden, with no time for the king to prepare, no farewells, no party for the monarch. "Till his hair was like eagle feathers." The idea is that he would be neglected until his hair would string about him like the feathers of an eagle, for "seven periods of time."

I want to dwell a little on the "time" named here. A certain prophetic interpretation called "the year-day theory" says, "All days are to be understood as years, months as thirty years, and years as periods of three hundred and sixty years." Now "a time" is undoubtedly, as most would agree, a year. "Times" would then be two years and a "half time" would be six months. Seven times would be seven years. If the year-day theory was true, it would apply here as well as elsewhere in the book. But, what would seven times three hundred and sixty years mean in this connection? It would amount to 2,520 years. In that case Nebuchadnezzar's madness is still going on, which is ridiculously impossible.

In every instance where any of these time prophecies have already been fulfilled and are clearly so stated in scripture, it is evident that days, months, or years were always fulfilled literally. For instance, God said to the antediluvians that their days should be 120 years, and in exactly that length of time the then-known world was overthrown with a flood.

Suppose the year-day theory had been held by Noah. He would have calculated that there could be no hurry in building the ark, since as the flood could not come for at least 43,200 years, or 120 prophetic years of 360 literal years each.

Another example would be when God told Moses that the children of Israel, because of their unbelief, should wander in the wilderness for forty years, according to the number of the days in which they searched the land. Now here, if anywhere, we might be supposed to have authority for this year-day theory, but on the contrary, we have the very opposite. Days mean days, and years mean years. In the book of Ezekiel the prophet is told to lie upon his side for 390 days, that he might bear the iniquity of the house of Israel, then God adds, "I have appointed thee each day for a year." This passage is often cited as evidence of the year-day theory in scripture. But this was a "special appointment" and gives no reason to assume that whenever times and seasons are specified in the prophetic scriptures the principle of a day for a year applies.

The great prophecy of the seventy weeks in chapter

nine might appear to be an example, but there, as we shall see, the time elements are evident. Each week mentioned is a time element that can easily be seen to be fulfilled. For example, the first seven weeks were designed to begin with the decree ordered by Artaxerxes in 557 B.C. when those who were sent were to restore and rebuild Jerusalem (Ezra. 7). At the end of this period would begin the sixty-two weeks to the time Christ would be born and sacrificed. We notice a period of forty years from this time until the last week would begin, for Christ died (Jewish calendar) AD 30. Then the last week would begin, and in the middle of that last week all sacrifice in the temple would cease, and the temple would be destroyed. We know the temple was destroyed in AD 70. Therefore, each day here represented a year, or a total of 490 years. Each text must be carefully considered. Daniel declared the king would be mad for seven "times," exactly seven periods (years) passed over him.

Verse 33. Now the Word concerning Nebuchadnezzar was fulfilled. The desire of God is to be accomplished when the king will repent and show his true status, God will bring him back and restore his kingdom. The significance of this humiliation can be applied to the nation of Jews until such time as they repent, or suffer the consequence of their sins. Here Nebuchadnezzar was to suffer and be humiliated; in chapter 9, the Jews are to suffer and be humiliated until destroyed.

Verse 34. The king's reason had been taken from him. Now his reason returns. For his recovery, and in humble acknowledgment of his dependence upon God, the praises here mentioned are those of a true penitent, deeply sensible of its faults. Nebuchadnezzar comes with a contrite heart. "And I praised and honored Him." By rendering thanks to God for restoring him, the earthly king was to recognize God as having the right to reign, and that his kingdom is over all kingdoms.

Verses 35-37. Nebuchadnezzar recognizes that the inhabitants of the earth are accounted as nothing compared to God, and that God does according to his own will. Man cannot ward off his hand of blessings or wrath. Great splendor was accorded the king; he was surpassed in greatness, but only after he had repented and recognized God as the ruler of all mankind. (Compare Job 42:10-17).

Observations on Chapter 4:
1. Mankind has no power to prevent the fulfillment of divine purpose.
2. God will accomplish his design in all things, whatever opposition man may make.
3. He controls all human affairs, and overrules all things to make them subservient to his own will.
4. God daily uses men to accomplish his divine purposes and plan of administration.
5. God humbles men through pitiable sufferings.
6. Daniel was used as God's instrument in the administration of Babylon's government. He served the king as governor of the province of Babylon, in the absence of Nebuchadnezzar; during the thirteen years Nebuchadnezzar laid siege to Tyre, warred against Egypt and other surrounding nations, and the third deportation of Judah. Daniel also reigned during the seven year period when the kingship was taken from Nebuchadnezzar. Dan. 4:26,31.
7. The prophet Zechariah in the first eight chapters directs his message toward the exiles while they are yet in captivity. Dan. 1:12,16; 2:1-7. "These seventy years," implies that the seventy years had not yet ended, 1:12. "Flee from the land of the north" indicates that the exiles were yet in Babylon, 2:6. "Escape you who are living with the daughters of Babylon," 2:7. These scriptures were given to the exiles, to show God's mercy for his people, and to give Zion the hope of return.
8. After the death of Nebuchadnezzar, Daniel is deposed. In the East, when a king dies, all his servants are released of authority. Daniel is not involved again until the time of the handwriting on the wall during the reign of Belshazzar, who was appointed by his father Nabonidus to reign in his stead, while he went about the conquered world gathering up all the gold and silver idols.
9. This chapter is the fulfillment of Jer. 27:2-8.
10. Each human is assigned angels. Jesus extended this thought in Mt. 19:10. "The angels of the Lord encamp around the man who fears God." Ps. 34:7.

DANIEL CHAPTER 5

Introduction

Chapter four closes the life of King Nebuchadnezzar, and chapter 5 begins with a new king on the throne of Babylon. Although the chapter begins with Belshazzar, there were other kings who reigned between Nebuchadnezzar and Belshazzar. They are listed below:

Evil Merodach, the son of Nebuchadnezzar, inherited the throne at the death of his father. He reigned for two years in an illegal manner, and a plot was laid against his life, by Neriglissar, his sister's husband.

Neriglissar succeeded evil Merodach and reigned four years.

Laborosoarchad, the son of Neriglissar, obtained the throne as a child and reigned only nine months. He was ill-tempered, and a plot was laid against his life. After his death the conspirators placed the crown on Nabonidus.

Nabonidus, after receiving the crown of Babylon, gave the kingship to his son Belshazzar, while he went about the subdued countries and collected the gold and silver idols from the land. Under Belshazzar the Babylonian Empire falls into the hands of Medo-Persia.

Nabopolassar, the father of Nebuchadnezzar, had begun the neo-Babylonian empire in 625 B.C. He sent his son Nebuchadnezzar into Judah in 606 B.C. to lay siege against Jerusalem. The siege lasted eighteen months, and Nebuchadnezzar returned to Babylon in 604 B.C. with the captives and the temple treasure. After a 21-year reign, Nabopolassar died in 604 B.C., leaving the throne to Nebuchadnezzar, who reigned until 661 B.C. As already recorded, he was succeeded by Merodach, Neriglissar, the child Laborosoarchad, all with short reigns. In the early part of 554 B.C. Nabonidus succeeded and reigned until 538 B.C. At that time Medo-Persia took the empire from Babylon and Darius the Mede became king, Dan. 9:1. *Josephus Complete Works,* "Against Apion," p. 614.

After General Gobryas Darius conquered Babylon and the empire had fallen into his hands, he sought to set over the kingdom 120 princes, and over these would be three presidents, of which Daniel would be first president, or vice king. Dan. 6:1-3. So Daniel prospered during the reign of Darius the Mede. Dan. 6:28.

The Jews had been in captivity 68 years, from 606-538 B.C. There were two years of exile remaining. But wait. God had decreed the captivity to be seventy years. They were not in captivity during the eighteen-month siege, were they? We must count the seventy years from the time they arrived in Babylon; therefore, we must account the captivity decree from 604 B.C.

When General Darius conquered the empire of Babylon, the Jews had four years remaining of their decree. Darius reigned as king over the Babylonian Empire for three years. During this period, especially for the first year of his reign, Daniel is concerned about his people returning to Palestine, so he prays, Dan. 9:1. Some scholars declare that this Darius is the one who came up after Cambyses. If this be true, then Daniel's prayer was in vain as Cyrus would have already released his people. Ezra 1:1-3.

The Darius of chapter 9 must by internal evidence be the Gobryas Darius of Daniel 6:1; 6:28. Obviously if Darius or Cyrus had made any decree respecting the exiles, Daniel would have known of it, since he was vice king. The time was at hand, but the seventy years was not yet completed. God spoke through Isaiah, and not only did he speak, but he looked into the future of Israel. He named by name the king who would reign in Persia over the whole world and who would offer the decree allowing the exiles to return to Israel and rebuild the temple, Isa. 44:28. Jeremiah also declared that when the seventy years were fulfilled, God would return them to the land of Israel. Jer. 29:10.

Likewise in Daniel, see Dan 9:1-23. Daniel makes a plea for his people, looking and hoping for their release, which had not yet taken place. In the second year of the reign of Darius God gave Zechariah a vision, Zech. 1:7-11, and in this vision God related a period of peace upon the earth, v. 11. History records that after the fall of Babylon, and during the period following, there was a peace among nations that had not been known before. Again, the Darius of Zechariah is the same Darius of Daniel. Look at the correlation of Daniel and Zechariah.

1. In chapter 9, Daniel prays for his people; he knows the seventy years are near to being fulfilled.

2. Zechariah 1:12, "Then the angel of the Lord answered and said, O Lord of hosts, how long wilt Thou have no compassion for Jerusalem, and the cities of Judah, with which Thou hast been indignant these seventy years?" Now notice the phrase, "How long wilt Thou have no compassion on Jerusalem." Such a phrase alone establishes the credibility of the correlation, and shows that Zechariah at this point is also concerned about the end of the seventy years. Because God had not yet had compassion on Jerusalem, it follows beyond any doubt that the exiles were yet in Babylon. Thus, when He had compassion on them He would stir up the mind of Cyrus, and in turn Cyrus would order the decree which would free the exiles.

3. "I will return to Jerusalem," Zech. 1:16. Future tense, He has yet not returned, therefore, the people must yet be in captivity. "My House will be built." Again future tense, indicating that the house will be built, but has not been built at this time. Therefore, the exiles must yet be in Babylon.

4. Zech. 2:6, "Ho there, flee from the land of the north." Obviously the exiles are yet in Babylon. "Ho Zion! Escape, you who are living with the daughters of Babylon," v. 7. The time of the decree is at hand, the people are being warned; when the decree comes, flee. Daniel was not given an answer to his prayer in 9:1-23, but the answer was given to Zechariah. Daniel was told by the angel what would befall his people in the last days of their theocratic nation.

The foregoing statements have been made to prepare the reader for interpreting chapter 5. God always explained through the prophets beforehand how He is the One who providentially manages both His people and all the other nations of the world. It is worthy of note that Isaiah predicted the downfall of Babylonia with words similar to Daniel.

1. An Oracle concerning Babylon. Isa. 13:1-22.
2. The Medes are to receive the Babylonian Empire. Isa. 13:17 (see Jer. 51:11 and Dan. 5:28).
3. Medo-Persia will come from a far country. Isa. 13:5.

4. The day of the Lord is near. Isa. 13:6.
5. The Lord is coming with burning anger. Isa. 13:9.
6. The stars, moon, and sun will not give light – this is symbolic of the governmental infrastructure and leadership of Babylonia falling from power (not the literal darkening of the heavenly constellations).

Verse 1. This chapter will close the history of the Babylonian Empire; we will see the last solemn scenes of the downfall of the head of gold. We will see the fall of the world's greatest empire, the result of its sin. In Revelation chapters 17-18 we have the fall of the second great Babylon, again because of sin. Throughout the first twenty-three chapters of Ezekiel we find that God very clearly sets forth the idea that Judah was more sinful than her sister Israel, yea, more than all the nations around her. In Revelation, Israel is set forth as the mother of harlots, after the order of Babylon.

It is proper to remark here that while the account given by Daniel of the destruction of the proud city on the Euphrates tallies in large measure with what has been left on record by Herodotus, the so-called father of history, and by other ancient writers, yet the scripture record is nevertheless challenged by a certain class of modern critics. They say it is unreliable because of alleged discrepancies between the biblical account and the inscriptions on some of the recently deciphered monuments. The chief question is the title given to Belshazzar, son of Nabonidus. To this objection, I will remark that Belshazzar was reigning jointly with his father at this time, and certainly was "King of Babylon" or "King of the Chaldeans" in the sense of being Prince Regent, with his seat in the Imperial City. The title "king" was not applied solely to the supreme monarch in that age, nor is it necessarily so used now. It will be noticed in chapter 2, when Daniel was honored by Nebuchadnezzar; the great king made him second ruler in the kingdom. But in this chapter Belshazzar appoints him to the position of third ruler, as he himself was clearly the second. So there is no discrepancy here. The liberal has a flimsy objection.

Babylon was at this time the most magnificent and luxurious city in the world, devoted to every vice, the center and mother of idolatry. From the days of Nimrod and the tower of Babel till it was blotted out from under heaven, Babylon was the headquarters for the heathen mysteries. Its walls, supposedly impregnable, were so broad that several chariots could drive abreast upon them. The Euphrates ran right through the city, passing under the walls, and, of course, upon that river the people depended for their support. Yet it was destined to become their enemy, for after an unsuccessful siege of many months, the Medo-Persian armies concluded the only way to force an entrance would be through the river bed.

A new channel was dug around the city without the Babylonians being aware of it. This channel connected with a nearby lake. On the very night the work of turning the waters of the river out of its course was finished the final assault was made. Belshazzar, utterly unconscious of the danger to the city, was keeping an impious feast with a thousand of his lords in honor of the heathen deities. It was not merely a feast that manifested the pride of his heart; it bore a far worse character than this. In insult to God, Belshazzar had ordered the golden vessels of the temple in Jerusalem, which had been carried down to Babylon, to be brought for use in their impious feast. Not only was this an insult to God, it demonstrated the king's approval of sin; his drinking before the thousands had its influence upon the warlord's. Such acts of sin will bring the fall of any nation. (See also Esther chs. 1-3).

Verse 2. As already mentioned, the vessels from the temple were brought forth. Thus they drank, praising the gods of silver and gold, of brass and of stone, and thus blasphemed the God of heaven. On this crowning act of impiety, their cup of iniquity being full, God's sudden and sore judgment falls. God never strikes, when he is dealing with nations in judgment, until that moment! He could not allow the people of Israel to take possession of the land of Canaan before the days of Moses because "the iniquity of the Amorites was not yet full." (Gen. 15:16). So it was with Jerusalem, their cup was not full until AD 70. Then God struck.

Verses 3-9. When the fateful moment arrived, Belshazzar was standing before his lords with one of the cups from Jerusalem's temple in his hand, praising his own vile demon gods. There came forth, in the full sight of all that multitude, the fingers of a man's hand, writing words of doom in letters of fire upon the plaster. God wrote them in their own language, but who could understand the four apparently unrelated terms: numbered, numbered, weighed, dividing? All instinctively recognized them as a message from the other world, but who could interpret the decree?

I think I see Belshazzar as he stands with the wine cup in his hand. I think I see the awful look of terror that comes over his countenance, the deadly pallor that overspreads his face. I see the cup fall from his nervous hand. I note the way in which he clings to the pillar to support his trembling limbs. The Word of God says, "his knees smote one against another."

He called for the astrologers, the soothsayers, and those learned in Chaldean lore. Great wealth and a position at the head of the Chaldean government was promised for the interpretation of the writing. But, like on previous occasions, they were unable to interpret the writings. Evil fails beside the power of God.

Verses 10-12. The queen mother (perhaps the widow of Nebuchadnezzar) entered and reassured the king. She told of Daniel, one that Nebuchadnezzar had appointed over all the magicians and wise men. Belshazzar called for Daniel, in whom was the "spirit of gods."

Verses 13-17. Belshazzar had been utterly indifferent to the man whom God had used in the days of his grandfather Nebuchadnezzar, but Daniel had gone on in a quiet, humble way, seeking the approbation of the One who is higher than the highest. Sent for in haste, he came in to rebuke by his very presence that godless multitude. Belshazzar addressed him in flattering terms, and promised him great honors and authority as third ruler in the empire, since Belshazzar was second and his father Nabonidus was first.

Notice here in v. 13, Belshazzar asks this question of Daniel, "Are you that Daniel who is one of the exiles from Judah, who my father the king brought up from Judah?" As the queen had said, Daniel had been made chief over all the wise men of Babylon by Nebuchadnezzar. Here I would conjecture that Daniel, on the death of that king, had been deprived of all authority given him before. As I have noted, when a Persian king dies, both his astrologers and physicians are driven from the king's court. The reasons behind such a move is, first, for not predicting his death, and second, for not preventing his death. If such was the etiquette in Babylon, and there is no good reason to believe it was not, then we have a satisfactory solution for the present king not having any knowledge of Daniel. Thus he asked, "Are you Daniel?" Daniel, having relinquished his office, may have lived privately on the wealth given him by the king he had served.

From this seemingly simple question asked by Belshazzar, many years of history are accounted for. Can we not say then, that many New Testament Scriptures and statements deserve just such consideration? Since history is not inspired, it is possible to forget that many unanswered questions remain hidden on the pages of some history book.

While Belshazzar was questioning Daniel, he knew nothing of the momentous events taking place in the palace. The waters of the river had been rechanneled. The armies of the allied kings, a mighty horde, were coming under the walls in the dry river bed, unnoticed and undetected because the watchmen of the city were all drunk. In the streets, as in the palace, the revelers were spending the night in godless sex and unclean orgies.

Daniel cared not for the reward, but makes his words to Belshazzar all the more solemn and serious. "Then Daniel answered and said before the king, let thy gifts be to thyself, and give thy reward to another. I will make known to the king the interpretation of the writing."

Verses 18-22. To convict Belshazzar of his evil deeds, Daniel recalls those events that brought about the change of mind in his grandfather Nebuchadnezzar and, with concern, tells Belshazzar that he is aware of these events. Now notice the fearful indictment of the wretched monarch before whom he stood. "And thou his son, O Belshazzar, hast not humbled thine heart, though thou knewest all this; but hast lifted up thyself against the Lord of heaven."

Daniel did not speak to Belshazzar as he had before spoken to Nebuchadnezzar. He could not have the same respect for him that he entertained for his grandfather. You will remember, when Nebuchadnezzar told his dream of the great tree, Daniel grieved to think of the suffering that he had to pass through, and said, "The dream be to them that hate thee, and the interpretation thereof to thine enemies." Tenderly and affectionately he besought him to repent of his evil ways.

But Daniel did not talk tenderly to Belshazzar. He knew the king's doom was sealed, his day of mercy had gone by. He saw in him only a wretched, impious degenerate who had sinned against the God of heaven, and deserved neither sympathy nor compassion. He realized that Belshazzar had gone steadily on in defiance of the God of heaven until the hour of his judgment. Isaiah the prophet foretold this judgment (Isa. 13:1-22). Here we see the fulfillment of that which God had decreed. Nothing now could avert the richly deserved wrath of the Holy One. Even while Daniel was speaking, the invading forces were drawing nearer and nearer to the palace gate, but the guilty king and his lords were altogether unaware of what had taken place down by the river.

Verses 23-31. Daniel explained the meaning of the words thus: "Mene" (numbered), "God hath numbered thy kingdom, and finished it." Belshazzar's days of probation were passed and gone. The day of his sentence had come. "Tekel" (weighed), "Thou art weighed in the balances, and found wanting." He who had exalted himself in his pride and folly was found to be "altogether lighter than vanity."

Then note Daniel says "Peres" (divided), a form of the same word (upharsin) which he read from the wall, but implying that the division had already taken place; for instead of saying, "God is dividing thy kingdom," he declares "thy kingdom is divided, and given to the Medes and Persians." It was as much as to say the blow had already fallen; it was not that God was about to do this, for it had already been accomplished. While Daniel was interpreting the writing, the kingdom had passed to other hands.

But the foolish and unrepentant king, despite all this, seems to fancy the idea that he is secure. He offers to Daniel worthless honors. But the awful chronicle of the Holy Spirit is, "In that night was Belshazzar the king of the Chaldeans slain. And Darius took the kingdom."

DANIEL CHAPTER 6

Introductory Remarks

Liberal interpreters offer several objections to the events of this chapter.

1. They contend that Darius the Petty was only a petty king, with no real authority, and Cyrus was really the king of Babylon. Daniel wrote, "It seemed good to Darius to appoint 120 satraps over the kingdom, to be in charge of the whole kingdom," Dan 6:1. Books like Daniel, which claim inspiration and have heathen writers accepting and using it, need to be recognized as true history, especially by Christians, without changing it to fit our own interpretations. Daniel is more credible as a historian than Xenophon or Herodotus.

2. If we accept the scriptures as being inspired of God, or God breathed, then we must accept the account of Isaiah: "Behold I am going to stir up the Medes against [Babylon]." (Isa. 13:17) Jeremiah said, "Sharpen the arrows, fill the quivers! The LORD has aroused the spirit of the kings of the Medes, because His purpose is against Babylon to destroy it; for it is the vengeance of the LORD, vengeance for His temple." (Jer. 51:11) Daniel says to Babylon: "Your kingdom has been divided and given over to the Medes and Persians." (Dan. 5:28). The Medes were to first receive the whole kingdom of Babylon; and then after a period of time the whole Median empire would blend into the Persian empire. To make the scriptures say otherwise is to deny their inspiration! Therefore, I must affirm that the Medes were the first receive "the whole kingdom" of Babylon, including Israel, Egypt, and the bordering countries. Therefore, Darius was king of the whole empire, while Daniel was vice king, and this reign must have lasted for several years, even during the period of Zechariah. By accepting the Word as inspired and accurate, it is possible to see that the Darius spoken of in Zechariah is indeed Darius the Mede. Any other interpretation falls into the trap of denying the inspiration of Scripture. Scripture is in harmony with properly interpreted history.

3. Third, had Darius the Mede not been in full power, he could not have appointed the satraps to rule over each province. The theory that Darius the Mede did not rule over the whole empire of Babylon is flawed. However, Darius did not rule over the empire of Persia, for at this time Cyrus ruled over the Persian Empire.

4. The above does not conflict with the prophecy of Isaiah which states, "It is I who says of Cyrus, he is My shepherd! And he will perform all his desire. And he says of Jerusalem, she will be built, and of the temple, your foundation will be laid," Isa. 44:28, also 2 Chron. 36:22. It was Cyrus, with the help of Darius, who fulfilled the prophecies of Isaiah, Jeremiah, and Daniel.

   It was Cyrus who became king of the lands, and who was named before his birth as the one who would give a decree allowing the Jews to return to Judea. While this is true, it is also true that God used the Medes to accomplish his will, Isa. 13:17; Jer. 51:11. King Darius' authority is established in Daniel 6, where he appoints governors over the whole Babylonian Empire.

5. Those ancient nations had a custom, so that when Jews went into foreign lands the people there would attach new names to them, and likewise when Median or Persian people were associated with Jews, the Jews would attach another name, a custom which showed their acceptance of the person. Even in America during the days of slavery, the slave holder would attach another name, usually the slave holder's last name. So it was in every country, and in this case we see by reading ancient history that Darius the Mede was also given other names, such as Gubaru, and others.

6. It is a scriptural fact that when Nebuchadnezzar died, Daniel lost his position as governor. Nabonidus appointed Gubaru (Darius) the Mede as governor instead. Gubaru served under Nabonidus' son Belshazzar. While Belshazzar ruled as vice king, his father went through the empire collecting the gold and silver, and writing the history of Babylon on stone. The question has been asked why did a Babylonian king appoint a Median to the empire? The answer is, to fulfill God's will. Isa. 13:17; Jer. 51:11; Dan. 5:28.

7. The Nabonidus Chronicles inform us that Gubaru (Darius) was the governor of Babylon on the very day

that Cyrus first set foot in the conquered land, Oct 27, seventeen days after its conquest by Ugbaru (or Gobryas). Ugbaru was charged with the conquest of Babylon and, according to Isa. 13:17 and Jer. 51, was a Median general. Gubaru, who once served as governor of Babylon, is now king of Babylon and continued his reign over the empire of Babylon throughout the lifetime of Satraps, and more than half the subsequent reign of Cambyses the son of Cyrus. The prominence given to Darius in the book of Daniel means he can be none other than Gubaru whose reign as king of the Babylonian Empire extended over a period of fourteen years (539-525 B.C.). See *Darius the Mede*, by Dr. John C. Whitcomb. ch. 2, pp. 10, 11.

8. A full translation of the Nabonidus Chronicles makes it possible to place King Darius at the head of the Babylonian Empire throughout the writing of Daniel, Haggai, and Zechariah. This brings more authentic meaning to the prophets Haggai and Zechariah.

9. The latest translation of the *Nabonidus Chronicles* clears up this much misunderstood subject. It mentions the installation of Gubaru as governor of Babylon, and later as king over the same regions. Gubaru was king of two administrative regions, Babylon and the regions beyond the Euphrates. The first, Babylon, was composed of Summer and Akkad, with the addition of the parts of Assyria proper which had fallen into the hands of the Medes through the partitioning of the Assyrian Empire, including the Mesopotamian connecting regions to the west as far as the Euphrates. The second, the regions beyond the Euphrates, were composed of Syria, Phoenicia, and Palestine down to the border of Egypt.

Verse 1. Evidently Darius means here to set rulers over Babylon, which had now received the whole Babylonian kingdom, according to Isa. 13:17; Jer. 51:11; and Dan. 5:23. The kingdom under Nebuchadnezzar had been divided into provinces, thus the satraps would act as governors, who would rule over states; therefore, Darius in appointing governors acted in the same manner as King Nebuchadnezzar. It was a measure of prudence adopted to maintain a vast empire.

Verse 2. The word president here denotes a high officer presiding over others who were responsible to the president. First in rank was the king, second in command was the prophet. It was common knowledge for Darius that Daniel served as president under Nebuchadnezzar, and most likely served as ruler during the seven seasons Nebuchadnezzar was disabled. It is also true that Daniel would have been the best choice for president under Darius. Further, this was in every detail God's plan.

Verse 3. Daniel was now set at the head and placed in rank over all the officers. It was an office of great responsibility; he would manage the affairs of the empire, and the office demanded integrity.

Verse 4. But the other officers were filled with envy, and they sought to find some pretext to prevent the appointment of Daniel to such a high office. Perhaps they reasoned among themselves that Daniel, being an exile and a captive, could not qualify to be a ruler over them. He would be a Jew ruling over a Gentile nation. Whatever their reason, it fit into God's plan, for the hammer soon fell, and their doom was at hand.

Verse 5. The officers admitted there was no charge against the character of Daniel, but were nonetheless determined to destroy him. They tried to find fault in his spiritual life. A good sermon can be found here regarding religion versus Christianity. Today many in the church practice religion, and they are the ones who protest against those who practice Christianity. Thus the officers proposed a law that for a limited time no one should be allowed to present a petition of any kind to anyone except to the king alone. The object of their evil would now be accomplished, for they knew Daniel would stand steadfast and worship his God. Little did they know they were instruments in God's hands, and their evil deeds would actually establish the credibility of Daniel as a ruler of the empire.

After the event of the lion's den, during the first year of Darius (Dan. 9:1), Daniel becomes concerned about the release of his people, and he prays on their behalf. Daniel says that Gabriel came to him in his extreme weariness. But Gabriel did not answer Daniel's prayer, instead, beginning in Daniel 9:24, Gabriel tells Daniel the time of the Messiah, as well as the utter destruction of Jerusalem and the nation of Israel.

Verse 6. When they proposed the new law, the conspirators came before the king together as a group. The Biblical and judicial idea of "two or three witnesses to confirm a matter" was necessary. One of them by himself would not have been able to accomplish this.

Verse 7. The committee knew this was an unusual request, one that might seem unreasonable to the king, so they used the force of agreement among themselves. "We have consulted together." The decree could only be established by the king himself, so to get rid of Daniel, they must show urgent concern and force to the king.

One wonders how often bad decisions are made because of this device of urgency. Evil forces know all the tricks, often working within to destroy God's children. "And thus consider ye throughout all ages that none that put their trust in Him shall be overcome." *Old Testament Apocrypha,* 1 Macc. 2:61, p. 144.

The evil officers included a mandate of thirty days for their decree, knowing very well that Daniel would not cease to worship his God, and they would have ample time to trap him. At the same time it would not deprive the kingdom for long of their habit of worshiping many gods. It would also test the king's strength among his subjects.

Verses 8-9. For the decree to become law, it had to have the king's stamp of approval. This could have been by his signet ring, a "seal" on the bargain that would prohibit the king himself from changing the law. A similar act in regard to the law of the Medes and Persians is recorded in Esther 8, where the king was unable to change or recall an order given to massacre the Jews. There, the king attempted to counteract his order by putting the Jews on guard, allowing them to defend themselves. When the king of Persia condemned anyone to death, no one dared to make intercession for him. Regardless of the cause, the command must be executed, for the law cannot be countermanded. Even the king himself could not altar it.

Verse 10. Daniel knew the king had signed the decree. He went into his house and made no changes in his habits. He bowed down in front of his open window facing Jerusalem, and worshipped. Daniel probably knew about the plot; but simply trusts God to work it out. It was not uncommon for a Hebrew to pray toward Jerusalem. Solomon did it, 1 Kin. 8:44-49, and so did Jonah.

Verses 11-12. At this time the guilty officers assembled, evidently to gain evidence against Daniel while he worshiped. After seeing Daniel bow to the God of heaven, rather than to the king, they came into the presence of the king. They first reminded him of the law he had just established concerning worship. Perhaps the king suspected that someone had violated this law, but there is no reason to assume he was aware the guilty person was his president, Daniel.

Verse 13. Notice the cunning way in which the officers refer to Daniel. Rather than refer to the exalted president, an officer to be honored, they refer to him as the captive Jew from Judah. Their speech was designed to aggravate his guilt and to raise the anger of the king.

Verse 14. Upon hearing that his president, Daniel, was the accused, the king was angered at himself for having established such law. No doubt the king realized he had made a decree without due deliberation. As yet there is no evidence that the king realized the decree had been proposed for the very purpose of destroying Daniel, but he was displeased with himself for acting hastily. Daniel would be ruined unless some way could be found by which the consequences of the decree could be averted.

Verse 15. Now the officers came before the king, eager for the law to be executed quickly. They may have thought that if the king was allowed to dwell on the consequence of this event, he might find some way to pardon Daniel. "Know O king the law says...." The point was so well settled that no question could be raised concerning the decree.

Verse 16. So the king gave orders that Daniel be thrown to the lions. The decree was executed, Daniel would no longer be in authority over them—or so the officers thought. But little did they know that the God of heaven would deliver Daniel. Little did they know that they were sealing their own doom! In his sorrow and grief, it appears the king loved Daniel and had great respect for him. Now he shows respect for Daniel's God, and trusts that God to deliver Daniel. Although it was common among the heathen to believe in the interposition of the gods in favor of the righteous, and particularly their own worshipers, nevertheless, Darius had confidence in Daniel and his God, and he expressed this to the last.

Verse 17. A stone sealed the mouth of the den, the entrance was sealed with the kings seal, and no one could open it until the prescribed time. The consequences of breaking the king's seal was punishment of the worst kind.

Verse 18. "The king fasted." His mind was troubled over what he had done. He would not eat his evening meal, which implies that Daniel had been thrown into the den in the afternoon.

Verse 19. "Then the king arose early the next morning." His remorse for Daniel led him straight to the den of lions, hoping Daniel would not be harmed, and he cried out to Daniel, "O Daniel, the servant of the living God, the God who has life, who imparts life, and who can preserve life." Daniel would have noted the king's concern for him when he was about to be thrown into the den, and probably had a good idea how it came about. By the time Daniel wrote this book, he was certainly aware of who had done all this to him, and how the King felt about it.

Verse 20. The king showed great concern for Daniel, which does him credit. Would that Christians today would show more concern for one another. What we note here is that Daniel, at all times, in all circumstances, even as a captive in a distant land, in places of honor and power, continued faithfully to worship the God of heaven. It is typical of Daniel that in this circumstance, he was the one who reassured the king! He kept his character, his humility, and his faith, even in the face of death. Not once did he speak against the evil forces or those who accosted him. This had been his consistent character, and it is fitting that the king should refer to it now, and to the God he served. Though it is not stated, it can be reasonably assumed that Daniel was not a man with worldly habits. He was not proud, nor a slanderer or gossip. He brought no charge against anyone except it be face to face, truly a preacher whom God loved. Daniel would have made an excellent Elder in the Lord's Church.

Verse 21. "Then Daniel said unto the king, O king live forever." Daniel pays homage to the king, and assures him that he is alive and well. God delivered Daniel for two reasons: 1) Daniel's faith led him to believe that God would deliver him; 2) It was part of God's plan to establish Daniel among the governments he served.

Verse 22. "My God hath sent His angel." Throughout the Old Testament we find that whenever a remarkable preservation was made, it was attributed to a God-sent angel. Here is another principle of interaction between angelic forces and mankind. God has not changed his way of caring for his children; we are today given blessings by forces unseen, things beyond our power to accomplish. Think then, dear reader, before you commit sin, that the holy angels are watching you. Think what shame it must bring to them when two people lay down to commit adultery in their presence! The angels carried Lazarus to Abraham's bosom, Lk. 16:22, and the angels of the Lord camp around those who fear God. Ps. 34:7.

Verses 23-24. The king rejoiced that no harm had come to Daniel, and restored him to his office. He would now exert even greater power in the government. The king put to death the men who had brought the charges against Daniel. The hungry lions made short work of them.

Verses 25-26. Darius now writes to all peoples in his empire, and for the benefit of future generations, asking that Daniel's God be honored and revered. He acknowledges Daniel's God as the One who lives forever, whose kingdom shall never end. It is not known if the preaching of Daniel had the same humbling effect on Darius in his latter years, as it had upon Nebuchadnezzar.

Verses 27-28. "So this Daniel prospered in the reign of Darius." Daniel had much influence during both Darius' and Cyrus' reigns. God had prepared Cyrus to take the kingdom so he might deliver the exiles. God had named Cyrus many years before his birth, Isa. 45:1-6, 13.

In the first six chapters we studied the history of Daniel and the kings he served. We can see God's plan developing for Israel. From chapter seven through chapter twelve we will study the future of Israel, its close, and the contribution Israel will make toward Christianity.

In the remaining six chapters of Daniel, we are concerned with symbols and figurative language. These chapters can best be understood when a standard interpretation is used, and when one recognizes that Jesus Christ died once for the sins committed in the past, and for every sin committed in the future. The visions in Daniel will move us from his days into the New Testament for their fulfillment, where the whole subject is bound up in the various eschatological discourses.

STUDY IN PROPHETIC SYMBOLS

Introduction

Symbolic language in the prophetic parts of sacred scripture require special care to interpret. Knowing the meaning of these words and phrases will help immeasurably in our understanding of the prophetic scriptures.

For the most part, the sacred Scriptures are their own best interpreter for both literal and figurative language. The interpretation of the following symbols is drawn, for the most part, from the scriptures themselves. However, I have consulted the *Eastern Oneirocritics*, handed down to us in the book of *Achmetes*, containing the acquisitions of the interpreters of the kings of India, Persia, and Egypt. The three great interpreters are *Bara* to the King of Persia, *Tarphan* to the King of Egypt, *Syrbacham* to the King of India. These men interpret nearly all the symbols in the Bible. Although they derive both the symbols and their interpretation from other religious sources, their information shows that during ancient times the symbols used in Holy Scripture were generally used among all peoples of the known world.

Words Used Symbolically in Prophecy

Angel. In symbolic language, denotes any agent or messenger which God employs in executing His will.

Air. Frequently used as equivalent to the heavens, a symbol of government, and an emblem of the kingdom of Satan. He is called "the prince of the power of the air." Eph. 2:2; cf. Eph. 6:12. A vial poured out upon the air denotes destruction of all existing governments under the influence of Satan. Rev. 16:17.

Ascension into Heaven. Symbol of the acquisition of political dignity and honor. "And the witnesses ascended up into heaven in a cloud." Rev. 11:12.

Balances. Symbol of justice. Balances joined with the sale of corn or fruits of the earth denote scarcity. Bread by weight is a curse. Lev. 26:26

Beast. As a symbol, denotes a usurping, tyrannical power. A succession of men exercising a lawless arbitrary power, whether civil or ecclesiastical. Beast coming up out of the sea denotes kings outside of Israel. Dan. 7:17.

Binding. Denotes forbidding or restraining from action. "To bind the dragon" is to restrain that cruel and tyrannical power represented by the dragon. Rev. 20:2.

Black. Denotes affliction, disaster, and anguish; anything sad, dismal, cruel, or unfortunate. Rev. 6:5.

Blood. Denotes war, carnage, slaughter. To turn water into blood is to embroil nations in war. Isa. 9:5; 15:9; 34:3; 34:6,7; Ezek. 9:9; 14:9; Joel 2:30.

Bow and Arrow, or *Quivers*. Denotes war and victory. Ezek. 21:21.

Burning. As a symbol, denotes destruction caused by God's wrath: "For our God is a consuming fire," Heb. 12:29. When directed to a mass of people, it signifies that God has looked into the future and has seen their rebellion, and warns them of impending destruction, Deut. 28:22, 29:23. God's anger kindled at Israel's arrogance: "The land is burned up, the people are fuel for the fire," Isa. 9:9. "Wail for the day of the Lord is near, every man's heart will be burned up," Isa. 13:5-7. "Behold the day of the Lord is coming with burning anger to make the land a desolation," Isa. 13:9. Notice this burning up is directed to the nation of Babylon, Isa. 13:1. It carries the same symbols as that of 2 Peter 3:12. To Israel, God said, "And the people will be burned to lime," Isa. 33:12. "For behold the day is coming burning like a furnace, and every evil doer will be set ablaze, and become chaff," Malachi 4:1-6.

Here it might be helpful to call the reader's attention to the following facts:

1. In directing His anger to Babylon in Isaiah 13, the land is destroyed, humans melt—they were set afire, the heavens suffer, the sun, moon, and stars will not shine. Heaven and earth and all therein is burned up. Was this literally fulfilled? Or was this merely symbolic language fulfilled by the destruction of Babylon by the Medes and Persians?
2. Isaiah 13 is directed only toward Babylon, Isa. 13:1.
3. Babylon was not literally wiped off the face of earth.
4. Now look at 2 Peter 3. The same symbols we saw in Isaiah 13 are used here. 2 Pet. 3 was not written to the whole universe, it was written to Jewish people, 1 Pet. 1:1-2; 2 Pet 3:1-2. Does the Bible not teach that if prophecy is not fulfilled in a reasonable time, it is no prophecy at all?

Buying, the act of buying. "No man might buy or sell." To give or receive religious instructions, or partake in the honors of the ministry, Rev. 13.

Book, the *sealing* of. Denotes the withholding of its contents until a later period, when the information will be revealed in full. Dan. 12:4; 10:14.

Candle, emblem of prosperity, success, joy. "His candle shall be put out," Job 18:6. "O that I were as in months past, as in the days when God preserved me; when His candle shined upon my head." Job 29:3.

Candlestick, or *lamp*, is sometimes the symbol of government, however in most cases it denotes spiritual authority, Zech. 4:2-6. It frequently affords instructions respecting the removal of ignorance, or calling for repentance Rev. 2:5.

Character, or *mark*, especially mark on the forehead, or on the hand. Denotes an open profession of allegiance to those whose name they bear, Rev. 13:16-18. Both servants and soldiers in ancient times were marked on the forehead or hands.

Cloud, an emblem of prosperity and glory. To ride on clouds is to rule and conquer. Daniel says, "One like the Son of man came with the clouds of heaven," to which our Lord adds an explanation of the symbol, "with power and great glory." Mt. 24.

Crown. Denotes dignity, power and honor. Esther 1:11; 2:17. It also may denote evil forces, Rev. 12:3. Each passage where the symbol appears must be considered.

Darkness. Denotes affliction. The kingdom of the beast was full of darkness, confusion and distress.

Day. In prophetic style, "I have given you a day for a year," Ezek. 4:5,6; Numbers 14:34. See also Dan. 9:24-27. Time, times, and a half time is equal to three and one-half years, Dan. 7:25; Rev. 11:2.

Death. A ceasing to be, the destruction of a life or a nation, a change of state, according to the nature of the passage. "Moab shall die with tumult."

Desert, or *wilderness*. Denotes paganism; the wild, savage manners of paganism. As the idolatry of the pagans was practiced in groves, woods, and waste places, so it became among the Jews the symbol of paganism.

Dew, and rain. Symbols of heavenly blessings. "The two witnesses have power to shut heaven that it not rain."

They will restrain the blessings of heaven from falling upon those who reject their testimony. Rev. 11:3-7.

Dragon. The well-known symbol of the old Roman government in its pagan persecuting state. The Egyptians, Persians, and Indians regard the dragon as the established emblem of a wicked monarch. The whole principality of the old serpent is denoted by it. In the Old Testament it is applied to the wicked monarch of the pagan nations. "Art thou he who has cut Rahab and wounded the dragon. I am against thee, Pharaoh king of Egypt the great dragon that lieth in the midst of the river," Ezek. 29:5.

Earth. In symbol language, always refers to a great body of people, in contrast with the government. The Hebrew words "Adarnah" and "Ara" denote land, soil and earth. However, when Isaiah calls for the inhabitants of earth to hear him, he says, "Listen O heavens, and hear, O earth." In Isa. 1:2 he uses the symbol of earth to denote its inhabitants. In speaking of Babylon, its land is burned up, Isa. 13:6-12. Zephaniah says that all the earth will be devoured, Zeph. 1:18, and in the same verse qualifies his statement by saying He will make a complete end to all the inhabitants of the land. Again in Zeph. 3:8, "For all the earth will be devoured by the fire of my zeal." Now notice v. 9, "Then I will give the people purified lips." If this was literal, there would be no lips left after the earth was devoured by fire. 2 Peter 3 denotes the same events as Zephaniah. See 2 Pet. 3:10, "The earth will be burned up." Then look at v. 13, "But according to His promise we are looking for new heavens and a new earth wherein dwells righteousness." What the symbol means in each case is that it represents an evil population which God will destroy, after which righteousness will dwell. In the case with Isa. 13, Babylon was to be destroyed. In Zephaniah 1 and 3, Judah was being destroyed. In 2 Pet. 3, Judah and Jerusalem were being destroyed by Rome.

Earthquake. A well established symbol of the political and moral revolutions and convulsions of society. "To shake the heavens and the earth" is explained by Haggai as denoting the overthrow of thrones, the subversion of the strength of the kingdom, Haggai 2:21,22. The Oneirocritics concur in affirming that "earthquakes" are signified by wars, slaughter of men, and the overthrow of kingdoms and nations.

Eclipse, or obscuring of sun, moon, and stars. The universe being the symbol of a kingdom or polity, the obstruction of the sun denotes the diminution of the glory of its sovereign. Thus the use of sun, stars, moon symbolize the potentates as is found in Gen. 37:9-10; Dan. 8:8-10.

Eye. The symbol of light or knowledge, as blindness is the symbol of ignorance. "I will open My eyes upon the house of Judah," Zech. 12:4.

Fire. Signifies fierce destruction, judgment while living, and that by the divine sanction of God. "For He is like the refiners fire" to consume the dross. (Mal. 3:2) "For behold the Lord will come with fire, to render His anger with fury," Isa. 66:15. "For by fire and sword will the Lord plead with all flesh; and the slain of the Lord shall be many," Isa. 66:16. To Babylon, God shall burn them; their hearts shall melt from the fire! The means of destruction, Isa. 13:1-13. In speaking to Judah and Jerusalem respecting the coming down of King Nebuchadnezzar in 586 B.C. God said, 'For all the earth shall be devoured by the fire of My Zeal," Zeph. 3:8. See also chapters 1-3. Ezek. 7:1-12, and Amos chapter 8 confirms the symbols of Zephaniah as pertaining to Judah and Jerusalem, therefore, the symbol stands as it is confirmed by three witnesses. 2 Thess. 1:1-10, and 2 Pet. 3:1-16 stands as a classic example of earth burning and the Lord coming in flaming fire, as a judgment upon the land of Israel in AD 70.

Fire from heaven. In Sodom's case, it was literal fiery destruction out of the sky (either thunderbolts or flaming sulfuric meteors). In Elijah's case, fire licked up the whole altar and sacrifice in front of the Baal prophets. At Sinai, fire from heaven came down visibly upon Mt. Sinai. In Jerusalem's case, it was the fiery tar and pitch-laden missiles and ballistae that the besieging armies hurled at her to destroy her gates and walls by fire.

Flood. Symbol of invasion by foreign armies. Daniel, when recording the message of the angel respecting the destruction of Jerusalem in AD 70 by the Romans said it would come like a "flood." Dan. 9:26

Fornication, or *whoredom*, denotes idolatry, departing from the truths of God and forming alliance with the enemies of God.

Hail. Denotes inroads of enemies, killing and destroying. Hail from heaven denotes destruction by the sword, Isa. 28:2; 28:17; Hag. 2:17.

Harvest. Cutting down grain is the figure of cutting down men. "The harvest of the earth is ripe," Rev. 14:15. The people are fit for destruction. And the harvest is the end of the age," Mt. 13:39. The end of the age would represent the closing of the second dispensation. See Heb. 9:26, the Lord died at the end of the age (world). "The tares are harvested and burned in the fire," Mt. 13:40. (Refer to the symbol of burning and fire). "A harvest is appointed for Judah," Hos. 6:10,11. "The harvest of the field is destroyed," Joel 3:13-16. It is inconceivable that the apostles and early church should have so utterly misunderstood our Lord's words when speaking of the tares, so as to see eschatology where He intended a divine social evolution! See G. S. Streatfield, *The Self Interpretation of Jesus Christ,* pub. 1866, Vol. 1, pp. 157-158. The synoptists shared the prevailing expectation that the Second Advent was imminent, and with this idea in their minds it is no marvel that, when they compiled the Lord's sayings about the future, they should have brought the destruction of Jerusalem and the final judgment into immediate connections. Note that Malachi 4:1-5 confirms what is being said in Matthew chapter 13 respecting the tares.

Heaven and earth, the whole universe, political or religious. Heaven is always the symbol of government, the higher places in the political universe. "Heaven and earth will pass away, but My words shall not pass away," Mt. 24:35. Here the Jewish power is represented as the heaven and earth, and the symbol denotes its passing away. "For truly I say to you, until heaven and earth pass away, not the smallest letter or stroke shall pass away from the Law, until all is accomplished."

One particular thing stands out regarding this symbol. Almost all Christians today regard this passage as the end of the world, when heaven and earth shall pass away. The same persons deny that we are still under the Law of Moses, so again we see inconsistency. Jesus said that no part of the Law would pass away until heaven and earth passed away! But if the symbol represents the passing away of Theocratic Israel, not at the cross, but in AD 70 when Rome left Israel without means of worship or national identity, we have perfect consistency. We know by fact, not by assumption, that we are not under the Law! The Law passed away as Peter described in 2 Pet. 3. The powers to be shaken in Mt. 24:29 would denote the rulers of Israel; no other meaning fits the context. Notice also that this shaking occurs at the Second Advent of Christ.

Professor Schwartzkop makes the following statement regarding this symbol, and its imminent climax." Here we have first the historical fact that the whole of early Christendom, without exception, most eagerly awaited the personal return of the Lord in their own day. The whole character of its practical life bears this peculiar stamp of hope for that event. This is an almost crushing fact for those who would spiritualize or explain away Jesus' predictions of his Second Advent in AD 70. That fact is reinforced by another, namely, that this universal belief of the early Christians is unquestionably derived from the apostles themselves." Schwartzkop, *Outlines of the Life of Christ*, p. 154.

The Prophet Isaiah confirms the symbol in dealing with Babylon. "They come from the end of heaven," Isa. 34:4. "All the host of heaven shall be dissolved." Jer. 44:15-20. See also Isa. 13:5; 15:10. In the context of these passages it seems clear that "heaven and earth" is connected with the nation and government.

Horns. "The great horn is the first king... the ten horns are ten kings." Dan. 7:24. The well-known symbol of a king. Rev. 17:12.

Horse. Symbol of war and conquest, the state, color, or equipage of a horse represents the condition of its rider. White denotes purity and victory. Black denotes distress and general calamity. Red denotes war and bloodshed, and fierce hostility. Pale is the symbol of death and destruction. See Rev. 6.

Jerusalem. Used as a symbol or figure of the Church of Jesus Christ, the Christian economy; the spiritual family of Abraham. Before the passing away of old Jerusalem, spiritual Jerusalem is said to be coming down from heaven to dwell among men. Rev. 21:1-3; Gal. 4:22-31. New Jerusalem is the sole lawgiver, and those who reside therein have received the promise made to Abraham and reign with Christ in the spiritual kingdom.

Lamb. Lamb of God, the symbol of the Messiah.

Lamp. Symbol of government, civil or religious.

Light. Well-known emblem of knowledge, except where it speaks of the true light, the Messiah. Gen. 1:2.

Locusts. Numerous armies of men pillaging and destroying a country, Joel 1:6. Achmetes, "If any king or potentate see locusts come upon a place, let him expect a powerful multitude of enemies there."

Olive tree. Trees in the prophetic scriptures are often the symbol of great men. Ezek. 17:22 speaks of the Messiah himself. Zech. 4:3, "the two olive trees." In v. 14 the two olive trees become anointed, they stand by the Lord of the whole earth. In Mt. 17:3 the two olive trees, and the anointed ones, are none other than Moses and Elijah. See Isa. 61:3, the "oaks of righteousness." In Jer. 11:16 the righteous Jews are referred to as olive trees.

River. Consolations are represented by rivers of living waters, the new covenant, the gospel of Christ, and the church. Zech. 13:1. "You would have asked Him, and He would have given you living water." John 4:10; 3:5; 13:14; Rev. 22:1; Ps. 46:4; Ezek. 47:1; Rev. 22:17.

Scarlet. Scarlet color denotes cruel bloodshed.

Sea. Gentile peoples, Dan. 7:2, 3,17. In Rev. 21:1 it can mean two things. (1) Since Israel, and especially Jerusalem, was the center of destruction in the book of Revelation, it can mean that there would no longer be the Jewish persecuting force. (2) It could mean that no longer would Satan have any power over God's people, he would be confined in his kingdom forever and ever. Rev. 20:10; Rom. 16:20; Heb. 2:14; 1 John 3:8, John 12:31; 16:11. Sometimes the symbol denotes an empire in agitation like the restless wind-driven sea.

Sun, moon, and stars. Symbol of authority in society, both political and religious. The sun denotes the chief authority. The moon next in authority, the stars are the nobles. See Gen. 37:5-10 for its original meaning. The Morning Star is a symbol of the Messiah. Stars falling from heaven denote the destruction of nobility, Dan. 8:10. Stars, moon, and sun not giving their light denote authorities having their rule taken away. Mt. 24:30. The sun, moon, and stars being turned into blood is found in Joel 2:28-32. Notice the following chronology of Joel 2:28-32.

1. V. 28, Holy Spirit poured out. See Acts 1 and 2.
2. V. 29, male/female receive the Spirit. Acts 2:16.

3. V. 30, wonders in the sky and on earth, blood and fire. See Acts 2:16.
4. V. 31, sun darkened, moon becomes blood, before the coming of the Lord. The argument here respecting the symbol is that almost all Christians say that these passages have not yet been fulfilled, yet Peter says in Acts 2:16, "But this is what was spoken of through the Prophet Joel." Peter is saying that the symbols of Joel was being fulfilled in his day. Notice Acts 2:16-21, Peter says that all these things will continue until the coming of the Lord. Now if the Lord has not returned, then we are going to have a hard time proving that the Holy Spirit is not with us today, and we will be pressed hard by the Pentecostals to prove that men and women do not possess the Holy Spirit. Tradition has almost wrecked the Lord's church, tradition leads to assumption, and assumption is sin. 2 Sam. 6:1-7. The result of assumption is irreverence for God.

Sword. Symbol of slaughter, Ezek. 5:17. Ezek. 7 depicts the type of slaughter, and to whom it is directed. Rev. 1:16 adds, "Out of His mouth went a two-edged sword," a double portion of slaughter. Rev. 1:1, 3 says it was then "at hand." See also Rev. 2:12.

Smoke. Symbol of the movement of armies; when associated with blood and fire it denotes God's wrath upon peoples, nations, or governments. Using the symbol for God's instruments, He tells Israel, "For smoke comes from the north," Isa. 14:31. "Be calm, have no fear and do not be fainthearted because of these two tails of smoking firebrands...." Isa. 7:4. Contrast Isa. 14:31 with Luke 21:20.

Thunder. "There were thunders and lightning," the symbol of sudden and terrifying destruction. As the coruscation of lightning and thunder shake the natural heavens, or air, so symbolic thunders and lightning shake the political or religious governments of men. Isa. 29:6; Job 39:25; 1 Sam. 2:10; Ps. 18.

Wheels. When associated with God, denotes the revolution and dispensations of God's government.

White clothing. Denotes innocence and purity.

Whore. Denotes the apostate church.

World. When used as symbol, it denotes an age or

dispensation. Empires and kingdoms were called worlds by ancient people. 2 Pet. 3:6 denotes the closing of the Mosaic dispensation, and the beginning of the dispensation of Christ. The KJV renders Heb. 9:26 as Christ who died at the "end of the world," the proper understanding is that Christ died at the end of the age, or the end of the dispensation then present. The same applies to the reading in the KJV beginning in Mt. 13:39-50, as well as Mt. 24:1-3. The end of the age is proper. If we understood the ancient peoples' definition of "world," then we would have no problem with the use of it in the KJV, especially in Paul's use of it in Eph. 1:21. There are only two ways to translate this text: (1) that God shall destroy the present world, and create a new world for His children, where they will live and reign with Him for a thousand years! (2) That Paul understands the proper use of the word, and applies its use to the passing of dispensations, at which time the church would be full grown, Zion will have been redeemed, and Christ will have made His promised second advent to bring his kingdom, wherein He would reign on His own throne. Mt. 16:27-28; Mt. 25:31; 10:23.

Zion. Denotes the Christian church in her impregnable and triumphant character. The symbol depicts the church in its first perfect state, in the Garden of Eden, then the symbol depicts the church in a lost state, and finally the church as being redeemed by Christ. There are three points here that beg to be considered.

(1) Before God created man, he made a plan for man, a plan of redemption. In brief, God knew from the outset that if he created man in his own image, as an intelligent free moral agent, there would not only be the possibility and probability of sin, but the certainty of it. Since man was created in a perfect and spiritual image of God, man was in total union with God, there was no separation from the presence of God. God walked and talked with his creation, and cared for their every need. In that state, the pair was without sin, and had they died, their soul would have gone into the presence of God. Therefore, the conditions of the garden of God presented a continuing cleansing from all sin. Therefore Zion, the garden of God, the assembly of God, was present in the beginning of the second creation, and remained so, until Satan, the prince of this world influenced the pair to submit to their free

agency, which resulted in sin. And sin brought about death for the pair, as well as all their posterity to the cross of Christ. The souls of all from Adam to the cross were held in bondage, Heb. 2:14, until Christ redeemed Zion and released them from bondage.

(2) The perfect state of Zion, as depicted in Isaiah chapters 51 and 52, implies that the garden of God was at that time considered as Zion. Then God moves on to show that he intends to restore to Zion all that was lost in Adam. Zion was lost in Adam, so in Isa. 52 God says he will redeem Zion through his Son. See Rom. 5:10-18. Therefore, through Jesus Christ and his blood, Zion was redeemed, and in Zion there is no condemnation (judgment), Rom. 8:1, a state just as it was in the garden. By obedience to Christ, God has created us anew, like Adam, in a safe state, Rom. 6:1-12.

(3) Abraham was promised the redemption of Zion through his seed and that his seed would enjoy the benefits of redeemed Zion. Note: For a thing to be redeemed, it first must have been lost. So Zion was lost at the time God made the promise to Abraham, which confirms that Zion was lost by Adam, and restored by Jesus Christ. This means the church was lost by Adam, and restored by Christ. Christ not only shed His blood for you and I, but for Adam as well. Jacob's dream of the ladder being taken back to heaven shows the church taken away from Adam and carried back.

Comments

Admittedly, many times traditional views cloud the real meaning of God's Word. For example, nearly all Christians believe that Jesus Christ is now reigning on His own throne, that He now has His own kingdom, that He is now our High Priest, that He now has all power and authority in heaven and on earth. One of our better scholars confirms this. "The point to be emphasized is that Christ is priest now; and therefore, He is sitting and ruling on His throne." Dr. Rex A. Turner, *Sound Doctrine* (quarterly periodical), Oct-Dec, 1980, p. 13. Published by Gospel Advocate, Nashville, Tenn.

There are many inconsistencies as a result of tradition. We all are aware that the Lord said in Mt. 25:31 that "when the Son of man comes in His glory, and all the angels with Him, then He will sit on His glorious throne." You see almost all Christians affirm that Mt. 25:31 speaks of the end of the world! No matter what period of history Jesus speaks of, his reigning on his throne was predicated upon his Second Advent, that much is clear. So what is the outcome? Well, if Christ has not come back already with all the angels, then he is not yet sitting on his throne. If he is not sitting on his throne, he is not King, and he has no kingdom, neither is he our High Priest.

Even more important, the writer of the Hebrew letter informs us that His second advent would be to bring full salvation to those who eagerly waited for Him, Heb. 9:28. Now, if the Second Advent has not yet occurred, then no one has salvation! We are yet waiting for it.

I suggest that the reader untangle the inconsistency of such teaching. As for me, I believe that the Bible, through pattern, types, shadow, and symbols teach that Christ died at the end of the age, and the tares were burned at the end of the age. Further, at the end of the age Christ made the promised second advent, at which time He brought full salvation, that He then became King, High Priest, and that he was then, and is now, reigning on his own throne. This idea of truth is confirmed in Mt. 16:27-28, where He promised to return with the kingdom before those to whom He spoke should die. If He did not return, we can put no confidence in anything else He has spoken. The alternative, if He did not return, would be that many to whom He spoke are still living! Even 2,000 years later!

Hopefully the foregoing study will in some small way aid the reader in his understanding of the symbols that appear in this survey. There is one important point that begs to be stressed: I can not say that I know exactly what every symbol means in every detail, so I can not make these things a test of fellowship. In the first place, I have not been given any authority to bind, or to judge anyone. I am under obligation to teach truth as I understand it, even if it is a nontraditional doctrine, Col. 2:8, therefore, it is not my desire to violate the autonomy of any church, or the personal opinions of anyone. I ask only that the reader without preconceived ideas study the survey, if what has been said can be scripturally refuted, then that person may help me by correcting me.

DANIEL CHAPTER 7

Introductory Remarks.

We now enter upon the second part of our book, and this chapter, as you will readily see, covers practically the same ground as chapter two. It covers the whole period of Gentile rule from the carrying away of Judah until the end time for Judah and Israel. Their end time was when Jerusalem was destroyed and Judaism abolished.

In the first section we were chiefly occupied with prophetic history viewed from man's standpoint. When a Gentile had a vision of the course of world-empires, he saw the image of a man—a stately and noble figure, one that filled him with such admiration that he set up a similar statue to be worshiped as a god. But in this section, in the opening verses of chapter 7, we find a new viewpoint. We see Daniel, the man of God, and his visions of the same empires. He sees them as four ravenous wild beasts, of so brutal a character and so monstrous, that no actual creatures known to man could adequately set them forth.

Daniel's vision saw each empire portrayed as a wild beast. Each wild beast characterizes the leading features of the empire it represents. Babylon is portrayed as a winged lion, which had its wings plucked, a man's heart given to it, and made to stand erect on its feet. This describes Babylon. Then we see a bear with three ribs in its mouth, which lifted itself up on one side. This represents Medo-Persia. The leopard represents Greece. The Roman Empire follows to the time of the end, the time when a new dispensation begins and the Jewish nation abolished.

The first vision portrayed the condition of the Jews and the end of their nation and religion, which would be replaced with a universal religion, into which all men from every nation under heaven could enter.

Chapters two and seven are parallel. Both speak of the fifth kingdom of the Messiah. Both present the arrival of the fifth kingdom as coming during the time of the fourth beast. Both speak of Greece being the third kingdom. Both speak of the survival of all the kingdoms until the ruin of the fourth. That is, they would be recognized as a nation, but would be under the rule and subjection of the fourth beast, Rome.

Verse 1. Daniel had a vision while sleeping, and he wrote the sum of it. It was customary among the prophets to record their predictions, whether communicated in a dream or a vision, or by words to them. Then there could be no doubt, when the event occurred, that there had been an inspired prediction of it. There would be a careful comparison of the prediction with the event.

When Daniel wrote the visions, he made a summary, briefly stating the contents, or the chief points of the vision, but only the chief points. The majority of Bible scholars agree that when the prophets described what was to occur to tyrants in the future, they conveyed their oracles in a comparatively dark and obscure manner, yet so as to be clear when the events should occur. The reason for this is obvious. If the meaning of many of the predictions had been understood by those to whom they referred, that fact would have been a motive to them, an incentive to defeat them. Since the fulfillment depended on their voluntary agency, the prophecy would have been void. It was necessary therefore, in general, to avoid direct predictions and the use of names, dates and places. Rather, they used symbols whose meaning would be obscure at the time of the prediction, but would be plain when the event occurred.

Verse 2. "And I saw the four winds of heaven." The winds blow under the heavens, or seem to come from heaven or the air. Compare Jer. 49:36 where the number of the winds where there is also four, blowing mainly from the four quarters of the earth. Nothing is more common than to designate them in this manner, from the east, the south, west, and north.

"And the great winds strove upon the sea." Notice the word strove. The Hebrew word means to rush forth, to break forth. It seems the winds rushed forth from all quarters, and met on the sea, causing a wild commotion, as a storm would churn the seas and cause great waves to lash out. (See Ezek. 32:2, Job. 38:8). Thus the Chaldeans break forth, to rush forth as the winds. The symbol here would naturally denote some wild commotion among the nations, as if the winds of heaven should rush together and cause confusion.

A heaving ocean, one tossed with storms, would denote nations agitated with revolution or rebellion. In the prophets and poets, hosts of armies invading a land are compared to flood waters, and mighty changes among nations as the heaving ocean during a storm. (Compare Jer. 46:7-8, Jer. 46:2. Isa. 8:7,8,17:12, Dan. 9:40, Rev. 13:1).

Verse 3. Though these beasts are said to come up from the sea, we are instructed by v. 17 that these are kingdoms that would arise from the earth. This would show that the succession of kingdoms would spring from the commotions represented by the heaving ocean.

It is not uncommon for the prophets to make use of animals to represent or symbolize kingdoms, or nations. Thus Isaiah spoke of the pharaoh as the dragon, crocodile, leviathan, Isa. 27:1. When the prophets use animals to represent kingdoms that are made up of other kingdoms, becoming one empire by means of conquest, they use monsters, fabulous beings made up of several others that will set forth the character of the kingdom.

In Rev. 13:1, Rome is represented as a power coming up out of the sea, having seven heads and ten horns. Thus the seven heads would be symbolic of the emperors of Rome, and the ten horns would be the symbol of ten kings ruling the provinces.

Since it was the policy of God to send a prophet years before a judgment was to be brought upon a nation or people, then in every Biblical case, a prophet was sent to say that the judgment was at hand, at the door. A perfect example is God sending Isaiah to Israel in 724 B.C. Hosea came just preceding the fall of Israel. Again, Isaiah spoke to Judah and foretold its fall. Just prior to, and during the fall, God sent Jeremiah. Now, God directs his anger at Israel through Daniel. Just before and during the fall of Israel in AD 70, God would send John.

God not only foretold "the end from the beginning," well in advance of a judgment, but also sent more prophets just before the events occurred, so that there could be no excuses. Such appears to be the case with John in the book of Revelation. God warned them through John the Baptist and Jesus, and then again right at the end, through the book of Revelation.

Verse 4. We saw in chapter 2 the huge image with its four parts, of which the head of gold represented Babylon. Here in chapter 7 the beast Daniel draws best represents Babylon. As a lion, ferocious and strong, Babylon had risen from a city state (not without God's intervention) to become a world power. Isaiah spoke concerning the rise of Assyria (Isa. 10:5-10, 24), telling the people they should not be afraid of Assyria, for Assyria is to receive judgment also. In the same passage, v. 26, Isaiah names Babylon as the scourge. Jeremiah promises the people will be given to Babylon, Jer. 22:25.

We are concerned now with the lion, having the wings of an eagle. The eagle is chief of all fowl, swift, and quick to snatch and carry off his prey. Thus will Babylon move against the nations which God had decreed to fall. Nebuchadnezzar was a tool in God's hand to bring about the fulfillment of prophecy concerning the Hebrew nation.

The plucking of the wing feathers from the beast would indicate two things:

1. When God had finished with the King of Babylon, He would cause him to retire in the palace.
2. Nebuchadnezzar's power was plucked away from him by the God of heaven, thus indicating that God would remove him from the throne, stripping him of his power.

The lion was made to stand upon his feet as a man. This symbol indicates the change of the kingdom under the successors, while Nebuchadnezzar was away for the seven periods. The beast was given the heart of a man.

We would do justice to the study at this point to notice that giving a man's heart was in fact after the plucking of the wings. Thus we have the following:

1. The wings plucked denotes the cessation of conquest; the empire would be extended no farther.
2. God controlled Nebuchadnezzar, sent him to his palace to live in peace, Dan. 4:4.
3. Nebuchadnezzar was sent into the pasture to live as an animal, something as uncommon as it would be for a lion to walk around on his hind feet.
4. The lion would no longer be lionhearted and ferocious, but would be humbled and recognize that God is supreme.
5. Since Daniel was second in command in Babylon, may we not say that Daniel was the heart given to the empire? Or that the heart represents the changed conditions of the king?

Verse 5. "And behold another beast, a second like to a bear." The bear is a well-known animal, and had properties very distinct from the lion and other animals. There was doubtless some reason why this symbol was employed to denote a particular kingdom, in which something corresponded with these peculiar properties. (See 2 Sam. 17:8, Prov. 17:12, Hos. 13:8.) The bear being raised up on one side would denote a kingdom that had been quiet and at rest, but that was now rousing up deliberately for the conquest of war. Having the three ribs in its mouth would denote the crushing of its enemies, and the devouring of much flesh. This beast, the bear, corresponds with the rise of Medo-Persia.

Thus Isaiah spoke concerning the fall of Babylon. (See Isa. 13, especially vs. 5-10) General Darius overcame the capitol city in one night, and the slaughter of prisoners was great, as Isaiah had predicted. For a complete history of Babylon and its rise and fall, see *International Standard Bible Encyclopedia*, Vol. 1. pp. 349-375. For the captivity of Assyria, the ten northern tribes of Israel, Judah, and finally Babylon, see *International Standard Bible Encyclopedia*, Vol. 1, pp. 569-576.

Verse 6. "After this... lo, another like a leopard." After the bear, another kingdom would arise, one like a leopard. The leopard here is Greece (Alexander the Great). Medo-Persia succeeded Babylon. The leopard with its bird wings describes the man born at Pella, for after the death of his father, Alexander, who in just eleven years ruled the world. The leopard is a very fast-moving animal; the added wings would denote swiftness that no hand but that of God could stop.

Alexander the Great was the only man in history who was able to destroy the island city of Tyre, which lay about one half mile off the coast of Tyre, and had walls so high and wide that no one could come into it without meeting certain death. But this man destroyed it, took the debris and made a causeway leading out to it, and caused such destruction that today the island cannot be seen. See *International Standard Bible Encyclopedia,* Vol. 5, pp. 3031-3032.

Compare the parallel of this history with the prophecy of Ezekiel. God stated that Tyre would fall and its debris thrown into the water, thus making the causeway that Alexander built out to the island city. Further, God stated that Tyre would never rise again, and would be for fishermen to cast their nets. See Ezek. 26:3-14. Thus the prophecy by Ezekiel was fulfilled by Alexander the Great.

Why not Nebuchadnezzar? He had laid siege to the city for thirteen years. The answer is simple: God was not ready for Tyre to be completely destroyed. God gave the people many years to repent (thus showing His mercy).

Perhaps now we can better understand that the leopard with bird's wings best describes Greece and Alexander the Great. The four heads denote the four generals under Alexander, to which the empire was divided after the death of Alexander: *Cassander, Lysimachus, Seleucus I Nicator, Ptolemy I Soter*. Mor of this in chapter eleven.

We are now concerned with the fourth beast, which is Rome, with its ten horns, and the rising of the eleventh horn, which can only be taken as eleven rulers in succession. The liberal view of the eleven horns will be dealt with later. Here we need to review the historical evidence about Rome as the fourth beast, and the eleven horns.

1. The horns seen by Daniel would be those rulers who would exert supreme power over the Hebrew nation, until their end came, for this prophecy pertains only to the Hebrew nation, and until its end would come, Dan. 10:14, 12:1-4.
2. God began to prepare the nation of Rome—the instrument of destruction—well before the Exodus from Egypt. God made provisions for their salvation, yet he warned them if they did not do all he commanded they would be punished. They had a choice, just as we have today. In Deut. 28:1-15 the promise is made for their well being, provided they do all that God commands. Then in Deut. 28:15-48 their first affliction is depicted in case they fail to do all that God has commanded; vv. 15-48 covers a period to include the captivity by Babylon and the seventy years. Deut. 28:49-68 depicts the final calamity upon Israel, if they continue to depart from God. The final calamity would, through Rome, bring about the end time for Judaism and theocratic Israel.
3. God was not being cruel toward Israel, for since creation man knew that when he rebelled against his

Creator, the penalty was destruction, so this event is nothing new. God simply informed the people of the manner of destruction. It was no afterthought for God; their destruction was well-planned. If they rebelled, their destruction was by their own choice.

4. As we move forward in time respecting this nation, we see that Israel during Isaiah's time had turned their back on God. Their sin has now come before God, and a just God cannot allow it to go unrequited. Isaiah informs the people that God has now chosen Assyria to come against the ten northern tribes, that they now must be punished for their rebellion. Isa. 10:5-10. Here we can see a portion of the prophecy made by Moses being fulfilled through Assyria. Yet Judah is not yet harmed; their cup of iniquity is not yet full. God is aware that Judah will also continue in sin, but until he is ready to punish, no harm will come to Judah; God will continue to protect them. We see this when King Sennacherib of Assyria attacked Judah, described in Isa. 37:30-38. The king's army was visited by the angel of the Lord, and the army was destroyed. The time had not come for Judah to fall. However, as sin progressed, God sent Jeremiah to tell them of their impending fall. After preaching to Judah without repentance, God said, "I have given you into the hands of King Nebuchadnezzar of Babylon." Jer. 22:25.

5. In scripture and in history we find all Israel in captivity in Babylon. Now they await the end of the seventy years appointed for their captivity, then we find them returning to their land as God had promised. However, it is not long before they rebel again. Here we see the real beginning of their end, the final end. Up to now, they always had a chance to return to God and be preserved, but that now changes. The time is described in Deut. 28:29 when they shall be oppressed evermore, and "no man shall save thee." Now God begins to prepare Rome, that nation from the ends of the earth, a nation whose language Israel knew not, the nation that would be the instrument in God's hands to destroy the covenant of Judaism. In Deut. 28:49 Rome is depicted as a nation, in Daniel 7:6 it is depicted as a beast, as it is in

Revelation. Our Lord refers to this nation, this beast, in Luke 21:20, the force that surrounds Jerusalem. "These are the days of vengeance that all things written must be fulfilled," v. 22. All things. The final destruction is sure and complete.

6. Daniel's prophecy is focused on the end of theocratic Israel, not the end of the world. Without inferring that our Lord knew nothing of what He speaks (as many do), and to be consistent with the whole Bible, I conclude there is nothing in the book of Daniel that should move beyond a point in history when Jerusalem is destroyed by Rome. There is perhaps no better scripture to prove this than Dan. 12:7. It adds credibility to the above statement: "And I heard the man dressed in linen, who was above the waters of the river, as he raised his right hand and his left hand toward heaven, and swore by Him who lives forever that it would be for a time, times, and a half time, and as soon as they finish shattering the power of the holy people, all these things will be finished."

In v. 6, the question is asked, "How long will it be until the end of these wonders?" The wonders are equal to "these things." What things? The things mentioned in this vision. Who were the holy people? The Israelites. When was the power of the holy people shattered? AD 70. And they were shattered by Rome. Therefore I suggest the Revelation letter is but a commentary on that which Daniel wrote: the end of the age, the end time, that great and terrible day of Jehovah God. I further suggest that the New Testament confirms the fulfillment of all which was spoken in the Old. To deny this is to deny that our Lord knew what he spoke of in Luke 21:22, "These are the days of vengeance that all things written must be fulfilled." The vengeance was the destruction of Jerusalem, v. 20. See Mt. 5:17; Lk. 22:37; 24:44, which confirm this.

Every major event mentioned in the New Testament was first spoken in dark language in the Old. For example, turn to Isa. 62:1-12. In v. 2, what do you see? God's people would be called by a new name: "Christian." Verse 4, "no longer will you be forsaken," Christ will be in your midst; you will "never be forsaken." You will be married to Him. He will become the bridegroom, and those who are righteous are the bride. In vv. 6 and 7, New Jerusalem is coming down out of heaven, and will be a praise in the earth. See also Gal. 4:22-31; Lev. 21:1-3. Verse 10 says, "go out and preach the good news of our Lord, preach it to the ends of the earth." Was this accomplished? According to Paul, it was (Col. 1:6, 23). After the gospel was preached to every creature under the heavens, then salvation was to come. Heb. 9:28 What was salvation, who was salvation? Was it Christ who was to come?

In v. 11 of the Isaiah passage, we see what happens when He comes. His reward is with him, and his recompense before him. What does this mean? Judgment! Zech. 14:1-5 confirms this. Note what our Lord says in Luke 21:20,22: When Jerusalem was destroyed, all would be fulfilled, including His coming (the "Second Coming").

Verses 7-8. These two verses relate to the events of vv. 19-28, which deal with the events of the fourth beast. We will cover vv. 9-14 later with emphasis on the subject of the kingdom. Verse 22 describes the coming of the Lord (the "second coming") and the transfer of the kingdom from the Jews to the Church composed of all nations.

Daniel saw ten major horns, and then another, a little horn, the eleventh. It seems the ten major horns represent Roman kings. The little horn could be something else. Here is a list of the first eleven Roman kings as history records them. See the chart on the next page.

Eleven Horns of Daniel 7.
 1. Pompey (52-49 BC) sole ruler of Rome
 2. Julius (47-44 BC)
 3. Augustus (Octavian) (31 BC to AD 14)
 4. Tiberius (AD 14-37)
 5. Caligula (Gaius) (AD 37-41)
 6. Claudius (AD 41-54)
 7. Nero (AD 54-68)
 8. Galba (AD 68-69)
 9. Otho (AD 69)
10. Vitellius (AD 69)
11. Vespasian (AD 69-79)

As stated before, it is only necessary to offer historical evidence to show that the first and eleventh rulers match the description here. The rest fall in line.

The *Fourth Beast* in Daniel 7

The "Beast" represents the Roman Empire
Its "Horns" represent the first eleven rulers:
1. *Pompey (52-49 BC) sole ruler of Rome*
2. *Julius (47-44 BC)*
3. *Augustus (Octavian) (31 BC–14 AD)*
4. *Tiberius (AD 14-37)*
5. *Caligula (Gaius) (AD 37-41)*
6. *Claudius (AD 41-54)*
7. *Nero (AD 54-68)*

8. **Galba (AD 68-69)**
9. **Otho (AD 69)**
10. **Vitellius (AD 69)**

*These three had very short reigns, less than a year – ***Vespasian** *"pulled these out"*

11. *Vespasian (AD 69-79)*
He ruled over theocratic Israel
only until August 10th, AD 70–
a very short reign (AD 69-70).

"Little Horn"
Vespasian

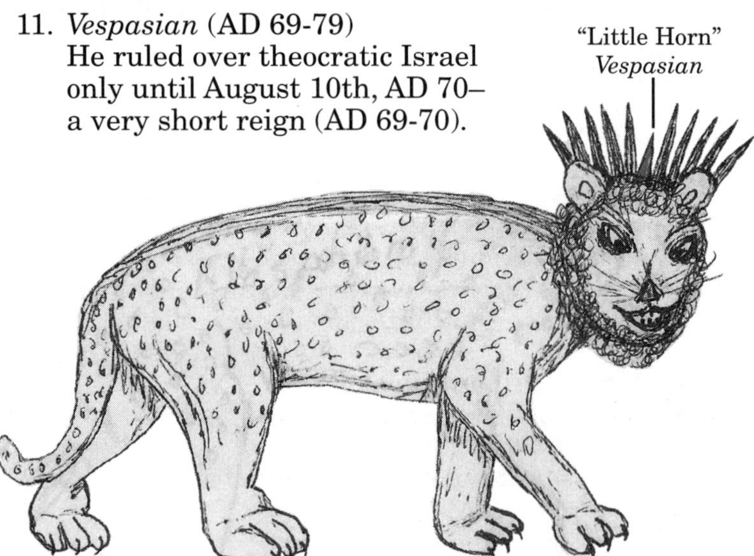

This "beast" is different from the 3 previous ones:
1. *Dreadful, terrifying, extremely strong and larger*
2. *Large iron teeth, and claws of bronze*
3. *Devoured, crushed, and trampled*
4. *Had ten horns at first, then another little one*
5. *Little Horn "pulled out" three before it*
6. *Little Horn had "eyes of a man" and a "mouth uttering great boasts"*

First, in reference to the chart on the opposite page, we look at the evidence to support Pompey as the first ruler. Pompey, along with Crassus and Julius, formed the alliance known as the Triumvirate (59 BC). This didn't last long. Caesar took his army to Gaul 58 B.C., leaving Pompey and Crassus in Rome. Crassus left to manage Syria and the eastern front, but was killed in the battle of Carrhae (53 BC), leaving only Pompey. Pompey was elected sole consul, from 52 to 49 B.C., until Caesar returned to Rome. Julius defeated Pompey in battle (48 BC). Pompey escaped to Egypt where he was killed (47 BC). Julius took control. *The Students Reference Works*, vol. 3, p. 1525, *Western Civilization,* p. 188.

Second, "Pompey [was] commissioned by [the Roman senate] to restore order in the empire in 52 B.C. and elected sole consul, [he] was virtually dictator of the empire until 49 B.C." *Illustrated World History*, pp. 238-247.

Third, The people and senate elect Pompey consul to regain power for the empire; Pompey agreed to repeal the obnoxious laws of Sulla.

Fourth, "The half century after Sulla's death was one of the greatest confusion and witnessed the final collapse of the Roman republic; sometimes the senate was in full control, sometimes the assembly, and sometimes, a strong man, or dictator; the strong man usually had the support of either the senate or the assembly, but always the army. One of these strong men...was Pompey until 48 B.C." *Man and His History*. A Roman Catholic textbook on world history and Western Civilization. p. 142.

Fifth, "Pompey by bribery won the election as Consul in 70 B.C. He had won universal admiration, and wondered why Rome waited so long to make him, in everything but name, a king. Pompey was given full authority over the navy. While in Cilicia, his friend Nanilius offered the assembly a bill transferring to Pompey full command of the armies and all the provinces. The measure was readily passed by the assembly after Marcus Cicero spoke before the assembly in the defense of Pompey. Thus Pompey had taken another step toward the sole leadership of Rome." *Caesar and Christ,* Vol. 3, pp. 138-145.

Sixth, "Caesar moves upon Gaul, Pompey and Crassus elected consuls. (*Ibid*. p. 176).

Seventh, "Crassus would have opposed the dictatorship by Pompey. Crassus was killed, and Pompey allies himself with the conservatives. His plans now for supreme power had only one obstacle, Caesar. Caesar removed to Gaul, Pompey secured decrees that continued his command until 46 B.C. In this way he would become master of Rome." (Ibid. p. 179).

Eighth, "Senate house burned, Pompey brought in to dispel the mobs; as a reward Pompey asked for and received consul, without colleague, one-man rule, dictator of Rome." (*Ibid.*, p. 180).

Ninth, "Pompey was looked upon as the new Democratic leader of the empire, was elected to consul, and had the support of his father-in-law Julius Caesar and the armies; he directed the change of new laws for Rome." *History of Nations*, Vol. 3, pp. 288-290.

With all this evidence, I cannot but see that Pompey was the first of the Roman rulers, or the first horn, in Daniel's vision. The evidence indicates that Pompey rose through the ranks from General to full power over the armies of Rome, as well as the provinces of Rome, then was elected by the senate as sole consul, ruling over all Rome as dictator. Other sources, not listed, show the same evidence. There can be no doubt that Pompey was the first ruler of Rome.

Most scholars do not accept Pompey as a ruler of Rome. Perhaps the question can be solved if we understand that Pompey did rise in power and become the sole ruler in his period, although Julius did not at the time approve of Pompey as sole ruler of Rome. Nevertheless the Senate approved of Pompey in the absence of Julius, and Daniel sees Pompey as one of the horns. Pompey was an important man in respect to the Jews; he was the one who brought Israel under the yoke of Rome in 63 B.C., and later was approved by the Senate as dictator.

Although I can see this explanation as being in harmony with Daniel's vision of the eleven horns, it will not fit the vision of John in Rev. 17:10. But there is no good reason to suppose that both visions must exactly match. Therefore, in John's vision he saw the kings as beginning with Julius, for he says, "Five have fallen, one is, the other has not yet come, and when he comes, he must remain a little while. He was speaking of Galba, who came to power in June AD 68 and was deposed in January AD 69. This is in harmony with the vision of Ezra, which is recorded in the *Old Testament Apocrypha*, 2 Esdras 12:15. Again there is no scriptural reason why the vision of John should be exactly like that of Daniel.

Since we will not give the history of the horns between Pompey and Vespasian, we will now be concerned with the eleventh horn of Daniel. First we must note those things recorded during the reign of Vespasian and compare them with scripture. We must consider the fact that the eleventh horn was the horn with which Daniel was most concerned. Daniel saw this horn as one who would bring an end to Judaism and his people. This is the one to whom God would give the people for a "time, times, and a half time," or three and one-half years. This period parallels the siege of Jerusalem.

A. The eleventh horn was to subdue three horns, or kings. There can be no doubt that Vespasian did subdue three kings, all small kings who reigned short periods. They were Galba, Otho, and Vitellius, who came up and went down in a year and a half, and were followed by Vespasian. Notice v. 20, "and the meaning of the ten horns that were in its head, and the other horn which came up, and before which three fell." What the interpretation is speaking of is this: before Vespasian comes to power, three small kings will reign each for a short period, and each will be disposed of in his own order. The eleventh horn can be none other than Vespasian. It cannot be watered down to mean someone else.

B. "He would speak out against the Most High." Not being a Christian, and being subject to Roman policy under Nero, not only did Vespasian speak against the saints, he persecuted them, routed them from their homes and places of assembly. It was common to speak out against those he had orders to destroy.

When Nero met Vespasian in Achaia, northwest of Athens, Greece, Nero gave the command to Vespasian and instructed him to destroy the Jewish population. This would also to a certain degree destroy the church. The route Vespasian would use would carry him from Achaia through Macedonia, Thrace, and into Asia Minor, then he would move upon Israel. So when John wrote the letters to the seven churches of Asia Minor (in Revelation), he warned them of the impending destruction as a result of Vespasian moving through this area.

C. "He was to wear down the saints of the Highest One." The book of Revelation was given as a warning to the people, and exhorts the seven churches to stand fast in the face of disaster. Those who overcame this trial would be given a crown. After having gone through the area of the seven churches, Vespasian continues the siege against the Hebrew nation by moving into Israel.

D. "He will intend to make alterations in times and in laws." Dan. 7:25. The historian *Suetonius*, Vol. 2, pp. 303-314, mentions the following:

1. He [Vespasian] recalled and freed those convicted by Nero.
2. Changed the law of the palace guard, a no-no.
3. Closed the temple of Janus, which was forbidden.
4. He was a plebeian, forbidden to hold king's office.
5. Roman law demanded all conquered countries to conform to the culture of Rome. Vespasian would not allow his native country to observe this law.
6. Nero, in making policy for the Roman emperors, decreed they should be worshiped and have control of all wealth. Vespasian (to his credit) would not be worshiped; he declared war on extravagance, and lived and ate as a very simple man.
7. The Law of Rome was that anyone found guilty of a plot to assassinate the king must die. Priscus laid a plot to kill Vespasian, the plot was exposed, and Priscus was brought before Vespasian. He was forgiven and restored to office.
8. Vespasian changed the law governing the choice of the Senate; he brought into Rome his own countrymen to fill the Senate, men from Patrician and Equestrian families. This change brought decency and order into the life style of Rome.
9. The law was changed regarding schools, teacher's pay, and retirement. All should be paid out of public funds, and after twenty years teachers should be retired.
10. Roman law stated there should be no one be-

tween the Caesar, the Senate, and assembly. Vespasian decreed that his son should share the throne with him, and delegated unlimited powers to him. Thus Vespasian changed the whole system of Rome.

E. "And they will be given into his hands for a time, times, and a half time" (or three and one-half years). On pages 24 and 25 I mentioned the reckoning of prophetic time, and stated that each must be considered in its own context. Since this text represents the eleventh horn, we must be able to state the events which occurred during the reign of the eleventh horn, and moving the "time, times, and a half time (or three and one-half years) from the reign of the eleventh horn is not authorized. After all, Daniel was shown only the first eleven horns, and his concern was with the eleventh horn. The angel's interpretation applied only to the eleven horns, and especially to the eleventh. This was the period when the Lord would come in judgment upon the world. Zech. 14:1-5; Mal. 4:1-6; Lk. 21:20-22. This period also encompassed the destruction of theocratic Israel. It was the "fullness of time" when all things would be summed up in Christ, Eph. 1:10. It was a time when Israel will be trampled under foot by the Gentiles. Lk. 21:24. A time when old Jerusalem would pass away and New Jerusalem come forth, Gal. 4:22-31. A time when the tabernacle of David would fully, and without competition, be restored. Acts 15:16-18. A time when a New Covenant would be fully given (it was not fully given when Hebrews was written). A time when the old would fade away and the new be fully known. A time when we shall be enrolled in the Church of Christ, a time when God will again shake the earth (not yet shaken when the Hebrew letter was written). A time when Judaism would be removed, and the kingdom fully established. Heb. 12:22-29. A time period when Christ would return in judgment upon the world. Dan. 7:22; James 5:7-9. A time when Christ would judge Israel. Ps. 50:1-9. A time when the mystery (gospel) of God would be completed, Rev. 10:7.

If Vespasian is not the eleventh horn, and the "time, times, and a half time" does not originate in this period of time, if "time, times, and a half time" represents, as some claim, 350 years, then the mystery of God, the gospel of Christ, the Church of Christ, the kingdom, and the passing away of theocratic Israel did not occur until AD 350. Consider the full implications of the 350-year theory! We can only fit into God's pattern by accepting Vespasian as the eleventh horn, and the "time, times, and a half time" as a time consummated during his reign. John said the holy city would be trodden down by the Gentiles, Rev. 11:1, 2. John again said that the holy city would be given to the beast for forty-two months (three and one-half years), or a "time, times, and a half time." And again the church would flee into the wilderness for forty-two months: "Time, times, and a half time" all refer to one and the same period of time. Vespasian received his orders while Nero was visiting Greece in AD 67, on Feb. 10. The war lasted until Oct 10, AD 70.

The above evidence gives credibility to the idea that "time, times, and a half time" means three and a half years, and was consummated during the reign of Vespasian. Further, the Gospels, and especially Matthew, are an expansion of the Old Covenant, which offers the book of Revelation as a full commentary upon Daniel and his visions. The gospel of the kingdom was not about indulgence. Judaism was such a gospel, and therefore would be destroyed–at the "time of the end."

F. Having the New Testament concealed in the Old is but a matter of truth, and being able to see the fulfillment of the old in the new is but fact. It contains also an implicit reference to truth, even through the human instruments who propagate it.

Propagate it we will, but will it be according to God's pattern and will? Have we prepared ourselves, as did Daniel, to look into the mysteries of God? Have we determined to teach God's ways rather than force upon others our own way? Do we pass the test of fellowship? I beg the reader's indulgence here as I give an example.

Look at Daniel 7, where four great beasts come forth from the raging sea. They are considered by almost everyone as four world empires, namely: Babylon, Medo-Persia, Greece, and Rome. Now, as we examine Daniel's concern, it was not for his people during the reign of Babylon, Medo-Persia, or Greece. Rather he was concerned what would befall his people during the reign of Rome, the fourth beast.

Just how far into Roman history did Daniel's vision extend? In Dan. 7:19-20 we see Daniel desired to know more about the fourth beast, and especially the exact meaning of the eleven horns. This was his concern. Why?

During the period of the eleven horns, Israel would be brought under the yoke of Rome. Pompey was the man who accomplished this, and later became sole ruler of Rome. The angel gave Daniel no interpretation beyond the eleventh horn and v. 27. But some will take v. 25 and move it 350 years beyond the eleventh horn. Does this propagate the truth of God's Word? Or does it propagate one's own selfish opinions, in order to find a future fulfillment for Revelation?

Since I have introduced Revelation into the body of material, it becomes necessary to examine the kings mentioned in Revelation 17:9b-10a. "The seven heads are seven mountains on which the woman sits, and they are seven kings; five have fallen, one is, the other has not yet come." We will consider only a few of the many proofs of who the woman and the kings were.

First, the woman who sat on the seven mountains was represented as a harlot, and Jerusalem was that harlot, not Rome. Rome was never at any time "the holy city." It was never in covenant relationship with God so as to come under God's covenantal wrath like Israel. After the captivity of seventy years in Babylon, there were times when Israel became very weak, and fell from the love of God. But there was never a time like the one when Antigonus took Jerusalem by storm, and the brutality began. Phasael dashed out his brains while in prison, then Antigonus cut off the ears of his other brother, so that he could never hold the office of governor.

Herod was in Rome, and here Anthony and Augustus crowned him king of Judea in 37 B.C. A short time later, with the aid of Herod, Augustus became emperor of Rome. Here is when Jerusalem, through the Herodian tree, became well known as the harlot who sits on seven mountains, and it is here that John begins the seven kings, with Augustus. The outrages in Jerusalem turned love into hatred, thus they were described as the mother of harlotry, and it was during the reigns of Herod and Augustus that this all began. It is no wonder that John would begin his signs of the end with kings well-known to everyone. The *International Standard Bible Encyclopedia*, Vol. 3. pp. 1378-1383.

Second, Rev. 17:2 speaks of the kings of the earth having committed immorality with her. Ezekiel 16 depicts Israel at an earlier time as a harlot who had committed immorality with every passerby. So here apostate Jerusalem, in broken relation with God, was given the mystic name Babylon, the mother of harlots. From generations past the execration of Israel had increased from the time of the prophet's reprobation in Isa. 1:21 to the Lord's lamentations in Mt. 23:29-39.

Third, the martyr Stephen laid upon Jerusalem the criminal charges of "betrayers and murderers," Acts 7:52. The descriptions given in Rev. 14:8, 17:1-6, 18:1,2 were but extensions of the continuing apostasies of Jerusalem.

Fourth, there was a series of immoralities of Jerusalem which would bring about their utter destruction. The Jews fared well under the leadership of Pompey and Julius. However, with the Herodian family and with Augustus, the calamity against Israel began.

John's concern was to show when immorality moved from a minor scale to a major one. Thus, his explanation counts Augustus, Tiberius, Caligula, Claudius, Nero, and Galba. This makes Nero, who died June 9, AD 68, the fifth, and Galba the sixth. This seems to fit precisely the passage of Rev. 17:10, "Five of the seven heads of the beast are fallen, the one, [Galba] is in power, the other, the seventh is not yet come; and when he cometh he must continue but a little while." This leads to the conclusion that the Apocalypse was written during the short reign of Galba, between June 9, AD 68, and January 15, AD 69. The seer in this chapter clearly distinguishes the beast as a collective name for the Roman Empire (so used also by Daniel) from the seven heads, kings, or emperors. Nero is one of the five heads who ruled before the Apocalypse was finished. He was slain by his own hand, and the empire fell into anarchy for two years, until Vespasian restored it, and so the death stroke was healed, Rev. 13:3. The three emperors between Nero and Vespasian were usurpers, and here represent an interregnum and the deadly wound of the beast.

Fifth, John did not recognize in his count those kings who did not play a great role in the destruction of Israel. He did not count Pompey and Julius, or the two little horns, Otho and Vitellius. He listed Galba because his release from Patmos was determined by Galba. Thus the seventh king of John 17:9-10 would be Daniel's eleventh horn, Vespasian.

Sixth, in defense of this postulate, I offer the following history to establish its credibility. "In AD 67 Vespasian was commissioned by Nero, while Nero was in Greece [AD 66-67], to suppress all Israel. Vespasian leaves his summer quarters in Antioch of Pisidia and receives his orders from Nero. He advanced into northern Galilee and by the end of AD 67 all Galilee was in the hands of Vespasian. Civil war and famine broke out in Jerusalem and all Judea." *Encyclopedia Britannica*, Vol. 15. pp. 400-402.

Nero visited Greece in late AD 66. At the end of the yearly games, Nero left Greece for Asia [AD 67], where he entered the temple of Diana at Ephesus and carried away all the valuables of the temple. "While Nero was in Asia, he sent two of his esquires back to Rome to bring him word of Paul's death." *Fox's Book of Martyrs*, p. 4.

The above offers the evidence that Vespasian received his orders from Nero, while Nero was on an extended visit to Greece and Asia in AD 66-68. Nero remained close by the battle front. After leaving Greece, he visited the cities of Asia, not for a friendly visit, but to kill and plunder. It may have been reported to Nero that John was a teacher of the hated sect called Christians, and that this is the reason Nero sentenced John to the barren rock called Patmos. There are many who have researched this matter and believe John was indeed banished to Patmos during the reign of Nero. I will mention only three of the best sources for this information: Kenneth Gentry (*Before Jerusalem Fell*), Foy Wallace (*The Book of Revelation*), and Arthur Ogden (*The Avenging of the Apostles and Prophets*). After leaving Asia in early 68, and returning to Rome at the insistence of his freedman Helius, Nero found Rome in civil war and strife. *Encyclopedia Britannica*, Vol. 19. pp. 393. 1911 edition.

Seventh, if John was banished to Patmos even before Nero left Rome for Greece in 66, John was dependent upon Galba for his release. If John was banished by Nero while both were in Asia, then John's release was determined by Galba. Since John said five have fallen, and one is in power, the obvious conclusion is that John wrote the Revelation before the destruction of Jerusalem in AD 70. And that makes the seventh king of John to be none other than Vespasian, the eleventh horn of Daniel, who would wear down the saints, change laws, speak out against God, disrupt the church, and who would be given the people for a "time, times, and a half time." They were in the hands of Vespasian from Feb. 10, 67 until Oct. 10, AD 70, precisely three and one-half years.

Eighth, from the evidence I must conclude that Vespasian was the eleventh horn of Dan. 7:25, and that the "time, times, and a half time" represented three and one-half years. Further, I conclude that the kingdom was to be given to the saints during the reign of the eleventh horn. I affirm that when Jerusalem was destroyed, every vestige of the Jewish nation was also destroyed, which meant that the kingdom could be received by the saints without religious competition from any source authorized by God. The church, or kingdom, at this time was full-grown. If "time, times, and a half time" meant 350 years, as some say, then the saints would not receive the kingdom until that time, for the scripture is very clear that the Lord would come in a physical judgment, and then the saints would take possession of the kingdom. Where is the prophecy, or historical account, of Jerusalem being destroyed in AD 70 and again in 350 AD?

This brings us to Daniel 7:22, where three outstanding points must be considered: (1) The coming of the Lord, (2) judgment, (3) saints receive the kingdom. We must ask ourselves some very pertinent questions. (1) Do I believe that we now have the kingdom? (2) Do I believe that Christ is now reigning in his kingdom? (3) Do I believe that Christ is now our High Priest? (4) Do I believe that Christ now has all power in heaven and on earth? Allow me to project some ideas here, and from these ideas perhaps we can answer the above questions.

Verse 22. "Until the Ancient of Days came, and judgment was passed in favor of the saints of the Highest One, and the time arrived when the saints took possession of the kingdom."

What was taking place and what would continue to happen until the Ancient of Days came? Verse 21 informed us "that horn waged war with the saints," the horn being the eleventh horn (Vespasian).

Are there other Old Testament passages which depict the "coming of the Lord" during the fourth kingdom, and especially during the reign of the eleventh horn? Perhaps we can show some that will give the reader insight into His coming. Turn back to Isa. 62:11-12, "Before the Lord comes, the Word must be preached to the ends of the earth." Paul tells us that during his lifetime the word was preached to every creature under heaven, Col. 1:6,23. After the word had been preached, then, according to Isaiah, salvation would come, and with Him would come rewards for the righteous, while His recompense went before Him [that is, judgment went before Him]. Verse 12 of Isaiah 62 indicates that after His coming, He would be the only name sought after, in other words the only one who could offer salvation. This is equal to Zech. 14:9, so Isaiah is saying that the Lord would come after the gospel had been preached to every creature, or to the ends of the earth. This coming is referred to as the "Second Coming."

In Joel 2:28-32 the coming of the Lord is called the great and awesome day of the Lord, v. 31. To see how this was carried over into the New Testament, look at Acts 2:16-21: Peter told the men of Israel, "But this is what was spoken of through the prophet Joel." What the people witnessed on that day and those following was fulfilled prophecy. But Acts 2:17-20 says that "the spirit" would be poured out, that prophecy would continue, that visions would not cease, that supernatural wonders would fill the earth, that there would be blood and fire, that the sun would be turned into darkness, and the moon into blood. But, notice the latter phrase in v. 20, "Before the great and glorious day of the Lord shall come." Is it not possible that a ten-year-old child could understand this? It simply means that all the above would continue in force "until the Lord come." Now this leads me to ask a question, if the Lord has not yet come, then we must affirm that there are those who now possess the gifts of the Holy Spirit, which included prophecy and visions, is that correct? Peter said these things would continue in use "until," or "before," the coming of the Lord. If the Lord did not come, then we still have prophets and visions, right?

Let us remember that in the Old Testament a thing was confirmed by the mouth of two or three witnesses. May we call the Apostle Paul to the witness stand, and see if he confirms what Peter has said. 1 Cor. 1:7-8, "So that you are not lacking in any gift, awaiting eagerly the revelation of our Lord Jesus Christ," v. 7, and "In the day of our Lord Jesus Christ," v. 8. What has Paul just said? That spiritual gifts would not be lacking until, or up to the coming of our Lord. I suggest that the prophecy of Joel quoted by Peter has just been confirmed by the mouth of a second witness.

Well, is there more? Yes, please turn to Zechariah 14:1-5. What is said here? (1) The day of the Lord is equal to the Lord coming. (2) The nations are gathered against Jerusalem to destroy it. (3) His feet will stand on the Mount of Olives. (4) The Lord will come, and all the holy ones with Him. The next verse, 14:6, is equal to Zech. 13:1 and Rev. 21:1, while the balance of the chapter depicts the church as Holy Zion, the city of God, the assembly of the church, New Jerusalem. See Heb. 12:22.

Now let's look at the first chapter of Zephaniah. It is said that this book depicts the carrying away of Judah in 586 B.C. by King Nebuchadnezzar. If it does, then there are questions in this chapter that God left unanswered. They are: Verse 2 says that God will remove all things. To remove all things means there should be nothing left upon the face of the earth, it was annihilated. Now I ask, was the earth annihilated in 586 B.C.?

When Paul said "old things are passed away, all things are become new," he was talking about what Christ was doing in His Church. (2 Cor 5:17) Were all things made new in 586 B.C.? No. Old things passed away and were made new in the period of Christ. Christ brought the final administration of God's redemptive work in the "fullness of time" to sum up all things in Himself and the Church. (Eph. 1:10)

Now we can understand the significance of the Lord's sacrifice in Zeph. 1:7-8. You see, according to the writer of the Hebrew letter, Christ was offered as a sacrifice only once. Heb. 9:26 and Zeph. 1:7-8 speak of this same sacrifice. And Zeph. 1:13 says their wealth will become plunder, and their houses desolate. Zechariah spoke the same words in 14:1-5, and he was not speaking of Jerusalem in 586, was he? Zeph. 1:14-18 is equal to 2 Peter. 3:10-13. In short, Zephaniah speaks of the Lord coming, of His judgment, and reward in AD 70.

I have already said that the "coming of the Lord" was equal to the "great and terrible day of the Lord." So now if we look at Malachi 4:1-5; what do we see? (1) The day is coming when the arrogant will burn in judgment. (2) The arrogant was none other than Israel. (3) There will be neither root nor branch of them left. (4) The righteous will shine forth. (5) We know that this speaks of Israel for v. 4 informs us of that. (6) Elijah will come before that great and terrible day of the Lord ("second coming.") Now the question arises, has Elijah come already, or is he yet to come?

Our Lord said in Matthew 11:11-14 that John the Baptist was Elijah. This is confirmed by our Lord again in Matthew 17:9-13.

James said during his lifetime that the "Judge" was standing right at the door. Jesus said in Matthew 16:27-28 that some of those to whom He spoke would live to see Him come back in the kingdom.

Our Lord informed the apostles that they would not finish going through the cities of Israel before He came back, Mt. 10:23. The same coming is named in Mt. 24:30. When our Lord was asked when He would come back (Mt. 24:3), this answer described the destruction of Jerusalem, which was to say that He would come back at that time. Is the evidence conclusive, or shall we deny the scriptures?

We find the same synthesis among the prophets regarding the subject of judgment.

When the Ancient of Days would come in judgment, "Judgment was passed in favor of the saints of the Highest One," Dan. 7:22. Malachi speaks of the same judgment, "Then I will draw near to you for judgment; and I will be a swift witness against the sorcerers and against the adulterers and against those who swear falsely, and against those who oppress the wage earner in his wages, the widow and the orphan, and those who turn aside the alien, and do not fear Me, says the Lord of hosts." Mal. 3:5. Verse 6 continues, "For I, the Lord, do not change; therefore you, O sons of Jacob, are not consumed."

It is quite obvious that the sons of Jacob are the righteous seed of Abraham, and they–the righteous ones–will not be consumed. This is equal to Daniel saying that judgment was passed in favor of the saints of the Highest One, and equal to the white throne judgment of Dan. 7:9-10.

Some may say, "the white throne judgment has not yet occurred." If the white throne judgment of Dan. 7:9-10 has not occurred, then we can throw away the book of Luke, for it records that Jesus said, "For I tell you, that this which is written must be fulfilled in Me." Luke 22:37. And "These are my words which I spoke to you while I was still with you, that all things which are written about Me in the Law of Moses and the prophets and the Psalms must be fulfilled." Luke 24:44.

Where and when did Jesus say these things would take place? "When you see Jerusalem surrounded by armies, then recognize that her destruction is at hand; for these are the days of vengeance that all things written may be fulfilled." Luke 21:20, 22. This means that the judgment of which Daniel spoke had to occur no later than AD 70 when Jerusalem was destroyed. If not, then we cannot place any credibility in anything Jesus says.

I suggest that Malachi and Daniel were prophets, and were recognized by our Lord as such. As true prophets, all they spoke would have its fulfillment no later than the destruction of Jerusalem.

John corroborates the time: "Now judgment is upon the world, now the ruler of this world shall be cast out." John 12:31. A judgment of the world, the same judgment seen in Dan. 7:9-10, in Dan. 7:22 and Mal. 3:5. At this judgment the ruler of this world is cast out (see Rev. 20:10), Satan and his works destroyed. Heb. 2:14; 1 John 3:8. "And He, when He comes will convict the world concerning sin, and righteousness, and judgment." John 16:8. Obviously the judgment was connected with His "Second Coming," at least that is what John says.

Judgment is clearly connected with the Second Coming. "...the coming [Gr. "parousia"] of the Lord is at hand, do not complain brethren, against one another, that you yourselves may not be judged; behold the Judge is standing right at the door." James 5:8-9. "But they shall give account to Him who is ready to judge the living and the dead." 1 Pet. 4:5. "Now it is time for judgment to begin with the household of God." 1 Pet. 4:17.

From 2 Cor. 5:17-19 it appears that for old things to pass away and all things to be made new, then judgment was necessary, if indeed there was a judgment, then the "coming of our Lord" is confirmed.

Note the correlation between Daniel and Jesus. "And the kingdom was given to the saints of the Highest One." See Dan. 7:18, 22, 27. Jesus said to the Jews "Therefore I say to you, the kingdom of God will be taken away from you, and be given to a nation producing fruit of it." Mt. 21:43. Was this kingdom given, or established, at Pentecost when Peter preached? Throughout the New Testament, it is spoken of as being future, yet "at hand." Notice Mt. 6:28 where the "coming of the Lord " is associated with the coming of the kingdom.

In Luke 21:31 the kingdom is at hand, and its arrival is associated with the coming of Christ, the judgment, and the destruction of Jerusalem. Let's put this "to the test." Paul said, "Every fact is to be confirmed by the testimony of two or three witnesses." 2 Cor. 13:1.

Let's call Isaiah to the witness stand. "For a Child will be born to us, a son will be given to us; and the government will rest upon His shoulders; and His name will be called wonderful Counselor, Mighty God, Eternal Father, Prince of Peace, there will be no end to the increase of His government or of peace, on the throne of David and over His kingdom, to establish it and to uphold it with judgment and righteousness." Isa. 9:6-7. (Some versions say justice, the two words are equal). So His kingdom will be established with judgment. Was there a judgment of the world at Pentecost? Or at AD 70, or yet to occur?

Remember, before discussing Dan. 7:22, I said there were some pertinent questions we should ask ourselves? May we list those again? (1) Do I believe that we now have the kingdom? (2) Do I believe that Christ is now reigning in His kingdom? (3) Do I believe that Christ is now our High Priest? (4) Do I believe that Christ now has all power in heaven and on earth?

I have shown evidence that the "Second Coming" was connected with His delivering the kingdom to a new nation, also that His Second Coming was connected with the judgment of the world. Now I suggest that if Christ has not made that "second appearing," then we have no kingdom, there has been no judgment, and while we await the "Second Coming," we also await the arrival of the kingdom, where He will be High Priest and will reign in His kingdom. If He has not yet come, then He is not on His throne, at least that is what Matthew said " But when the Son of man comes in His glory, and all the angels with Him, then He will sit on His glorious throne." Mt. 25:31. Other scriptures that confirm Jesus, as the High Priest are Heb. 3:1; 3:17; 4:14; John 2:1,2.

Matthew said that Jesus must first come with all the holy angels, then He would sit on His glorious throne. One may say, "but, is this confirmed by the prophets?" Yes, Zech. 14:5. If the prophets were fulfilled, as Lk. 22:37; 21:20-22; and 24:44 all indicate, then the "coming" with all the holy ones must also be fulfilled? Yes. "All power is given me in heaven and on earth." Mt. 28:18.

Eight Horns from the perspective of John.
1. Julius (47-44 BC)
2. Augustus (31 BC to AD 14)
3. Tiberius (AD 14-37)
4. Caligula (AD 37-41)
5. Claudius (AD 41-54)
6. Nero (AD 54-68)
7. Vespasian (AD 69-79)
8. Titus (AD 79-81)

John's vision (in Rev. 17) does not include the three that Daniel's eleventh horn was to uproot, namely, Galba, Otho. Vitellius, nor does it include Domitian.

Notice John states that the seventh king would reign but a short time; and here we have the seventh, namely Vespasian who reigned for ten years. In no way can this mean a short time. To get a ruler who must reign but a short time, we must strike Julius Caesar, and begin with Augustus Caesar, which puts Vespasian on the throne at the time when John writes, and states, "Five have fallen, one is." Namely Vespasian, who reigned 69 to 79, and then the next who came up would reign but a short time, namely Titus, who reigned for two years.

There is no little dispute over the eleven horns of Daniel, and the eight kings of John. Yet there is one most important point to remember, and that is that regardless of what his name was, the sixth ruler of Rome was in power during the time John wrote the Apocalypse: "Five have fallen, one is." So the sixth, whether Nero or Vespasian, would still mean the Apocalypse was composed before the fall of Israel.

The eleven horns have been covered quite thoroughly, so I will now move back to the judgment scene in vv. 9-10.

Verses 9-10. "I kept looking until thrones were set up, and the Ancient of Days took His seat, His vesture was like white snow, and the hair of His head like pure wool. His throne was ablaze with flames; its wheels were a burning fire. (10) A river of fire was flowing and coming out from before Him; thousands upon thousands were attending Him, and myriads upon myriads were standing before Him, the court sat, and the books were opened."

Since this series of visions pertained to Daniel's people, there is no good reason to assume that this scene of judgment did not also pertain to Israel, as indicated in Dan. 10:14. The fact is that John also saw this judgment scene, in Rev. 20:4. Notice the following:

1. Dan. 8:26: Daniel is told to keep the vision secret, for it pertained to many days future.
2. Dan. 10:14: "I have come to give you understanding of what will happen to your people in the latter days, for the vision pertains to many days yet future."
3. Deut. 31:29: "Evil will befall you in the latter days."
4. Deut. 28:49-68: "The Lord will bring a nation against you from afar, from the ends of the earth, as the eagle swoops down, a nation whose language you shall not understand."
5. Dan. 12:1: "Now at that time Michael, the great prince who stands guard over the sons of your people, will arise. And there will be a time of distress such as has never occurred since there was a nation until that time; and at that time your people everyone who is found written in the book, will be rescued."

6. Dan. 12:13: "But as for you [Daniel], go your way to the end; then you will enter into rest and rise again for your allotted portion at the end of the age.

7. Zech. 14:1-4: "And I will gather all nations against Jerusalem."

8. Mt. 23:29-39: "Behold your house is left to you desolate."

9. Mt. 24:15: "Therefore when you see the abominations of desolation spoken of by Daniel the prophet, let the reader understand."

10. Lk. 21:20: "When you see Jerusalem encompassed with armies know that her desolation is at hand."

11. Rev. 5: the books of curses opened against Israel.

12. Rev. 20:12: "And the book of life was opened."

13. Gal. 4:22-31: "Israel cast out."

From the preceding passages I observe the following:

1. The judgment scene of Daniel 7:9-10 pertained to the judgment of Israel in AD 33 or from the cross until the Jewish temple was destroyed in AD 70. Further, that the resurrection began just after Christ's, Mt. 27:52-54, and that every man in his own order received resurrection, 1 Cor. 15:12-23. At least some of true Israel was looking forward to some kind of resurrection on the third day after the death of the Messiah. Hosea 6:1-3, cf. Mt. 27:52,53.

2. The scenes of Daniel 7:9-10 and Rev. 20:4 are looking at one and the same judgment, that of Israel.

3. The tribulation Daniel spoke of and the one Christ referred to in Mt. 24:22 is one and the same tribulation. Further, the apostle Paul confirms this in 1 Thess. 3:4 when he states, "We warned you about the tribulation, and now it has come to pass, and you know it." See also 2 Thess. 2:5.

4. That the book of curses opened in Revelation chapter 5 is the material that Daniel was told not to write, to leave it "sealed up until the end time." The end time referred to here was the end of the Mosaic age when Judaism would be abolished. And those books that Daniel sealed up until the end time is revealed by John at the end time.

5. Daniel saw the book of life opened 12:1, and those

of his people who had throughout the ages re-mained righteous would from this book be judged, Rev. 20:4. Jesus made it known who would sit in judgment against Israel. Mt. 9:28. James, writing to the Jews scattered abroad, made clear the judgment by saying, "Behold the judge is standing right at the door," Jas. 1:1. There can be no question who James was speaking to. Peter confirms this: "The end of all things is at hand." 1 Pet. 4:7. Then he qualifies his statement: "Now it is time for judgment." 1 Pet. 4:17

Verse 11. "Then I kept looking, until the beast was slain, and its body was slain and destroyed in the burning fire." The eleventh horn of v. 8 is here referred to as the beast. Daniel moves from the judgment scene to say that he kept looking and saw the beast destroyed.

Daniel's concern was the eleventh horn, which here is represented as a certain ruler rather than the empire itself. The eleventh horn was the one that would bring destruction upon the commonwealth of Israel, and cause the temple to be destroyed. Thus the abolishment of Judaism would naturally follow. It was God's plan that Christianity should no longer have religious competition, and especially that of divine origin.

It is not the empire that Daniel sees destroyed here, but the beast who was given power to persecute and to destroy. The passage does not infer that when the beast is destroyed, all persecution will cease, but when the beast had consummated God's will. Just as in the case with Nebuchadnezzar, God had no further need for him, thus he was destroyed. It was not because God foreordained him to hell, but because the beast made that choice.

Verse 12. "As for the rest of the beasts, their dominion was taken away." The rest of the beasts here represent the three empires who would fall before Rome came up, Babylon first, Medo Persia second, and Greece third. When Medo Persia overran the Babylonian Empire, the government of Babylon was abolished; their dominion was taken from them by Persia. And when Greece came into world power, Greece took dominion from Persia.

So it was that the people of these countries remained,

but they had lost their identity as Babylonians, or Persians, or Greeks. When Rome became a world power, then all nations came under the government of Rome. So Daniel saw the first three world empires taken away, in accordance with King Nebuchadnezzar's dream of Daniel 2.

Verses 13-14. "One like the Son of man was coming, and He came up to the Ancient of Days." This is an Old Testament resurrection verse, and Daniel here sees the Son of God ascending back to the Father, after His resurrection from the dead. "Men of Galilee, why do you stand looking into the sky? This same Jesus who has been taken up from you into heaven, will come in just the same way as you have watched him go into heaven." (Acts 1:11).

Israel had no problem with the resurrection from the dead, they had been taught the importance of the resurrection, their problem was the time, and what part they would share in it. See Hosea 6:1-3. Daniel was promised a part at this time also. Dan. 12:13. They all had their part in the resurrection, but only after Christ had broken the seal of resurrection, Mt. 27:52-53. After the resurrection of Christ the first fruit, then every man in his own order, 1 Cor. 15:12-23, until the end, 1 Cor. 15:24. After death comes judgment, Heb. 9:27. It stands to reason that the dead must be raised out of Hades first and given some kind of bodily form, so that judgment could take place. *New Testament Commentary on Hebrews,* by Robert Milligan, p. 265.

> "And to Him was given a kingdom, dominion, glory and power." Here Daniel sees the fulfillment of his interpretation of Nebuchadnezzar's dream, "And in the days of those kings the God of heaven will establish a kingdom, one that will never be destroyed." Dan. 2:44. This is the fifth kingdom that Daniel saw, this was to be unlike the four, which were earthly kingdoms, the fifth was to be a spiritual kingdom, "Not of this world."

It is clear the fifth kingdom was to be established in the days of the Roman kings, the first eleven Daniel saw. Dan. 7:20-25 indicates when the saints will receive the kingdom of God, and reign therein without religious competition. It was established during the days of "those kings" in AD 33 Roman calendar, and was relieved of any divine religious competition when the temple in Jerusalem was destroyed in AD 70.

In Mt. 16:18, Jesus informed Peter, "Upon this rock I will build my Church." And again, "And unto thee I give the keys to the kingdom." Church and kingdom are interchanged here as the same spiritual institution. It is called the house of the Lord in Isa. 2:1-3. It is called the church in Romans 16:16, and the Church of the Lord in Acts 20:28, where all those souls who received baptism on Pentecost, as well as those who were being saved daily, were added to the church, Acts 2:47. Paul stated that he had been transferred from the domain of darkness to the kingdom of God's beloved Son. Col. 1:13. John, in his letter to the seven churches of Asia Minor, said, "I, John your brother and fellow brother in tribulation and in the kingdom."

The kingdom was no afterthought on the part of God. It was in the scheme of redemption, planned before the creation of man, Mt. 25:34.

Yet there are those who deny the clear teaching of God on the subject, and therefore teach that the kingdom has not arrived and that Christ will establish that kingdom when he makes his second appearance. And further, they teach that Christ had come to establish his kingdom, but upon being rejected by the Jews established the church instead, then at His second coming will establish the kingdom and reign therein for a thousand years.

This doctrine has been brought about by the abuse of the book of Daniel, and especially 9:24-27, where the time element is abused and falsely applied. Then the book of Revelation has received no little abuse.

Verses 15-28. This section deals with the kingdom from the vantage point of the saints. Christ is the King who receives the reign from the Father. He rules over this kingdom which is given to the saints. Let's look more closely at this kingdom that is mentioned here and especially in the New Testament writings.

The following dissertation will set forth the true character of God's Word, and show the great error that ensues when one has the idea that God has not yet established his kingdom.

Scripture shows that the kingdom would be established at the time of the "Second Coming." But we have been so influenced by tradition, we did not notice what scripture really says. The kingdom is indeed predicated upon the "Second Coming," so setting a future date for the Second Coming forces many other things to be put in the future, things which we absolutely cannot still place in the future. Note:

1. His reign in His own kingdom, predicated upon "Second Coming." Mt. 25:31.
2. Having His own Throne predicated upon "Second Coming." Mt. 25:31.
3. Judgment of the world, predicated upon "Second Coming." Mt. 25:32.
4. Being King, and having all power, predicated upon "Second Coming. Mt. 25:34.
5. Jerusalem destroyed and cast out, predicated upon "Second Coming." Zech. 14:1-5.
6. New Jerusalem coming down from heaven predicated upon "Second Coming." Gal. 4:26,31, Rev. 21:2, Heb. 13:14, Mt. 16:28.
7. The changing of powers in heaven, when God abolished all rule and authority, received His kingdom, and gave Christ all power in heaven and on earth, at the "second coming" when the enemies were destroyed, 1 Cor. 15:23-24.
8. Full salvation, without competition, and promise, predicated upon "Second Coming." Heb. 9:28. Remember Peter said in Acts 2:39 that the promise was to the Jews, their children, and to those afar off. Promise of what? These people were charter members of the kingdom, like Paul in Col. 1:13 and John in Rev. 1:9. Obviously the kingdom was still future, Luke 21:31.

Before discussing the problems of a postponed kingdom, let's look at some scriptures which nail down the *time* of the "Second Coming."

1. Zech. 14:1-5. Time of the destruction of Jerusalem.
2. Mt. 10:23. Before the apostles could finish going through Israel.

3. Mt. 16:28. During the lifetime of His disciples.
4. Mt. 24:1-30. During the physical casting out of Jerusalem.
5. Mark 8:38, 9:1. During the lifetime of those who stood around Him, and heard Him preach.
6. Luke 21:1-32. During the destruction of Jerusalem.
7. John 21:21-24. During the lifetime of John.

Some say that the kingdom was established at Pentecost. This idea comes from Mark 8:38 and 9:1, which says that the Holy Spirit would establish the kingdom with power. Note the kingdom would be established with power, not by power. And further, the kingdom was to come when Christ came. Therefore Christ would be in the wrong place at the wrong time if the kingdom was to come at Pentecost. According to Acts 1:11, Christ was taken up before Pentecost, and according to Acts 2:33, Christ was at the right hand of God pouring out the Holy Spirit.

Now for the problems associated with a future coming. If Christ did not come when the scriptures say, then we yet await the kingdom, we yet await Him to become our High Priest, and we yet wait for Him to sit on His throne. He is not our King, and we have no salvation. Can you see how inconsistent some teaching becomes?

This subject of the kingdom is where many varied opinions arise. Some say that the saints possessed the kingdom of Rome, others say we have not yet received the kingdom, and still others say the kingdom was established on Pentecost after Christ's death.

In the following, I hope to set forth scriptural thoughts which will serve to add credibility to the idea that the kingdom of Christ was not fully established until the time when Judaism was taken out of the way.

A. Jesus in Lk. 22:28-30, Mt. 19:28 informs his chosen disciples, that He will appoint them a kingdom, wherein they may eat and drink at His table, and where they will sit on thrones, and judge the twelve tribes of Israel.
    1. If we affirm this text represents the establishment of an earthly kingdom, wherein the disciples would reign as judges, then we are looking at the same doctrine the Jews held. They were

looking for a physical kingdom. It must be a difficult subject to understand, for the disciples before Pentecost did not understand. Acts 1:6

2. In Dan. 2:34, the stone is said to be cut out without hands, indicating that which is spiritual. Therefore, Dan. 2:44 gives the proper interpretation of Dan. 2:24, "kingdom."

3. 2 Cor. 5:1: for we know that if our earthly tent which is our house (body) is torn down, we have a house from God, not made with hands, which awaits us in heaven. Again, not made with hands signifies that which is spiritual.

4. The kingdom which is to be appointed to the disciples, where they would judge the twelve tribes of Israel, signifies a spiritual kingdom. Matthew taught this when he said, "And Jesus said to them, truly I say to you, that you who have followed Me in the regeneration when the Son of Man will sit on His glorious throne, you also shall sit upon twelve thrones, judging the twelve tribes of Israel." Mt. 19:28

B. Since Jesus is to sit upon his glorious throne, Mt. 25:31, where is his throne located? Zech. 14:9 states that the Lord would be King of the whole earth, which includes his kingdom. Zech. 14:1-8 says that the Lord being made King of all the earth was predicated upon the destruction of theocratic Israel. If Christ now reigns in his own kingdom, where is that kingdom located? We find the answer in the scriptures. Since Christ has all power on earth, Mt. 19:28, is it possible that anyone else could have any power? Zech. 14:9-10 states that the Lord would be the only one, and His name the only name. Does this leave Satan any power at all? Would Rom. 16:20, Heb. 2:14, 1 John 3:8 help us to understand this question? Would we not deny the very purpose of the death of Christ if we affirmed that Satan and his kingdom still exist on earth? Please look to Zephaniah 3:14. "Zion is being redeemed."

The Kingdom of God, of Heaven, and of Christ

Respecting the kingdom in Dan. 7, I submit these questions which I believe are very important to an understanding of the Kingdom as it is dealt with in both the Old and New Testaments.

A. What is the difference between the kingdom of God, and the kingdom of heaven?

B. Does Paul make a distinction between the two kingdoms? In Col. 1:13 he informs the Colossians that he has been transferred out of the domain of darkness into the kingdom of His beloved Son. Is the kingdom of Christ different from the Church of Christ? Or were the two one and the same institution? According to Col. 1:25 Paul was made a minister in the Church of Christ. Is this what the passage states? Or was Paul in two different institutions?

C. Did Christ come to His own (the Jews)? And was He rejected as being their King? Luke 19:14. Did He not say that He would build His church? Was He speaking to the Gentile world at this time? Did He promise the Jew the church? Did He promise that they would retain the kingdom? If the kingdom and the church were the same spiritual institution, then the Jews had the kingdom before the Gentiles received it, for Christ said after He had been rejected, that He would take the kingdom of God from the Jews, and would give it to a nation who would produce fruit of it. Mt. 21:43. Was it this kingdom that the saints were to possess in Dan. 7:22? Or was it the kingdom of Rome the saints of Dan. 7:22 were to possess? If indeed it was the kingdom of Rome, would that not make Christ the king of the Roman Catholic Church? There is a popular doctrine which states that the saints took possession of the kingdom of Rome in the fourth century, and that because of their taking that kingdom, it would be judged, and its dominion would be taken away, it would be annihilated and destroyed forever, Dan. 7:26. Isn't something wrong here? Is not the Roman Catholic Church the most powerful in the world?

D. May I suggest that when we rearrange the time, times, and a half time in Dan. 7:25 to be other than the time when the horn would make war with the saints (being the little horn that came up after the ten, making it the eleventh), we are inviting all kinds of strange doctrines? Our minds are then prepared to see doctrines which are not yet fulfilled, and which clouds our minds with traditionalism? Christ said that when theocratic Israel was destroyed, "all things which are written are fulfilled." Lk. 21:20-22

Is it an unfair question to say then that he spoke the absolute truth, and all things have been fulfilled? I suggest it is not nearly as unfair as it is to say that the Old Testament is not fulfilled, or was not fulfilled until the fourth century!

It also seems that Apostle Paul made a distinction between the kingdom of Christ and the kingdom of heaven.

A. What does 2 Tim. 4:18 really teach?
B. Did Paul acknowledge that he was in the earthly kingdom? See Col. 1:13.
C. Did Paul know the difference between the kingdom on earth and the kingdom of heaven?
D. 2 Tim. 4:18, "And will bring me safely to His heavenly kingdom."
E. Does this imply that Paul was looking forward to being with God after his physical death? If so, then again we must consider the resurrection.
F. Is this passage equal to Eph. 3:14 and Phil. 1:20-24?
G. If not, then there is no family in heaven and Rom. 8:19-21 can be removed from the Book.
H. But if there is a kingdom of heaven, then can we understand Mt. 25:34? And can we understand that we inherit this kingdom after having been found righteous, and after physical death?

Paul stated that he was in the kingdom, Col. 1:13. Paul was flesh and blood, yet through the blood of Christ he was made to be a spiritual being, yet he said it was better to depart the flesh and be with Christ, Phil. 1:21-23. Paul infers that before entering the kingdom of heaven one must put on immortality, 1 Cor. 15:50-54. Peter said that greater blessings awaited us in heaven, 1 Pet. 1:4. There must also be a kingdom of heaven. The two promises made to Abraham were intended to be the basis of a twofold relation to God, and the foundation of two distinct religious institutions, called "the Old Covenant and the New." Two covenants, one a covenant of promise. Two kingdoms, the first with temporal and typological connections, the final kingdom as the spiritual fulfillment.

Two good reasons may be offered why Matthew, the oldest Christian writer, generally prefers "kingdom or reign of heaven" to the phrase "kingdom or reign of God." I say "generally" for he occasionally used both designations. Mt. 6:33, 12:28, 19:24, 21:31,43. He also found a good reason in the idiom of the Jewish prophets for using the word heaven (both in the singular and plural form) for God. Daniel told the Babylonian monarch that his kingdom would be sure to him when he would have learned that "the heavens do rule"; yet in the preceding verse he says, "till thou knowest that the Most High rules in the kingdom of man." Thus Matthew was authorized from the Jewish use of the word to regard it as equivalent to God. If, then, Matthew had meant no more by the phrase "kingdom of heaven" than the "kingdom of God" he was justified, by the Jewish use of the word heaven, to apply it in that sense.

Some may object to these remarks about Matthew's manner, and say it was Jesus Christ and the preachers He commissioned who called it the kingdom of heaven, and not Matthew Levi. To such I reply that the other sacred writers uniformly, in reciting all the parables and incidents, use the phrase "the kingdom of God" and never the phrase "the kingdom of heaven." From the use of the phrase "kingdom of God," we must, I think, regard him as having special reference to the "kingdom of God." He does not say the kingdom of heaven shall be taken from the Jews, but "The kingdom of God shall be taken from you, and given to a nation bringing forth fruits of it." Although Jesus here implied the Jews already had the kingdom of God in some sense, it could not be said they had the kingdom of heaven as described in Matt. 21:43. Accordingly, the Jews had the temporal kingdom of God, and they were to prepare themselves by righteous living to inherit the kingdom of heaven. According to Jesus Christ, it was the kingdom of God that was taken from the Jews and given to the Gentile nations. (Mt. 21:43)

When compared with the earthly kingdom of God among the Jews, it is certainly the kingdom of heaven, for Jesus alleges that his kingdom is not of this world; and Daniel affirmed that in the days of the last worldly empire the God of heaven would set up a kingdom unlike all others then on earth. Paul taught that God's people are now "blessed with every *spiritual* blessing in heavenly places in Christ." (Eph. 1:3)

Evidently the kingdom of heaven is "the kingdom of Christ and of God." Eph. 5:5 It is the kingdom of God, because He set it up. (Dan. 2:44). He gave the constitution and the king, and all the materials out of which it is built. Jer. 31:31,34. It is the kingdom of Christ, because God the Father gave it to Him as His Son, who is the heir of all things, and therefore, "All that is the Father's is mine," says Jesus, "and I am His." (John 17:10) "God created all things by Jesus Christ and for Him."

God is the author of the constitution of the kingdom of God and of heaven. He propounded it to the Word that was made flesh, before the creation of mankind.

The earth is now the Lord's, the present temporal territory of his kingdom; the heathen people are given to Him for His inheritance, and the uttermost parts of the earth for His possession; all the ends of the earth are His. All that He redeems are His seed, His subjects in the kingdom of God and Christ. (Zech. 14:9)

Heaven and the kingdom of heaven are not the same thing. God is not the kingdom of God. But, as the kingdom is something pertaining to God, so the kingdom of heaven is something pertaining to heaven, and consequently to God. The kingdom of heaven is the last abode of the righteous redeemed from earth through the temporal kingdom of God and Christ. (1 Pet. 1:4)

The following conveys a classic example of the kingdom of this world, and the kingdom not of this world. When speaking in Judea, Jesus said, "There are some of you standing here who shall not taste death until you see the Son of man coming in His kingdom." (Mt. 16:28). For sure, Jesus intended to return to earth, and He would come in His kingdom, and the subjects of the kingdom of heaven would come with Him. Further, this coming in the kingdom would not be long after His death, because He promised that some of those who heard Him speak would still be alive. Many authorities say this passage represents the end of the Christian age! If so, then we have somewhere in the world a group of Jewish people yet alive and waiting the return of Christ in the kingdom of heaven. Further, they would be nearly 2,000 years old. We know this for sure, because Jesus promised that some of them would not die until He came in His kingdom. The answer to this absurdity is that Jesus did come in the kingdom of heaven in AD 70, when He brought wrath upon the earth, and removed the temporal kingdom of God. Zech. 14:1-5; Malachi 4:1-5. Luke 21:20-32 also confirms this very thing.

The key to understanding. We must understand the type, or we cannot understand the antitype. We must understand the natural before we can understand the spiritual things. God deals with man in ways that man can understand, in order to reveal the spiritual. The Bible is a spiritual book. It has answers for every spiritual question. We do not understand the natural, or the type; therefore, we look to the Bible for physical answers.

A classic example of this follows. Isaiah chapter 13 speaks of the Lord coming, and of great calamity. He will come in fire, and the fire will be so severe that it will melt the flesh of the people. The stars, moon, and sun will be darkened in that great and terrible day of the Lord. This chapter is given in physical terms and we accept it as such, and apply our reading to the end of all time. But look at v. 1: "An oracle against Babylon." This is given in natural terms so that we might understand the spiritual. God was here foretelling the fall of Babylon, not the end of all time. Isaiah chapter 34 uses the same language. Throughout the New Testament this type of language is used. 2 Peter 3 is an example in the New Testament. The physical is shown in order to reveal the spiritual.

We do not understand the kingdom of heaven because we do not understand the kingdom of God, the temporal kingdom. The kingdom of God and Christ is but the door to the kingdom of heaven.

Concluding Observations on Chapter 7

1. Dan. 7:4, From this verse, and from Jer. 22:25, I observe that Babylon was indeed the first of the four beasts seen by Daniel.
2. Further, the four beasts of Daniel would only encompass the time period of the Hebrew nation, from the time King Nebuchadnezzar came down into

Judah, according to God's direction, and end with Rome utterly destroying Old Israel.

3. Dan. 7:5 (cf. Isa. 13:17; Jer. 51:11) From these texts I observe that the second nation to be used by God as his instrument was the Medes. At this point there is no mention of Persia. (See also Dan. 5:28; 8:3)

4. Dan. 6:6; 8:8-9; Ezek. 28:7; 30:11; 26:11-14. From these passages, I observe that the third beast was Greece, with Alexander the Great as its leader. Further, I observe that King Nebuchadnezzar laid siege against Tyre for some thirteen years, however, he did not destroy Tyre. Therefore, God gave Egypt to Nebuchadnezzar as his wages, Ezek. 29:17-19, so it was Greece who was ruthless. Ezek. 28:7

5. Dan. 7:7-8; Deut. 28:49; Isa. 5:26-30; Isa. 7:8-25. From these passages I observe that the fourth beast was Rome, in whose hands God had entrusted the utter destruction of Israel. But, someone asks, how about Isa. 7:8-25? Well, think for a moment, "In that day" God will bring about the birth of the Messiah, and in "that day" God will destroy Israel. Notice Isa. 7:17, a passage related to Mt. 24:21. Isaiah depicts the birth of Christ. In Isaiah's day the Northern Kingdom of Israel had a change of governmental covenants during King Ahaz, symbolic of the national disaster that would come in AD 70.

6. Dan. 7:9-10; Dan. 12:1; Mal. 3:5; Isa. 62:11; Mt. 12:49; John 12:31; James 5:8-9; Rev. 1-22. From these passages, I would observe that Zech. 13:7-9 and 14:1-5 speak of the white throne judgment. It would appear from Luke 21:20,22; 22:37; 24:44, that at the time in which Rome destroyed Israel, all Old Testament prophecy would be fulfilled. If it was not, then Christ knew little of that which He predicted.

7. Dan. 7:13-14; Lk. 19:11-15, Christ was caught up to heaven (Acts. 1:11), where the Father would present Him with the kingdom, and with all power in heaven and on earth, Mt. 28:18. I also note that at His "second appearing" He transferred the kingdom of God to other nations, Mt. 21:43. The kingdom could not have been established on Pentecost, for Christ had just been taken up to heaven (Acts 1:11), and at the very time of the outpouring of the

Holy Spirit and the birth of the church, Christ was at the right hand of God, Acts 2:33. Christ was in the wrong place at the wrong time for the kingdom to be established at Pentecost.

8. Dan. 7:15-21. I observe there are ten horns, then a little horn, making a total of eleven horns. These are the eleven rulers of Rome from the period in which Pompey brought Israel under the yoke of Rome and became the empire's first universal ruler, until Vespasian the eleventh who destroyed Israel.

9. Dan. 7:22. I observe that this passage sets forth the time in which Christ, the New King, will make His "second appearing," transfer the kingdom, render judgment to the world, and afterward He would sit on His own throne, Mt. 25:31. This would depict the fullness of time, Eph. 1:10.

10. Dan. 7:23-25. The fourth kingdom is to tread down the whole earth, and ten kings will arise, namely, Pompey, Julius Caesar, Augustus Caesar, Tiberius Caesar, Caligula Caesar, Claudius Caesar, Nero Caesar, Galba, Otho, Vitellius. Then Dan. 7:24 says another will arise. According to Dan. 7:21 it is this horn, the eleventh, that actually makes war against the saints. Nero declared war on Israel Feb. 10, AD 67 and sent General Vespasian (who would become the eleventh horn). It was this horn that waged war for the "time, times, and half time," three and a half years, until Sept. 10, AD 70. The evidence does not support a date later than AD 70. To make the "time, times, and a half time" fit some event 350 years later would discredit the words of Christ in Lk. 21:20,22 and 24:44. A later date would place the "coming" of our Lord at a time when *all* of those He spoke to in Mt. 16:28 would be dead, *some* of whom Jesus promised would still be alive at His return. And John would have been nearly 400 years old by that time! John 21:20-23 implies that John would remain until the Lord should "come." It would also discredit the testimony of James who said that the Judge was standing right at the door, Jas. 5:8-9.

11. Daniel 7 speaks of a judgment where a court will sit, confirming verses 9-10 of Dan. 7, and accordingly would be during the period of the eleventh

horn. And yet, when the court sits, his dominion will be taken away, annihilated, and destroyed forever. From this passage I observe the following:

a. That God would at "Christ's coming" abolish His power, after having received His kingdom, and would give Christ all power in heaven, and on earth 1 Cor. 15:24.

b. That "his dominion" really refers to the dominion and power of Satan being annihilated at the "second appearing." Further, that the evidence points to the destruction of Satan cast into his kingdom in the lake of fire, never to arise again. John said, "Now judgment is upon the world; now the ruler of this world shall be cast out," John 12:31. Paul informed the Roman Christians that "The God of Peace will soon crush Satan under your feet (during their lifetime). Rom. 16:20. The writer of the Hebrew letter said, "That through death He might render powerless him who had the power of death, that is, the devil." John corroborates this in 1 John 3:8. John also saw in the Revelation, chapter 20, the Devil being bound, evidently the binding took place at the cross as per Gen. 3:15. Rev. 20:7-9 shows that Satan was released for a short period, and v. 8 informs us as to the purpose of his release.

Accordingly, Satan was used as God's instrument for the three and one-half-year war with Israel, for v. 10 (of Rev. 20) informs us that the devil who deceived them was cast into the lake of fire, forever and ever. Now the same John in John 16:11 informs us that Satan now has been judged. Satan had the power of death, so says Heb. 2:14, but just before Paul's death, he says that death has been abolished. 2 Tim. 1:10

Therefore, Dan. 7:26 can mean either A or B above, and most likely means both, since both occurred during the period of His "Second Coming."

DANIEL CHAPTER 8

Introductory Remarks

This chapter gives an account of a vision seen by Daniel during the third year of Belshazzar's reign. Like many of the books of both the Old Testament and the New, the book of Daniel is not in chronological order. To be sure, chapter 5 looks to the end of Belshazzar's reign, while chapter 8 is given during the third year of the reign. However, to account for this, the book has been divided into two sections, the first a history which ends with chapter 6, and the second section of visions and prophecies beginning with chapter seven.

While chapter seven showed in v. 1 that Babylon was the empire in power, and was the first beast, Chapter 8 begins with the second beast (8:3) which would overthrow Babylon and govern the Babylonian Empire. The meaning of v. 3 is very simple, the ram had two horns, and one horn was longer than the other. Therefore, the short horn depicted the Median Empire, which was according to God's plan to receive the Babylonian Empire before Persia, Isa. 13:17; Jer. 51:11; Dan. 5:28. The long horn would depict the Persian Empire, and Daniel says that the long horn (Persia) would come up last.

Only after several years did Darius the Mede allow the Median Empire to merge into the Persian. We have no record that Darius the Mede sought to enlarge his empire by war, nor that there was any uprising during his reign; it was a time of peace. However, as soon as Persia gained full control, nations began to rise up against one another in rebellion.

In this chapter Daniel relates the terms of the vision and the interpretation given by the angel Gabriel. Gabriel instructs Daniel to know that the vision pertains to the time of the end (not the end of time). Daniel no doubt is shown much respecting his people, the nation of Israel, that he cannot tell them. He was to "keep the vision secret." Perhaps to know their fate in advance would have caused a loss of faith, and would have incited the people to even greater rebellion against God.

At the beginning of this introduction I stated that this chapter begins with the Median Empire coming against the Babylonian Empire, and that the Medes must retain the empire until God decides that they should merge with that of Persia. In v. 5 we see the male goat (Greece) coming up against the ram. The male goat was victorious, and magnified himself. But very soon the large horn (Alexander the Great) was broken from the male goat, but in its place came up four horns. That is, Alexander the Great met his death soon after he had been victorious over the world and in his place of power came his four field generals. These were Cassander, Lysimachus, Seleucus, and Ptolemy Soter, who was to gain control of the vast Grecian Empire, and who would divide the kingdom four ways. While Cassander would fight for Macedonia, Lysimachus would seek Thrace and Asia; Seleucus would gain Syria, while Ptolemy Soter would receive Egypt.

From vs. 15-27 we must understand that Daniel, and the angel, speak of two distinct time periods, and we must be able to separate the two with understanding. Notice vs. 17 and 19 speak of the final indignation against Israel, and uses the phrase, "time of the end." This refers to the final wrath poured out during the destruction by Rome. Then in v. 20 Daniel quickly returns to the events respecting Antiochus Epiphanes IV.

Verse 1. "And I saw in a vision." This vision seems to have occurred to Daniel while he was awake. Daniel sees the following events in a vision, and he contemplated it with earnestness to properly understand what is seen. Since Daniel was among the exiles he perhaps thought that the result of this vision would bring relief to the oppressed Jews, about whom he was much concerned, but instead he is told it pertains to his people in days yet future, Dan. 10:14.

"A vision appeared to me after to the one which appeared previously." Although chapter eight is the first recording of visions, it follows that the chapter is not in proper chronology. It should appear before chapter seven, for chapter seven is the third vision seen by Daniel. Verse 1 indicates that Daniel had two visions under Belshazzar, or more, for in v. 26 Daniel is told to keep the vision of the morning and evening secret; thus it is very possible that Daniel had more than two visions under Belshazzar.

Verse 2. "And I looked in the vision, and it came about that while I was looking I was in Susa." Daniel could have been carried away to Susa for the vision, or he could have already been in Susa. Why Daniel was in Susa is unknown, but he was on the king's business, for after the vision and the sickness passed away, Daniel continued to go about the king's business, v. 27. Daniel could have been sent to Susa among the exiles to give them hope of returning to their land after the seventy years was fulfilled, Jer. 29:10, or there could have been an uprising among the exiles. Or the father of Belshazzar, Nabonidus, could have sent Daniel to Susa to remain there while he, Nabonidus, was going about the land gathering up all the golden idols for his treasure. This could account for Belshazzar's not knowing Daniel, and had to be informed of him by the wife of Nebuchadnezzar who at this time was yet living.

Verse 3. "A ram which had two horns was standing in front of the canal." Daniel saw a ram with two horns, one longer than the other. There can be no mistake about the interpretation of this ram, v. 20 tells us that it was the kings of Media and Persia, and one horn was longer than the other. Persia was the long horn. Soon after Babylon fell, the kingdom of Media merged into Persia and Media was known only in history. Here the united power of the kingdom was denoted by the ram itself, and the two horns denote great power. The one high horn who springs up last would be the sole ruler of Persia. While the Median or Assyrian was older, Persia is now the mighty.

Verse 4. "I saw the ram pushing northward and southward"; this would denote the conquests of the United Kingdom of Persia. The east here is not mentioned. The Persians did not extend their conquest to the east. They were from the east, and nothing could better express the conquest of the Persians. On the west they possessed Babylon, Mesopotamia, Syria, and Asia Minor. To the north through Armenia, and all the area around the Caspian Sea. To the south the Persians conquered Palestine, Egypt, and all the area to the south. Isaiah represents this great power as coming from the east, Isa. 41:2. *Guizot's Ancient History*, 1844 ed., article "War of the Persians", p. 59.

The description given by Daniel in 7:5 of this kingdom is here being fulfilled as directed by the providence of God. This is the kingdom that will furnish Cyrus as king, who in turn will allow the Jews to return to their land, Isa. 44:28. Cyrus also would order that the temple be rebuilt, and the state reestablished, 2 Chron. 36:22,23.

Verse 5. "As I was considering the vision." It is natural to suppose from this statement that the vision was one of great calamity. It was one that could not readily be understood; it evidently denoted some combined power that was attempting conquest of the world.

Now a male goat is seen (Greece). No doubt Daniel was frightened, and much concerned. Like the vision of chapter 7, this was yet future. While Daniel is receiving visions of Greece mounting for war, and making this known to those within his reach, Zechariah is telling the exiles in the wilderness of Babylon the same thing. Zech. 9:1-7. "And behold he came from the west." Notice v. 21 where it is called the rough goat, the king of Greece. The goat represented the power of Greece when Alexander the Great went forth at God's appointed time in his subjugation of the vast Persian Empire.

At the height of the Persian Empire, only Greece remained unconquered, that is, a willing subject to Persia. Greece caused much trouble to the Persians and some nine years after the battle of Marathon, Xerxes the son of Darius assembled the largest army recorded in history (5 million men) and attempted the conquest of Greece, but lost the battle. God was not willing that Greece be conquered, for this was the next nation in His plan to be used against the Persians. *Guizot's Ancient History,* pp. 108-112. 1844 Ed.

Even now God was preparing Greece, a small nation with but little force, for the conquest of Persia. God was directing this preparation of Greece. The city state of Rome, the fourth beast of Daniel 7, was also being prepared to conquer Greece at God's appointed time. God had told the Hebrew nation that if they continued to rebel against him, He would in the last days bring a nation against them, one from afar, from the ends of the earth, one whose language they would not understand. Deut. 28:49-68

Verse 6. "And he came to the ram." The fair meaning is that the goat, which was Greece, came to the ram, which was Persia, and the goat made war and ran into him with the fury of his power. Here Alexander is represented as a fast-moving and fearless warrior. Alexander attacked the Persians at the Granicus at Issus and overran the Persians in their own country. "And I saw him come close to the ram," the ram was standing in the heart of the Persian Empire, and the goat is now seen to attack the ram in his own dominion. The goat was moved with great wrath and anger. The old sores of war that Persia had inflicted on Greece were being remembered by Alexander, and with anger he is to repay a debt long to be remembered by the people of Greece.

Young and ambitious, Alexander became a world leader, conquering as he went. He laid siege to the port city of Tyre. He gave orders for the debris to be cast into the sea, making a causeway out to the island city of Tyre, which lay from the shore about a mile. This city had withstood Nebuchadnezzar for thirteen years, but the causeway was constructed, and Alexander and his troops crossed it and destroyed the city. *History of Nations, Vol. 2* by P. F. Collier and Sons, pp. 483-510.

Nebuchadnezzar had a much larger army than that of Greece, so why could Nebuchadnezzar not conquer Tyre? The answer is simple; God was not ready for Tyre to fall. That would come in the period of Greece under the leadership of Alexander. He would make a complete waste to Tyre, fulfilling the scriptures, Ezek. 26:11-14. After Alexander left Tyre, the island sank beneath the waters, never to be seen again.

"And there was no power in the ram to stand before him." Throughout their reign, the Persians continued to meddle in the politics of Greece and continued a warfare against Greece. The wrongs inflicted on the Greeks were never forgotten. *Wycliffe Historical Geography,* p. 441-443.

Verse 7. Undoubtedly the remembrance of these afflictions caused by Persia would be a powerful motive driving Alexander the Great onward and adding force to his armies. Now the ram could not stand before the goat. The providence of God was assisting Alexander, and no power could stay his hand. It was now time for Persia to fall. God had so decreed. The Persian Empire was trampled to the earth.

"And there was none who could deliver the ram out

of his hand." No earthly power, no nation could come to their aid, no allies were left. The Decree of God was here being fulfilled. When Babylon fell to Persia, no earthly power could deliver them, it was decreed by God. Now Persia falls to Greece, and God's plan is fulfilled.

The angelic watchers informed king Nebuchadnezzar, "This sentence is by the decree of the angelic watchers, and the decision is a command of the holy ones, in order that the living may know that the Most High is ruler over the realm of mankind, and bestows it on whom He wishes, and sets over it the lowliest of men." Dan 4:17. So God had set Alexander over the kingdoms of mankind, and no one could stop him.

Perhaps all this was being done in such a way as to afflict the Jews and cause them to return to God before the final afflictions that would be brought on by the fourth beast, Rome. At that time the Son of God would be manifested in the flesh and would establish His spiritual kingdom. It would seem that all the visions of Daniel are pointing to one period of time, the end of Judaism, and the establishment of Christ's kingdom.

Verse 8. "Then the male goat magnified himself exceedingly, but as soon as he was mighty, the large horn was broken." The Grecian power, especially under Alexander the Great, became very strong. In the period of its greatest strength an event occurred that broke the horn, the horn where all the power of Greece lay. At no time was the empire so strong as it was prior to the death of Alexander the Great, but God said the horn must be broken and the empire divided. Alexander the Great had reigned only twelve years when death came unexpectedly. Alexander was thrown from his horse and died of the fever shortly afterwards in 323 B.C. He was married and had one son. They were both killed by power seekers, who removed every obstacle that might hinder them from seizing the throne. The horn of power was broken. *Guizot's Ancient History,* "Article History of Greece," pp. 139,140. *The Life of Greece* by Will Durant pp. 545-551.

The vast empire created by Alexander's unparalleled conquests was brought down by the struggle for power and the wars of his successors. Before the close of the fourth century B.C., his empire was broken into many fragments. However, four well-defined and important monarchies rose out of the ruins. The boundaries were rearranged following the decisive battle of Ipsus fought in Phrygia in 301 B.C. The four principal states were ruled by Lysimachus, Cassander, Seleucus Nicator, and Ptolemy Soter. Each assumed the title of king. Cassander governed Macedonia and Greece; Seleucus ruled Syria and eastward; Ptolemy ruled over Egypt; Lysimachus ruled Thrace and the western part of Asia Minor. *Guizot's Ancient History,* Article, History of Greece, pp. 145-147. *The Life of Greece* by Will Durant, pp. 540-551.

Verse 9. "And out of one of them came forth a rather small horn." From one of the four field generals of Alexander would come forth one whose son would spring up and become a persecuting power, a power later directed against the Jewish nation. This one who sprang up "waxed exceeding great." This one would cause the sacrifice in the temple at Jerusalem to cease. This "one who would come forth" does not infer a direct son of the General, but rather a grandson. This one was none other than Antiochus Epiphanes IV.

He would cause the Jews to worship idols; he would plunder the temple, taking all the riches from the treasure. *Old Testament Apocrypha* 1 Macc. 1:7, 9-10.

Chapter 8 is a brief of this period. Chapter 11 will give the full details of this period and the persecution of Antiochus IV. God keeps his promises. At the beginning of this nation God had warned Israel not to depart from him. If they did, the result would be unlimited tribulation, and here it is foretold again.

Verse 10. "And it grew up to the host of heaven." The host of heaven was the holy host of God who served in the temple at Jerusalem, the priesthood, the rulers of God's people. Thus Antiochus would grow very strong, and be lifted up with pride. He would exalt himself as a god, one who would change God's laws respecting worship. Antiochus carried his conquest to Egypt and to the east, and into Egypt for a second time. After his defeat in Egypt, he entered the Holy Land, and made war on the holy army of God, priest and worshipers, "The host of heaven."

"And caused some of the host and some of the stars to fall to the earth." This symbolic language can best be understood using the appendage inserted between chapters 6 and 7.

Antiochus did not literally cause the literal stars of the literal heaven to fall to the earth. Did this man actually make war with the holy angels in the realm where God abides? Did his power actually become as great as that of God? Of course, not! Then what is meant? "The host of heaven" meant the host of Israel, "heaven" meant the place of God's people, and the host was God's people. By "the stars falling to earth" what is meant? "The stars" were the rulers of Israel, and they would fall to earth, their power would be taken away. Why? Israel as a nation had again rebelled against God, the promised tribulation, the recompense for rebellion, had now come.

Do these symbols apply elsewhere? Yes, the Hebrews knew and had knowledge of such symbols. Such symbols had been used before, and they would be used in the New Testament. Do the symbols mean the same everywhere they are used? The symbols must be considered in each context; for the most part, they retain the same meaning.

An example is Mt. 5:18, where Jesus said, "Until heaven and earth pass away, not one jot or tittle shall pass from the law." What did Jesus mean by "heaven"? Until heaven passed away, no part of the Law of Moses will be abolished. Either the heaven here means the same Israel, and that Israel would pass away before the law would, or we remain under the Law of Moses.

The temple at Jerusalem was destroyed in AD 70. At that time the destruction of Jerusalem served to confirm the fact that the Law of Moses was forever destroyed. In just the same way the resurrection served to confirm Christ as being the Son of God, Rom. 1:4. The resurrection was necessary; the destruction of Jerusalem was also necessary. It furnished solid proof that the heaven spoken of in Mt. 5:18 had passed away. Babylon was depicted as a heaven in Isa. 13:1-17. I observe a pressing need for the careful study of Hebrew symbols, first observed in the Old Testament, and followed up in the New Testament.

Daniel is looking at the second physical judgment that will come on Israel, the first being by Nebuchadnezzar in carrying away Judah in three episodes, ending in 586 B.C. The second is by Antiochus IV. Yet this still does not finish God's wrath against the wicked Jews. The prophets were sent, they were rejected. Christ had to come to this nation in the flesh and give them the last chance to return to God and accept the New Covenant.

All the prophets of the Old Testament foretold the end of Israel. Like Daniel, they may not have fully understood that which they foretold. Isaiah gave no comfort to Israel when he foretold their end. Notice the following:

1. Isaiah 24:1-5. The inhabitants of the earth scattered, the earth laid waste, all people become equal. What makes all people equal? The earth mourns, the world fades, and the exalted people will fade away; the earth polluted by sin.

2. Isaiah 24:6-11. A curse devours the earth, the inhabitants are burned and few are left (sounds almost like 2 Pet. 3), the vineyard decays, the music-makers stop, the taste of wine is bitter, the happiness of earth is banished, replaced with sorrow; desolation is left in the city.

3. Isaiah 24:13-18. The great desolation will be in the midst of the earth. I recall Palestine as being in the middle of the earth, there will be a great shaking, and when the desolation is over they will shout for joy, they will cry out for the Lord. Then glory to the Righteous One will be heard, but the wicked will cry out in pain, they are to be burned, v. 6. Only terror will confront the wicked.

4. Isaiah 24:18-23. No escape for the wicked, the windows of heaven are opened, and judgment is poured out, the earth shakes, the earth is broken! The earth is split, the earth reels to and fro like a tree on a windy day! The earth totters! Sin is heavy upon the earth! The earth will fall, never to rise again!

   So it will happen in that day. The Lord will punish the host of heaven (the wicked) and the kings of earth. And all will be gathered together (Zech. 14:1-4, also a gathering). The moon and sun will be ashamed of the sin of earth! After this, the Lord will reign on Mount Zion in Jerusalem.

Pertinent to this chapter are the following questions:

1. To what period of history does Isaiah relate this desolation? The Northern Kingdom of Israel in 722 BC, the southern kingdom of Judah in 586, Judah

under the bonds of Antiochus IV in 186 B.C., or to the final overthrow of Israel in AD 70? This could be typical of any of those periods. But the point to be made is, whatever period is under consideration, it is expressed in symbols. If taken literally, then you have the end of the world in verse 20! Is this not a similar passage with 2 Peter 3, regarding the same nation?

2. From these observations it will be clear that Daniel 8:10 is not referring to the literal stars falling from the literal sky. (Isa. 24:21) Instead, Isaiah refers to the government and leadership of Israel as the host of heaven. Where was Israel? The kings of the earth represented the kings of other nations. Look at Isa. 34:4, where the "heavens "were to be rolled up like a scroll. Did Isaiah refer to Dan. 8:10, which refers to the host of Israel, and not to the literal heaven?

Verse 11. "It magnified itself equal with the commander of the host." The idea here seems to indicate that Antiochus would consider himself both a ruler of civil affairs, and that of a religious leader, and would think of himself as being equal or above the high priest or perhaps equal to the God of Israel. In so doing he would become the master of the host of heaven, he would be minister of religion, meaning that all authority was invested in him, and no one could worship any gods other than those he prescribed. To this end Antiochus commanded the Jews that they should not worship as before, but should comply with his orders and should burn sacrifice to the idol gods. He forbid the Jews to circumcise their children. Those found guilty of doing so were punished on the spot, their child killed and hung around the neck of the mother for many days. The Book of God and the Law of Moses were to be searched for and burned where found. *Old Testament Apocrypha*, 1 Maccabees 1:41-64.

Verse 12. "And on account of transgressions the host of heaven will be given him."

Again we come upon the host of heaven, or rather the host of Israel. Already I have covered fully the symbol use of the words "the host of heaven," and already we have seen that this expression can mean only the people of Israel, and not at the end of the world. We have already seen that the same symbols are used many places in the New Testament, and there, when speaking of the Jews, has the same meaning "the host of Israel."

Here we have the reason for the "host of Israel" being given into the hands of Antiochus: sin. Israel had again transgressed God's law for man, and now they must suffer the consequence of that sin. The host of the Jewish people were given into his hands at the time of the daily sacrifice, the sacrifice and the people passed into his hands at the same time. God gave up the "host of heaven" and their temple, and gave them into the hands of Antiochus as punishment for prevailing iniquity.

Joshua chapters 6 and 7 reveal sin in the camp. Israel was not successful in battle because of sin. Furthermore, Israel could not progress. Neither can the church, when sin is present.

Verse 13. "Then I heard a Holy One speaking, "How long will the vision about the sacrifice apply." The vision was now ended, and Daniel represents himself as hearing the angels speak among themselves. He asks how long this desolation will apply, how long will the "host of heaven" be given into the hands of Antiochus, and how long would it be before the sacrifice would be restored?

It appears here that one angel had more knowledge about the impending event than the other, and one seeks to know the details of the desolation upon Jerusalem and the temple.

Verse 14. "And he said to me, for 2,300 evenings and mornings, then the holy place will be restored." The question of the angel is here answered, as the other angel refers the statement to Daniel. Respecting the period that the "host of heaven" would be given into the hands of Antiochus, the angel says that 2,300 evenings and mornings will pass before the holy place will be restored. Each of the "evenings and mornings" here must be considered as a twenty-four hour day. Thus the whole period of time would be near seven years, and this time would pass before God would allow the holy place to be restored.

We are not to confuse this event with that of Daniel 7:25, where the scripture speaks of the saints being given into the hands of the eleventh horn which came up from the fourth beast, or the kingdom seen by Daniel. In Daniel ch. 7 he makes it very clear that he is much depressed about the fourth beast and the eleventh horn. Therefore, chapter 8 does not deal with the fourth beast, which is the empire of Rome. Again, if we applied Dan. 7:25 to the period of Antiochus IV, then we would have Christ coming in about 168 B.C., and the kingdom established in that period. This would not fit either Biblical or secular history.

Some have understood this text to mean that after the 2,300 days, the Jews would return to the temple to worship. If this is true, then it would mean that Christ came in the period of restoration, and instead of establishing the kingdom, He established or restored the physical temple, and this would make the scriptures of the New Testament dealing with the spiritual kingdom ineffective and void. That would mean that we are still under the Law of Moses, awaiting the final return of Christ when he will establish the kingdom! Absurd.

Verses 15-27. Within the commentary already given, I have covered the angel's interpretation of the above. In the following verses the angel gives to Daniel the interpretation of those things seen and heard in the vision. However, I will make a full display of vs. 17-19 following. Beyond that I shall refer the reader to the interpretation given from vs. 1-14.

Verse 17. "But he said to me, son of man, understand that the vision pertains to the time of the end." In the future time when the divine indignation shall be manifested toward the Hebrew people, the beginning of these calamities would therefore bring forth the end, seen in chapter 8 as beginning with Antiochus. It therefore pertains to a series of events which are to introduce the latter days, when the kingdom of God (Christ) will be established, and Judaism abolished. In justification of this statement compare 1 Cor. 10:11, "Now these things happened to them as an example, and they were written for our instruction, upon whom the ends of the ages have come."

It is everywhere represented that these calamities would come upon the Jews, and would occur as proof of the divine displeasure in sin, and Judaism would at the end time be abolished. Compare Dan. 9:24-27; 11:35; 10:14; 12:4. 2 Macc. 7:33. There is a divine and definite plan of

God, and when the time for it arrives, the end of all this will take place. The affairs of the world under the Mosaic dispensation will be wound up, and a new order of things will exist.

Verses 17-19. The end meant here cannot be the time of Antiochus IV. When the end comes, it will close out the Mosaic Law. What begins here is the time of extreme calamities upon the Jews, which will result in bringing about their end. Legally that time came when Christ was on the cross, Heb. 9:26. But by God's plan and purpose, the Jews were given some forty years to merge into Christianity before they were destroyed. The destruction of the temple confirmed the kingdom of Christ. It ended the national religion of the Jews. That is the time the angel in vs. 17, 19, referred to.

The "end" cannot mean the ultimate end of time when Christ will deliver up the kingdom to the Father. Such is contrary to the revealed plan of God. If such were true, then according to Dan. 8:14, we would be worshiping in the temple, not the kingdom, and we would still be under the Law of Moses. If this verse proves anything, it proves that after Antiochus destroyed the temple at Jerusalem, then after seven years it would begin to be rebuilt, and the Jews would return to temple worship before the coming of Christ to establish His kingdom.

Verse 26. "And the vision of the evenings and mornings which has been told is true; but keep the vision secret, for it pertains to many days in the future." Daniel admits that this vision was subsequent to the one which appeared to him previously, v. 1. The angel in v. 26 tells Daniel he is to keep the visions of the evenings and mornings secret. Just how many visions Daniel received up to this point is uncertain, for he saw and heard things that he was instructed not to write. He was not to reveal all the visions.

Not everything was revealed to the Jews in Daniel's writings. Look at chapter 10:1, "In the third year of Cyrus King of Persia a message was revealed to Daniel, who was named Belteshazzar, and the message was true and one of great conflict, but he understood the message and had an understanding of the vision."

First we have Daniel giving the description of himself, and then a full description of the angel. Then the angel speaks to Daniel and tells him "Now I have come to give you an understanding of what will happen to your people in the latter days, for the vision pertains to the days yet future." Then Daniel reveals that the vision was such that he became speechless and fell down. Then the angel touches him, and he stands upright. But, where is the vision that was so terrible? See vs. 15-18.

The vision is not here revealed. This record of this vision under Cyrus was perhaps the last vision Daniel received, closing this chapter under Cyrus. The angel returns to Persia to fight against the prince of Persia, and prior to leaving Daniel informs him, "However, I will tell you what is inscribed in the writing of truth."

Now look at the beginning of chapter 12. The angel, before leaving Daniel, tells him the final outcome of all the events he had just foretold. In Dan. 12:4, Daniel is told to seal up the book, leaving the things he is not permitted to write sealed up until the end time (meaning that these sealed-up things would not be more clearly revealed until the end time, the close of the Mosaic age, when the Messiah would come). Therefore, chapter 12 seems to be a continuation of chapter 10. And chapter 11 seems to deal with the same events as chapter 8. See our comments elsewhere on the reign of Darius the Mede, which occurred before Cyrus came to the throne.

If these visions were not to be revealed to the Jewish nation at this time, then when were they revealed? And in what book?

Respecting the end time and those things which Daniel was not permitted to write, the angel said, "There will be a time of distress such as never occurred since there was a nation." Dan. 12:1. In Mt. 24:21 Jesus said, "There will be a tribulation." Paul says in 1 Thess. 3:4 that the people were in the tribulation. Could it be that the book of Revelation reveals that which Daniel could not?

DANIEL CHAPTER 9

Introductory Remarks

In Chapter 7, we saw the prophecy which began to foretell the utter destruction of Judaism and the Hebrew nation, as well as the beginning of universal Christianity. Chapter 9 deals with matters which greatly concerned Daniel, and his prayer was not answered in such a way as to give him relief. Rather, when the angel came to him, the angel brought more distressing news of his people and their nation. Here I feel a need to review some of the more pertinent points of chapter 7, which in turn, will better prepare the reader for chapter 9.

    A. The concern of Daniel is over the ten horns, and then the little horn which would wage war against the saints. I have already shown many events which would occur during the period of the eleventh horn, namely: "Coming of the Lord, judgment, giving the kingdom to another nation without competition from Judaism, a time when He would sit on His own throne, becoming King of kings, as well as being High Priest, a time when the Father would abolish His rule and authority, and appoint to His Son the Messiah to all power and authority in heaven and on earth.

    B. So the reader not be confused respecting the "coming of the Lord," it is necessary to say that the scriptures reveal the Lord's coming as one which would result in judgment, and not to annihilate the earth. To explain this notice the following.

        1. In Genesis ch. 3 where "the Lord comes," the result is judgment upon Adam and Eve.

        2. In Genesis ch. 6 when Jehovah God visits Noah and informs him of the impending judgment upon the world, and that for sin, the event is called a "coming of the Lord."

        3. In Genesis ch. 18 and 19, a "coming of the Lord" resulted in judgment upon the cities of the plain.

        4. In Exodus 3:8 a "coming of the Lord" resulted in freedom for the exiles, and judgment upon the land of Egypt.

        5. In Isaiah 19:1 a "coming of the Lord" is another

judgment upon Egypt.

6. These are only a few of the many passages which depict a "coming of the Lord." Both Old and New Testaments are full of such "comings." Perhaps this will in a small way help the reader understand the "coming of the Lord" named in the book of Daniel.

C. The reader should also understand that this chapter is highly controversial. There are several varied opinions respecting vs. 24-27, and this survey makes no pretense of being the final authority on the subject. The reader should remain free to search the scriptures, and decide for himself which is right. I have no authority to judge another person's writings as error, or to castigate that writer for what he believes is correct. Only Jehovah God has that right, through His Son the Messiah.

D. There is a most important study in Dan. 9:1. The chapter was written during the first year reign of Darius, the son of Ahasuerus the Mede, who was made king over the Chaldean empire. It is necessary to relate some facts respecting this king. It is alleged that Darius the Mede did indeed receive the empire of the Chaldeans, however, the same doctrine states that Darius the Mede was not the king who overran Babylon, further that the Median empire was not the instrument in God's hand who would destroy the empire of Babylon. Instead the doctrine says that it was King Cyrus, and Darius the Mede was not the Darius of Haggai and Zechariah. Therefore, I give the quotation from the source which is generally accepted by the church:

> "It was Cyrus who brought about the fall of Babylon and ended the New Babylonian Empire in 539 BC... He was 'the battle axe' with which Jehovah was to shatter Babylon (Jer. 51:20), and as he proceeded on his path of victory, the unknown Seer whom we call the Second Isaiah, welcomed him as the liberator of his people... (Isa. 44:26-28)." *International Standard Bible Encyclopedia,* Vol. 1, p. 575, Article 18.

> This statement by itself, without a disclaimer, can

cause much confusion to those who believe in the inspiration of Holy Scripture. For example, notice Isa. 13:17; here is the battle ax, and neither Cyrus nor Persia is mentioned. Notice Dan. 5:28, "The kingdom has been given over to the Medes and Persians." Accordingly, the Medes were to receive the kingdom first, then the Persians. Notice now Dan. 8:3, the long horn was to come up last, which was Persia. Now notice Jeremiah 51. Since the writer of the above article has used this, may we notice the whole chapter? In v. 11, it is the kings of the Medes who become the battle axe in God's hand. To the king of the Medes He says, "You are My war club, My weapon of war, and with you I shatter nations." In v. 20, Persia is just not mentioned. In vs. 24-28 the kings of the Medes are the instrument of destruction against Babylon, not Persia.

Notice what another scholar in the same encyclopedia says about it: "This identification is supported further by the fact that there is no other person known to history that can well be meant. Some indeed have thought that Darius the Mede was a reflection into the past of Darius Hystaspes the Persian; but this is rendered impossible inasmuch as the character and deeds and empire of Darius the Persian, which are well known to us from his own monuments and from the Greek historians, do not resemble what Daniel says of Darius the Mede." *International Standard Bible Encyclopedia*, Vol. 2, p. 788.

Things we can observe from this information:

A. Neither Haggai nor Zechariah refers to Darius as the Persian.
B. The deeds and events of Haggai and Zechariah reflect those of Daniel.
C. Therefore, consistent study will show that the Darius of Daniel is indeed the Darius which both Haggai and Zechariah write under. Again, the purpose in showing the above is to show the inconsistency of writers. Perhaps our problem arises when we do not search the scriptures thoroughly enough, and allow someone else to influence our thoughts, thus allowing for tradition, a thing Paul condemns, Col. 2:8.

As we sum up this introduction, we notice the following:
1. Daniel was studying the scrolls of Jeremiah.
2. Daniel sought to learn when the captivity would end for his people, and from Jeremiah he learned that the time of release was near, Jer. 25:11-12.
3. Daniel was filled with the deepest solicitude; he was filled with anxiety in regard to his people.
4. The return of his people was positive, and was the reason why he should pray, and was the reason why he prayed so earnestly at this time.
5. The prayer which Daniel offered is an illustration of the truth that men will pray more earnestly when they have reason to suppose that God intends to impart a blessing, a strong incitement to prayer.
6. Daniel's prayer is frank, it is appropriate, it is done in the name of his people, and becomes a confession of he and his people.
7. The long captivity of nearly seventy years, the desolations of the city and temple during that time, the many privations and evils to which they had been exposed all demonstrated the degree of the sins for which these calamities had come upon the nation.
8. And now Daniel confesses the sins of the nation before God, and asks for mercy.
9. Daniel recalls the curse that God promised upon this nation, Deut. 28:15-48. Daniel reckoned that what this nation was enduring was the fulfillment of those curses spoken by Moses.
10. Now, it is remarkable that the angel approaches Daniel, and does not give an answer to his prayers. What is told Daniel seems to have no bearing upon his prayer. He is told the city of Jerusalem would be rebuilt, the temple restored, but then he looks ahead to a more important event: the closing of the Jewish state, the coming of the Messiah in judgment against Israel. And a more enduring destruction to the temple, wherein the city also would be destroyed.

    Remarkable also, is that the angel tells Daniel how long the nation would endure from the time of the decree to rebuild and restore Jerusalem until their end would come. At that time they will have the free choice to receive or reject Christ and His kingdom. And they chose to reject him, Lk. 19:14.

Verse 1. "In the first year of Darius." We would expect this prayer and visit by the angel to be well after Daniel's ordeal with the lions, at a time when Daniel had composed his spiritual life.

Verse 2. "I, Daniel observed in the books the Word of the Lord to Jeremiah." Daniel observed in the book of Jeremiah where God had informed the prophet that this people would suffer captivity, Jer. 25:11-12. Daniel no doubt during his travels as vice king secured the book of Jeremiah, for when Daniel was carried away in 606 B.C. the book of Jeremiah was not finished.

The words here employed by Daniel would suggest that Daniel referred to his own collection of sacred books, rather than those in some world library.

Verse 3. "And I set my face unto the Lord God." It was a Jewish custom when praying to turn toward the city of Jerusalem where God once dwelt. Just as we face the person we are addressing. So when Daniel prayed, it may be described as "setting the face toward God."

Daniel evidently set aside a proper time for prayer, and prepared himself by fasting and humbling himself in sackcloth and ashes. This prayer was a solemn occasion, a prayer when mercy was implored, and the mind must be prepared for earnest and fervent communication with God. The occasion was of great importance, and it was proper to prepare the mind by fasting. Daniel recalled the sins of his people for which they now suffered, and fasting was appropriate. Pouring ashes on the head denoted great grief and sorrow, as well as humbleness before the God of heaven.

Daniel's preparation for prayer should give the Christian an idea for approaching God in the right frame of mind for making petition. Daniel had a reason for prayer, the concern and well-being of his people. I suggest there were divine principles here which governed Daniel's prayer. Notice the following:

A. Undeniably, some prayer requests are denied, fervent pleas do go unanswered, Ps. 88:13. There are likewise cases where a repeated petition is refused for reasons which may never be understood this side of heaven.

B. Why Daniel's prayer was not answered by the angel we do not know; yet we do know that Daniel met the

principles of prayer.
1. Heb. 11:6 and Mt. 17:20 indicate that prayer avails only as it is made in faith.
2. 1 John 5:14-15 indicates that prayer avails only when it is made in keeping with God's will.
3. Mt. 6:12-15; Jas. 5:14-16 make it clear that prayer avails only as it is made by a forgiving heart. Our Lord repeatedly indicates that unforgiveness is a fatal hindrance to effective prayer.
C. Daniel met all these principles except for the one about God's will. It was not God's time to reveal the answer to his request. He had the answer in the book of Jeremiah, "When seventy years was ended."

Verse 4. "And I prayed unto the Lord my God." From the evidence here, we are to understand that Daniel offered his prayer, and at a later time recorded the summary of it.

"And made my confession." Daniel not only offered the confession of himself, but on behalf of the nation of Israel, and in their name. The nation could not but be aware that these calamities had come upon them on account of their sins, and that these calamities could not be removed except by confessing their sins before God.

If we attempt to vindicate ourselves and justify our deeds, we have no hope that God will remove any physical judgment directed against us. We must do as Daniel did, admit our sins before God to avert judgment.

Verse 5. "We have sinned and rebelled." Daniel pleaded for his people, but he could not plead that his people had been obedient or had any claim to the divine favor of God. But he could cast himself and the people on the mercy of a covenant-keeping God, who would remember his covenant, who in times past forgave their sins, but only when they came in repentance before Him.

Though Daniel was alone, he spoke in the name of Israel. No doubt Daniel recalled the long list of crimes of the nation which had preceded the captivity, and which was the direct cause of the people being in exile, and the cause of the ruin of the city and temple.

The mind, in a true state of repentance, dwells on its sins and crimes committed against God. In Daniel's confession he multiplies the expressions of regret and sorrow over the transgressions of himself and his people.

Daniel does not at any point place any blame on anyone else, or on God, for what has happened to his people. Daniel is ready to admit before God their transgressions.

Verse 6. "We have not listened to Thy servants the prophets." Those prophets had called upon them to turn from their sin and advert the impending judgment. They had made known God's will, and had foretold the judgments that Daniel and his people were suffering. God, in speaking to the first prophet of this nation, Moses, advised him that He knew the hearts of the people, and how they would rebel against Him. To that people God had stated He would turn His face against them and allow the curses to take their course, Deut. 31:16,17.

The prophets spoke to all classes of people, from kings to the lowest of the nation. But these admonitions had been unheeded, and the people now saw clearly that these curses had come upon them because they had not hearkened to the voice of the prophets.

Verse 7. "Righteousness belongs to thee, O Lord." The one who is making prayer to God should always ascribe God as being righteous, and ascribe to Him justice. Here Daniel feels that God has been right in dealing with this people. God had promised that when this people sinned against Him, He would punish them, and God cannot lie. Here the people are to suffer the consequence of transgression against God, and here Daniel ascribes to God justice and righteousness. Daniel here takes all the shame and blame of the people.

There is no murmuring or complaining on the part of Daniel. He does not say "why us, Lord" as if God had been wrong in His judgment upon the nation. We see rather the utmost confidence in God and His government. This is a good attitude in which to approach God when we are afflicted and stand in need of God's intervention.

"To the men of Judah, and all Israel." Daniel here excludes none. After the revolt of the ten tribes, they became known as the kingdom of Ephraim, because Ephraim was the largest tribe. It is sometimes called the kingdom of Israel. The other portions of the people were known as the kingdom of Judah, and is here referred to in Daniel's prayer first, because Daniel was from the kingdom of Judah, and was of the seed royal. The prophets had already foretold the carrying away of the people and their scattering among the countries of the east. Deut. 28:36-41; Isa. 10:5-12; Jer. 22:25.

Verses 8-9. Daniel here excludes none, all have been guilty of sin, all came under the curses which were the consequence of sin. All were to share the righteous judgments of God. No sin can go unrequited and God remain a just God. God had laid carefully the plan of judgment against the nation in the event they rebelled against Him. Since they did rebel, and they would not repent, the judgment was inevitable. And thus Daniel prayed and confessed in the name of all the people.

Verses 10-11. The commands of God through the prophets had not been obeyed, and the people had not turned from their sins. God loved this people and was longsuffering, and had sent many prophets into this land to proclaim His will. God spoke through Jeremiah and said, "Turn, O backsliding children saith the Lord, for I am married to you; and I will take you one of a city and two of a family, and I will bring you to Zion," Jer. 3:14.

God likened this people as a wife unto Him; but they had committed adultery, they had played the harlot with other lovers, and yet God said, "Yet return again to me saith the Lord, Jer. 3:1.

God also likens Judah and Israel as two daughters of one mother; they were His. But they committed adultery with other gods, Ezek. Ch. 23. Daniel here recalls all these warnings and transgressions of the people, as he makes his plea to a righteous God. Refusal to obey the commands of God resulted in the curses being poured out upon the people like rain. Deut. 28:15-48.

Here we might add that beginning with Deut. 28:49-68 we see the prophecy dealing with the last curses that will be poured out on all Israel, and deals with the end time of the Hebrew nation. We should observe carefully here that v. 49 will in no way fit into the system of judgments seen in Assyria or Babylon. Notice Isa. 10:5-12 where God foretells that Assyria will come against Israel; and later in Isa. 10:24-32 God states he will bring a scourge against Assyria and Babylon. Both these nations were to the north and bordered Israel. These two nations fit the prophecy given by Moses in Deut. 28:15-48. But, notice, if this exile does not turn the hearts of the people and turn them to God, there will be the severest consequence. If they continue to rebel against God, then He will bring against them a nation from afar, from the ends of the earth, who will swoop down as an eagle, one whose language they will not understand–Rome. This nation will bring about the end of the Hebrew world. This beast and its kings is what Daniel sought understanding of. And now, because of the knowledge that Daniel possesses, he pleads with God on behalf of his people. Nehemiah, like Daniel, was also concerned about the welfare of his people and mourned for days over their condition. (Neh. 1)

Verse 12. "Thus He has confirmed His Words spoken against us and our rulers."

Again we begin with the curses found in Deut. 28:15-48. "That oath which was written in the Law of Moses." All He had threatened in the event of transgression would be brought upon the people. Daniel saw there was a complete fulfillment of all that God had decreed to come upon all Israel. All the prophets had only enlarged upon that which Moses spoke. Now, after God had been longsuffering toward all Israel, Daniel could not complain. Respecting the captivity, the slaughter, and the complete desolation to the temple, no one of Israel could doubt now that God was a covenant-keeping God.

Now those whom God chose to save could tell about the great judgment, the children could tell their children, for generations. Ezekiel records that God sent an angel into the city, and marked those who were mourning over the condition of Judah. Those whom the angel marked would escape death, but not tribulation. Those who received not the mark would be killed. Ezek. 9:3-11.

The same parallel is found just prior to the last destruction of Jerusalem and the temple in Rev. 7:1-3. It was God's hope that the 70-year captivity would cause the people of Israel to remain faithful unto Him; however, in the event that they again committed spiritual adultery, He had in the beginning of the nation prepared also their end. Deut. 28:49-68. Respecting the marking mentioned in Revelation, Joel foresaw and spoke of the last event upon Israel, stating that those who were faithful would escape the great tribulation prepared for this day. Joel 2:28-32. Malachi spoke of the event as a burning of the chaff, a day that God was preparing. It would set them ablaze, but for those who fear the great name of

God; they would skip about like fatted calves in a feeding stall. Malachi 4:1-5. Jesus, quoting from the Old Covenant on the same subject, related it to the tares. Mt. 13:36-50. Once more, if we can understand the type and the natural, then we can understand the spiritual application.

Both Joel and Malachi mention that the righteous would be saved, just as those were in Jerusalem in 586 B.C. And both associate the destruction of the wicked with fire, saying they will be set ablaze. Malachi states in 3:2-4 that it will be a burning of the wicked as a refiners fire! The time was when Jesus would come in the kingdom of heaven to purge the temporal kingdom of God and Christ. Mt. 16:27,28. Is it possible that Jesus was pointing to the same event when He spoke of the tares in Mt. 13:37-50? And could it be that Paul was referring to the same event when he spoke to the Thessalonians in 2 Thess. 1:4-10? Correlate the scriptures, and notice to whom this judgment was directed, and what kingdom was to be purged— and it would occur in their own lifetime. Mt. 16:27,28; Matt 24:34; Lk. 21:20-32; James 5:7-8,9. According to the pattern of scriptures, these are one and the same event. If so, then Peter when speaking to the same nation, and to the same temporal kingdom of God, when he said, "The time is now that judgment (purging) must begin at the house of God." 1 Pet. 4:17. Then in 2 Pet. 3, Peter like Isaiah in Isaiah chapter 13, gives the natural or physical to represent the spiritual. If such is type and antitype, natural and spiritual, then Peter refers to the burning of the tares in Mt. 13:37-50; see Malachi 4:1-5 and Zech. 14:1-5 where the heavens represent nations. If in Isaiah chapter 13 the heavens represented the nation of Babylon, then why could it not represent the nation of Israel in 2 Pet. 3, Gal. 4:22-31 and Heb. 8:13?

What did Jesus really mean when He said in Mt. 5:18, "For verily I say unto you, until heaven and earth pass away, not one jot or tittle shall pass from the law of Moses?" Is it possible to view this passage in a literal sense, without recognizing that the literal heaven and earth would pass out of existence before the Covenant, or Law of Moses, passed away? For sure the literal heaven and earth have not passed out of existence. Thus, if viewed literally, this would mean we are yet under the Law of Moses, and should be offering sacrifice rather than observing the Lord's supper. The following is a classic example of how the word "heaven" is used. Isaiah chapter 13 names an oracle against the nation of Babylon. In v. 5 the Medes are represented as coming from a far country, from the end of heaven and v. 17 confirms this. Now v. 10 says that the stars shall not give their light, the sun shall be darkened, and the moon shall give no light. In v. 5 the heaven represents the Median Empire. In v. 10 the word heaven represents Babylon, who is being destroyed; the stars, moon, and sun represent the powers of that nation. (See Gen. 37:9-10).

I recognize that my viewpoint in these matters differs from that of our forefathers, and many times it is said that we are "straying from the old paths." There is a strong inference by those who make this statement that the "old paths" are sacred, and any deviation is dangerous and sinful. I personally have great respect for our forefathers, and I know that much prayer, study and long hours went into those things written. Have we by our deeds and actions credited these men with having answered all Bible questions relating to past, present, and future? We are afraid to question their thinking, therefore we have parked our brains, and allowed ourselves to become stale and unmoldable in the hands of the Messiah.

Our forefathers, the restoration leaders, never claimed to have arrived at all truth. Therefore, to park our brain where they left off would be to disregard the request of God to "study," to "seek knowledge." In the times of restoration, people used oil lamps, but today we have advanced, and therefore, would not, except in dire circumstance use oil lamps. Why not advance also in Christianity? If we can do better, and learn more, why not? This is not to suggest that the old paths are wrong, simply that any of them should be open to question, and that question be received without impugning the character of those great men in our past. Who should we fear?

Verse 13. "As it is written in the Law of Moses." Moses wrote many laws and gave much advice, but this verse refers to the spiritual law contained in the song of Moses, Deut. 32. Like Deut. 28, God here warns the nation; this song they were to memorize and sing at every sabbatical and jubilee festival. Deut. 31:10-19 This song promised both coming blessings, and eventual doom.

Daniel here remembers those matters written where Moses pleaded with this stiff-necked people to repent of their sins and beg for mercy. Now Daniel recalls that his people are in captivity as a consequence of their sins. He pleads, "That we might turn from our iniquities." Since Daniel had the books of Jeremiah, he must also have had the book of Hosea, for it seems that both Daniel and Hosea were pleading for their nation, and both seem to have been an object lesson for Israel (see Hos. 1:1-11, Amos 5:1-24).

Verse 14. "Therefore the Lord has watched upon the evil." This means He has kept the curses in store for the wicked. God had watched them sin; now he executes the afflictions and watches for their reaction. Ezekiel is prepared to go among the exiles as their preacher while in captivity; it was Ezekiel's duty to dispel any false hope of a fast return to their land, and remind them that God is a righteous God, a God of justice, and that He had promised their return predicated upon their repentance. Thus Ezekiel was to turn their hearts back to God. To the faithful, God would watch over them to safety, Jer. 31:28. God had not slept, but had carefully kept an eye on them, and had observed the course of events. The fact that God knows all prompted Jesus to say that, "every idle word would be accounted for," Mt. 12:36-37. How can the mind of man be so twisted as to commit sin, knowing that not only God but the holy angels are watching every move, and listening to every bad word?

"For the Lord our God is righteous in all His works." This is the language of a contrite heart, always used by one who properly fears and worships the Sovereign God. God is holy and righteous in all his ways, even in His discipline upon the Jews in exile. Jesus said, "Those whom I love, I reprove and discipline," Rev. 3:19. We are disciplined to effect our repentance. This will be found to be true always; it seems to be God's established pattern, that we suffer the consequence of sin that is not repented of. When repentance produces a contrite heart, God erases the sin from his book, and remembers it no more forever. But it seems that this people could not forgive each other, how then could they ever expect God to forgive them? Daniel is teaching that all have sinned, and need to confess our error, not only to God, but to each other, since we have sinned against man. Mt. 10:32; James. 5:16.

Verse 15. "And now, O Lord our God, that hast brought thy people forth out of the land of Egypt." Daniel here seems to be reminding God that this is yet the same people that He brought out of Egypt. Daniel seems to be calling to God's attention that the people sinned at that point; they rebelled against Him, creating an image of gold and worshiping it even while the law was being given, Ex. 32:1-12. At this time Moses made a plea to God concerning what the heathen world say should God consummate His plans to destroy all the people at this time. It appears from the argument by Moses that the anger of God was cooled somewhat, and from this can be seen that God will listen, and be reasonable toward the righteous man. Here God allowed Moses to make the proper punishment. And it seems that here Daniel is making the same type of plea as did Moses, suggesting these matters for God's consideration. The arguments Daniel urges are those derived from the divine mercy and faithfulness of God: from his former dealing with this people, from their sins and misery, from the great sacrifice made for sin, from the desire that his name should be glorified. In his prayer, Daniel properly refers to the former divine interposition in favor of the Hebrew people, and he recalls the deliverance from Egypt as a reason why God should now interpose and save the people.

Verse 16. "O Lord, according to all thy righteousness." Perhaps Daniel now recalls the time when the people of Israel had sinned against God, and Moses went before God on their behalf. When God heard the prayer of Moses and his request, and granted remission of their sins up to that point, these sins were erased from the Book of Life, never to be remembered against them anymore. Ex. 32:30-33 Without doubt the mind of Daniel is fixed upon what God had formerly done, and upon his character of justice and mercy and goodness, upon the faithfulness of God to His people, and as Moses pled with God, so Daniel pleads on behalf of his people Israel.

"And let thine anger and fury be turned away." Daniel having in his possession the books of the prophets, he could recall the anger of God when Moses told this same people that God was a jealous God. "The anger of the Lord will be kindled against you, and you will be wiped off the face of the earth." Deut. 6:15. "Let thine anger be turned away." The anger of God was against those who caused the captivity, the destruction of Jerusalem and the temple. Now Daniel pleads with God to remove his anger.

"The holy mountain." The meaning is that God once lived among this people in the temple at Jerusalem; thus when God made his abode there, it was holy. But God removed himself from that temple. Ezek. 9:3; 10:4; 11:23.

Verse 17. " Now therefore, O God, hear the prayer of thy servant." On behalf of the people of Israel, Daniel pleaded for his people and their country, entreating the Lord to be merciful. His argument seems to be based on the confession of sin and on the character of God, on the condition of Jerusalem and the temple and of the former interposition of God in dealing with his people.

"For the Lord 's sake." Meaning that whatever God does, it would be done for his sake and for his glory, that his name might be glorified. God related to the people through Ezekiel and said, "And there you will remember your ways and all your deeds, with which you have de-filed yourselves, and you will loathe yourselves in your own sight for all the evil things that you have done... Then you will know that I am the Lord when I have dealt with you for My names sake." Ezek. 20:43,44.

Verse 18. "O My God incline thine ear, and hear." Daniel is here pleading earnestly for God's attention and his favor. This reminds us of the prayer of Nehemiah when he inquired concerning his people who had gone back to Jerusalem under the decree of Cyrus. Nehemiah was told they were in great distress. When told of their sad condi-tion, he sat down for days and mourned over his people, the country, and the city; and in v. 6 of chapter 1, begs that God would be attentive, His eyes open to Nehemiah's prayer. Neh. 1:2-11.

"And the city which is called by Thine name." Ear-lier I spoke of God dwelling in the temple in Jerusalem. When punishment was due, God removed himself from the city and the temple. It was the place of His sanctuary, the city where His worship was celebrated, and which was His dwelling place on earth. Ps. 48:1-3; Ps. 87:3.

Verse 19. " O Lord, hear! O Lord, forgive! O Lord, listen and take action for Thine own sake." Although this verse is almost identical to v. 17, Daniel is not being repetitive, but is using every form of earnest expression to God in prayer. This shows a mind intent on the object of his prayer, a heart greatly interested, an earnestness that cannot be seen today. There is no mention here as to the length of time Daniel prayed. It is not unreasonable to assume that perhaps the greater part of the day was consumed in prayer, and there is no sign of vain repetition in Daniel's prayer. It could be said that the time consumed in prayer would show the interest of the person praying, and not only this, it would show the faith of he who prayed this length of time.

Verses 20-21. "Now while I was speaking and praying, and confessing my sin, the man Gabriel came to me." Gabriel, evidently in heaven, had received commandment to go to Daniel and to communicate a message to him. Gabriel had borne the message very swiftly, and appeared before him as one who is wearied of a long trip. The reference is to the rapidity with which he had come on the long journey, as if exhausted by his journey. Daniel, perhaps exhausted from the long prayer, relates how his weariness in the evening was much encouraged at the appearance of Gabriel.

Verse 22. " And he gave me instructions." That is, the angel gave Daniel intelligence and understanding about his visit. The information Gabriel was to give to Daniel was what would occur to his people at the end time, that is, their end time.

Verse 23. "At the beginning of your supplication the command was issued." We are not informed as to the exact time when Daniel began to pray, but it would be natural to assume that he began in the morning and used the greater portion of the day in prayer, for he had fasted, not eaten his normal food, but instead was engaged in prayer. The angel Gabriel came in the evening of the day. The Word of God was given to Gabriel as to those things he should make known to Daniel respecting the future of his people. It is fair to say that Gabriel left heaven and the presence of God as soon as Daniel began to pray.

"I have come to tell you... So give heed to the message." The message was of such importance that the angel Gabriel warns Daniel to give heed, to understand the matter, and consider the vision. The mention of the vision no doubt would be the continuation of the vision in chapter seven, where Daniel was much concerned about the events and the action taken for his people.

Verse 24. We are here concerned with the last four verses of this chapter, where there has been much abuse of scripture. However, as was stated in the beginning of the book, I have little if anything to say about the varied opinions resulting from the abuse of the book of Daniel. But, here I must show some of the abuses in order to set forth the full truth.

In chapter 9, Daniel did not receive a new vision, but was spending time in prayer to God about what God had already revealed to him. Therefore, Gabriel referred to the previous vision of chapter 7, and verses 24-27 of chapter 9 are but a further amplification of the things revealed in chapter 7. Perhaps a review of ch. 7 would be helpful.

A. Four beasts were seen arising from the sea; these were four kingdoms, namely Babylon, Media Persia, Greece, and Rome.
B. Daniel was concerned with the fourth beast and the eleventh horn, or eleventh king.
C. The court was set, the books were opened.
D. A national judgment was seen, both on Israel and on the beast.
E. The eleventh horn would make war with the saints, the period of this war would be, time, times, and a half time, or three and one-half years.
F. During this period the Lord would come to render the judgment upon Israel, and the beast.

The question is asked, why was Daniel shown only eleven horns? God saw fit to reveal to Daniel the period when Israel would be destroyed, along with its national religion. I am acutely aware of the scholars who disregard the rightful rulers as Daniel saw them. Some move up to Julius Caesar to begin counting the eleven horns, and some begin with Augustus Caesar. This is all done to try and make these horns fit the vision of John in Revelation 17. I personally feel that this is a mistake. It is not necessary that the two be in complete harmony, as each lived in a different period of time. Since Daniel lived some six hundred years before the event, he was shown the eleven horns, which would bring the end of Israel to a close during the reign of Vespasian. John lived near to the event and he saw eight horns. Regardless of how the scholar renders the number of horns, Jerusalem fell during the reign of Vespasian in AD 70. And further, if all the kings of Rome are seen from the time of Pompey there would be eleven including Vespasian.

Daniel 8:26; 9:24-27; 10:14; 12:1-4 all seem to indicate that all the visions pertained to the Hebrew nation as the one which would receive the physical judgment. No other nation can be classed as the people of Daniel. But, the "errorist" would make an abuse at this point and teach that the desolation spoken of by Daniel is not yet fulfilled, that the tribulation is in our near future, at which time the nation of Israel will begin to be restored before God. But, the book of Daniel does not anywhere teach such.

As Gabriel begins to relate the interpretation of that which Daniel is much concerned about, Gabriel uses the day-year system, just as God used in Ezek. 4:4-8. There God himself designated the system of heavenly keeping of time, where each day was equal to one year, and since Gabriel is here as the messenger of God, no other system of keeping time is recognized. But the errorist here makes another mistake, they have a system worked out whereby the time mentioned of seventy weeks will end in this century, and then will come the tribulation, which they say we are shortly to incur, and there we shall receive the mark of the beast. But Daniel does not teach such!

Since I have made a point of speaking of the errorist in this chapter, I shall move upon two other points which warrants careful consideration, they are:

A. That God promised through Daniel a kingdom for Israel, which to this date has not been established, and therefore, is yet future.
   1. Although I have already burdened this survey with the subject of kingdom, I will again approach it now from a different direction, in hopes that at least one approach may make it clear.
   2. It is perhaps possible that today we have done as the Jews did in the first century. They thought that all religious matters had been settled by their forefathers, and therefore anyone who said anything, or

taught a matter different than their forefathers, was branded as a false teacher. Christ himself was thus branded, castigated and killed because He did not follow the set traditions of the forefathers! We see some today in this same rut.

Jesus said "I have come in my Fathers name, and you do not receive Me; if another shall come in his own name, you will receive him. How can you believe when you receive glory from one another, and you do not seek the glory that is from the One and only God? Do not think that I will accuse you before the Father; the one who accuses you is Moses, in whom you have set your hope. For if you believed Moses, you would believe Me; for he wrote of Me. But if you will not believe his writings, how will you believe My Words?" John 5:43-47.

The point that I wish to make from this quotation is that we—like the Jews—do not believe what Moses wrote, and therefore, we do not believe what Christ in His person spoke! Well, you say, but you are wrong, I do believe. Well then, respecting the kingdom, allow me time to present that which the scriptures teach, and which is written plainly.

3. Was the kingdom established in AD 33 on the first Pentecost after His resurrection? Many think so. But what saith the Word? Luke 19:11-15 clearly shows by parable that the Lord would go away to receive the kingdom at His ascension. Dan. 7:13-14 shows that Daniel saw One like the Son of man coming up to the Father to receive a kingdom.

Again, in Luke 19:15 the Lord says, "And it came about when he returned (Second Coming) after receiving the kingdom." It was already said He would go away to receive the kingdom, and after receiving it, He would return.

In 16:28 Matthew records that when the Lord returned, He would come in his kingdom. The words are plain that the "Second Coming" and the establishment of the kingdom must be at the same time. The doctrine of a "second appearing" at Pentecost fails for lack of evidence. It cannot be sustained by scripture.

4. Acts. 1:11 shows Jesus Christ being caught up to

heaven. Acts 2:33 shows that at Pentecost He was at the right hand of the Father. Phil. 2:9 shows that God exalted Him at His right hand. 1 Pet. 3:22 says that Jesus Christ was, at that time, at the right hand of God. In Eph. 1:20, Paul says that at his writing, Christ was at the right hand of God.

Now I suggest that Christ could not be at the right hand of God, and at the same time be in Jerusalem establishing the kingdom. Someone says, the apostles were to establish the kingdom. But, the scripture says that the kingdom would come when Jesus came. I suggest that Christ did not come at Pentecost, therefore, the kingdom was not established on Pentecost. However, there are other pertinent questions to be answered respecting the kingdom before we decide the matter.

5. When did Jesus Christ obtain all power and authority on earth and in heaven? Mt. 26:18. In Eph. 1:22 Paul says it happened when "God received Him at his right hand." Phil. 2:9,10 says "after the Resurrection." Col. 2:10 says He was head over all rule and authority "when he sat at the right hand of God." 1 Pet. 3:22, "after going into heaven all power and authority was subjected to Him." John 17:2, "all authority," and in John 17:3, Jesus knew that "God had given all things into His hands." Again, John 3:35, "all things are given into His hands."

It would appear, from Matt 3:16, that at His baptism Jesus received power and authority on earth. However, I suggest that there was more to receive, for the scriptures indicate that after being seated at the right hand of God, He became head over the church. And there is yet more. At His "second coming" He shall sit on His own throne, Mt. 25:31. After receiving a throne He will have the authority to judge, Mt. 25:32. And after His "coming" He will be the King in His own kingdom, Mt. 25:34.

Although it was destined for Christ to have all power, it would appear that it came over a 40-year period, from His baptism until His "second appearing" when His own kingdom would be established. It is impossible for two kings to reign over the same kingdom; one must be taken out of the way. Is this what Paul referred to in Gal. 4:22-31? See Heb. 8:13. If Paul had in mind the casting out of the old kingdom in Gal. 4, then we have a complete answer to the problem in 1 Cor. 15:23-24. Notice: "But each in his own order: Christ the first fruits, after that those who are Christ's at His coming, then comes the end, when He (Christ) delivers up the kingdom to the God and Father, when He (God) has abolished all rule and authority and power."

6. Now we ask, when did He come, or when will He come? Zech. 14:1-5 informs us that it would be during the destruction of Jerusalem. Mal. 4:5 said that just before that great and terrible day, Elijah would come. Mt. 11:11-14 tells us that John the Baptist was Elijah, and this is confirmed in Mt. 17:11-17. Jesus told his disciples they would not finish going through Israel before He came (Mt. 10:23). Matt. 16:28 also says it would be during the lifetime of those who were listening to Him speak. Matt. 24 says it would occur at the time Jerusalem was destroyed (see parallels in Mk. 13 and Lk. 21). James 5:9 says it was "at the door" at the very time James wrote. Luke 21:31, the kingdom was "at hand." The fact is that if He did not come at that time, and fully establish the kingdom, then we have no kingdom, we have no King. That would make Christ a false prophet and false teacher with no power and no authority. If he hasn't "appeared a second time unto salvation," we are not saved. Heb. 9:28

B. There is a school of thought which believes only some portions of Daniel were fulfilled in the fourth century AD (when Constantine freed the Church from Roman persecution), and that the rest of Daniel is yet to be fulfilled. They rely heavily upon Daniel 2, 7, and 9.

1. Respecting Dan. 2:44, it is affirmed that the kingdom the saints would possess was not the kingdom of God. True, that kingdom would be set up during the period of the diverse beast, but it is untrue that this kingdom was the one the saints would possess, as is often contended. The fact is that the saints of God—who were in the kingdom of God, the church—had conquered Imperial Rome by AD 313, not with the arm of flesh, but through righteousness."

    2. The time, times, and a half time is merely a way of saying three and one half, which could be three and one half days, or weeks, or months, or years, or centuries. The meaning is determined by the context, and the context in the case of Dan. 7:25 might suggest three and one half centuries.

    3. It is said of Dan. 7:26, "It is to be understood in the light of the saints having undermined paganism through their proclamation of, and dedication to, the gospel of Christ that the diverse beast ceased to exist as a world power."

C. There are three points here which need clarification.

    1. First, if the saints were not to possess, or receive, the kingdom of God, and were indeed to possess the kingdom of Rome, where might we find the evidence of fulfillment?

    2. If "time, times, and a half time" means three and one-half centuries, how does it fit Mt. 5:18; Lk. 21:20,24; 22:37; 24:44; Isa. 63:4-6; Gal. 4:22-31?

    3. How can Dan. 7:26 be understood to mean that the saints will assemble the heavenly court, sit in judgment over Rome, take away their dominion, annihilate their dominion, and destroy it forever, when the same doctrine says that the saints will possess the kingdom of Rome? Is there inconsistency present when the scripture states that 'his dominion' shall be annihilated, and destroyed forever, and man's doctrine states "That the saints will possess the kingdom which 'his dominion' encompassed"?

D. To clarify these three questions (under C. above), I offer the following. Beginning with question C. 1. above.

    1. *Question One.* Here we must give careful consideration to the text from which the question arises. See Dan. 7:22 which says, "Until the Ancient of Days came, and judgment was passed in favor of the saints of the Highest One, and the time arrived when the saints took possession of the kingdom."

        a. Judgment, and possession of the kingdom, was predicated upon the coming of the Lord. At least that's what the scripture says.

        b. Judgment, possession of the kingdom by the saints, as well as the coming of the Lord, was to be during the period when the eleventh horn was making war with the saints. Verse 21. The eleventh horn was none other than Vespasian.

c. Mt. 21:43 states that the saints would receive the kingdom from the Jews, not from Rome. Mt. 16:28 says that both the "coming" and the kingdom would be during the lifetime of those to whom Jesus preached. Luke says the kingdom comes at the destruction of Jerusalem, Luke 21:31, "Even so you, too, when you see these things happening recognize that the kingdom of God is near." Then in v. 32 he adds, "Truly I say to you, this generation shall not pass away until all these things take place."

d. Jesus said in Luke 21:20-21, "But when you see Jerusalem surrounded by armies, then recognize that her destruction is at hand. Because these are the days of vengeance, in order that all things written may be fulfilled."

e. I suggest that if any part of the prophecy of Daniel was delayed until the fourth century, then we have a contradiction in the Holy Scriptures respecting the time of fulfillment. The words of Jesus cannot be counted as trustworthy, and inspired, if indeed there is a contradiction on His part. In short, there is no evidence which indicates that the saints were to, or did, or ever will receive any kingdom other than the one promised in Dan. 7:13-14.

f. In conclusion, I suggest that the phrase found in Dan. 7:22, "The saints took possession of the kingdom," and that found in Dan. 7:18, "but the saints of the Highest One will receive the kingdom and possess the kingdom forever and ever," is one and the same event. I believe it names the kingdom of God, rather than the kingdom of Rome.

In the event we choose to go with the kingdom of Rome as being the one the saints received, then we must admit to the Roman Catholics that they are God's chosen people, for they are the ones who received the literal kingdom of Rome, and they possess it to this day!

Further, I suggest that "The other horn which came up," of v. 20, is the same horn as "that horn" in v. 21, and the same as "another will arise after them" of v. 24, and the same as "he will speak out against the Most High" of v. 25.

2. *Question Two.* There is no basis for "time, times, and a half time" being three and one half centuries. Such reasoning defies the inspiration of Mt. 5:18; Luke 21:20,22; 22:37; 24:44.

Further, Dan. 7:22 says, it was "that horn," meaning the one which came up after the ten, which in turn made him the eleventh horn, and it was this horn that made war with the saints for "time, times, and a half time."

To show any consistency at all, should we hold the meaning of centuries, we must affirm that the eleventh horn reigned for some 300 years in order to get him into the fourth century. There is no inference which shows that the Roman Empire was designated as the eleventh horn. The eleventh horn was not the beast, but was a ruler, a designated ruler in the empire of the beast, therefore, the eleventh horn did not wage war against the saints for 350 years, the beast did.

3. *Question Three.* First, the saints had nothing to do with the events of Dan. 7:26. Secondly, it was not the saints who commanded the court to sit in Dan. 7:26. Outside of the twelve apostles, Mt. 19:28; Rev. 20:4, no earthly being was ever promised to make a universal judgment; the judgment of the twelve was limited to only Israel. In the third place, Rome is not implied in Dan. 7:26. The fact is, the phrase "But the court will sit for judgment" is seen first in Dan. 7:9-10 where the white throne judgment is foretold, and where the court sat. The court sitting in v. 26, and the court sitting in v. 10, is one and the same event. "And his dominion shall be taken away" does not refer to the Empire of Rome. The court that sat was the heavenly court, and "his dominion" refers to the dominion of the prince of this world, or Satan's dominion, that is being taken away from him, destroyed and annihilated forever.

May we now observe evidence of this judgment and the casting away of Satan? During Paul's lifetime he wrote to the Roman Christians and informed them that "The God of Peace will soon crush Satan under your feet," Rom. 16:20. The writer of the Hebrew letter said, "Since then the children share in flesh and blood, He Himself likewise also partook of the same, that through death He might render powerless him who had the power of death that is, the devil." Heb. 2:14. The meaning of this passage is that Satan once had power to hold departed spirits in the earth, and therefore, the death spoken of here simply meant the separation from God. Well, the passage informs us that Christ abolished this sentence of death, which began with Adam. But in spite of what the passage says, we are daily informed that the spirit is yet held in bondage, away from God, and thus there has been no resurrection. Such doctrine defies the plain teaching of Christ. Next John 12:31 informs us that judgment is upon the world. You see in Dan. 7:26, Daniel saw the Court sit, John says that now judgment is upon the world, and the ruler of this world (his dominion) shall be cast out (destroyed forever, Dan. 7:26), taken away, Rev. 20:10. In 1 John 3:8 we read, "The one who practices sin is of the devil, for the devil has sinned from the beginning. The Son of God appeared for this purpose, that He might destroy the works of the devil." As I recall, Daniel said that his dominion would be destroyed, his works, his power, his influence. Well, that is what the scripture says. I am only doing the survey.

In Rev. 20:8-10, Satan was bound at the cross, but released during the period of the eleventh horn, Dan. 7:20-27. According to Rev. 20:8, the purpose was to stir up the nations against the saints and the beloved city, Rev. 20:9. After this war was over, according to Rev. 20:10, Satan was cast out of this world, his dominion taken away, destroyed, annihilated forever. Now when we move back to John 16:11 we see that the ruler of this world (Satan) has been judged. Well, Dan. 7:26 says the same thing.

In short, consistently the scripture shows Satan being judged, cast out, destroyed, and annihilated forever. Rome is just not mentioned. But again, if we move the fulfillment of any part of Daniel into the fourth century, we defy the fact that Christ said that when Jerusalem was surrounded by armies, these were the days of vengeance, that all things which are written must be fulfilled. Jerusalem was totally destroyed by Rome, and the eleventh horn in AD 70, not AD 350.

Respecting v. 24, Gabriel sets forth the objects for which the temple and the city were to be rebuilt. It was the responsibility of the priest and temple to prepare Israel for the Messiah.

a. "To finish the transgression." As the first object to be accomplished, the 490-year period would, according to the angel, finish transgression. The meaning of "to finish transgression" is that by the end of the 490 year period the gospel would be preached, and sin and iniquity would be shut up. This is a figurative description of the forgiveness of sins by the blood of Jesus Christ.

b. "To make an end to sin," meaning that by the end of the 490-year period, Christ would have made His sacrifice of blood atonement, where sins could be removed by obedience. "An open fountain for the house of Israel," (Zech. 13:1), and "a place of refuge," (Isa. 2:2-3).

c. "Make atonement for iniquity," meaning that by the end of the 490-year period a means would be made for the full and final atonement of the curse of sin guilt that had been on mankind ever since man's sin in the garden, an atonement through which men could finally be reconciled back to God. The Jews had been promised a better covenant (Jer. 31:31-33). This, according to Isaiah, was the new heaven and earth prepared by God (Isa. 65:12-19). All the Old Testament prophets looked forward to the coming of the Messiah. Daniel 9:24-27 says they would have 490 years to prepare the nation for the arrival of the Messiah and the cleansing of sins He would bring. Jesus stated, "He that believeth and is baptized shall be saved, but he that disbelieveth shall be condemned." (Mk. 16:16, ASV)

d. "To bring in everlasting righteousness." To cause to bring in, meaning to cause true righteousness to finally be manifested to the world, so they could be truly righteous in God's sight, to recognize the arrival of the Messiah, to teach true righteousness to the world. Therefore, to "cause to come" denotes a direct agency by which that righteousness would come, and would be introduced into the world, thus placing the subject of morals upon a better foundation.

There appears to be some very important events connected with the phrase everlasting righteousness; notice first that the verse is connected with the "last days," that is, the last days of the Jewish economy, which is to say the days when the Messiah will come and establish His kingdom. This kingdom is that which shall be "everlasting." There will not be another. This kingdom is the only one Christ will ever have.

The fair meaning is that the kingdom of Christ was now, at the expiration of the 490 years, the only means of approach to God. For Judaism was a national religion and was to be abolished in favor of the universal religion that the kingdom would offer. This alone should discourage the Jew as well as others that Christ will not come back to establish an earthly kingdom. Israel could be saved only in the kingdom of Christ, Isa. 51:4-8; 45:17.

e. "To seal up vision and prophecy." To "seal up" is to close up, bring to an end. Whatever is being sealed is full; it is to stop, put forth no more. Since the bringing in of righteousness moves upon the kingdom of Christ, and the agency for that being God, we are to understand that the sealing up of visions and prophecy would not occur until the kingdom had been fully confirmed by the destruction of the temple by God. We know that visions and prophecy did not cease at the death of Christ. Therefore, when Jerusalem and the temple were destroyed, all Old Testament prophecy was fulfilled. Luke records the following, "These be the days of vengeance that all things written be fulfilled." Lk. 21:22.

Respecting the New Testament visions and prophecy, the apostle Paul had some things to say about the sealing up. "Love never fails, but if there are gifts of prophecy, they shall be done away; if there are tongues, they will cease; if there is knowledge, it will be done away with... For we know in part, and we prophesy in part... But when the perfect comes, the partial will be done away." 1 Cor. 13:8-10. The word "perfect" as used here does not mean Christ, the word is neither masculine gender or feminine gender, but rather neuter gender, meaning a "thing." So when the Bible was finished, we had the sealing up of visions and prophecy. All the apostles had written prior to the destruction of Jerusalem AD 70, with perhaps the apostle John writing later, as some scholars claim; but even so when his book the Revelation was written, according to Paul, visions and prophecy would cease.

f. "And to anoint the most holy place." The phrase would denote the consecration of the cornerstone, Christ. God at one time dwelt in the temple, that was the holy place. God promised a new covenant, Jer. 31:31-33; the Messiah was promised, Isa. 7:14; the government would be upon His shoulders, Isa. 9:6-7; He was to be the head, Col. 1:18. Therefore, when man accepted the New Covenant, and came into worship, it became the holy place, for Christ dwelled there, Mt. 18:20. Thus Christ was to be anointed as King of His kingdom, and recognized as ruler over His Empire of believers.

Daniel was not able to see clearly how this would be done, but we who now have the complete revelation of the method by which God removed sin, can understand how this was accomplished by the blood of Christ. Through our baptism into Christ, our sin is covered and forgiven. There can be no doubt that "Whosoever believes and is baptized shall be saved, but whosoever believes not shall be condemned." Mk. 16:16

"Come to Mount Zion, the city of God, the heavenly Jerusalem, the church of the first born," Heb. 12:22-25. "And I saw the holy city New Jerusalem... The tabernacle of God is among men." Rev. 21:2-3.

Verse 25. "So you are to know and discern, that from the issuing of a decree to restore and rebuild Jerusalem." We are now concerned with a particular decree, one concerning the rebuilding of the city of Jerusalem. Evidently Gabriel wanted to awaken the interest of Daniel by the assurance that, if he would pay close attention, he would gain an understanding of that which Gabriel was about to give. The first period of seven weeks was evidently to be characterized by something different from that which would follow, or it would reach some important point. Then would follow a continuous period of sixty-two weeks, and afterward would be the remaining week when the nation of Israel would come to its end time. This would complete the total of seventy weeks. Notice the chronology of events below. It is assumed here that the decree which began the 70 weeks sequence would be counted from the issuing of the decree by King Artaxerxes in the seventh year of his reign. Ezra 7:1-24

    A. It is said by many scholars that King Artaxerxes gave the commission to Ezra to write the law. Admittedly, Ezra was a priest and scribe, but where is the verse that states that Artaxerxes commissioned him to establish that law? According to the scriptures, it was Ezra's intent to establish the law before the decree was issued. The king's decree amounted to the giving of silver and gold to purchase bulls, rams, and lambs. All silver and gold left over could be spent on whatever Ezra chose.

    B. Verse 20. The king tells Ezra that the rest of the needs for the house of God should be shared by the royal treasure and free-will offerings of the people. When has any city been rebuilt without the aid of silver and gold?

    C. Nehemiah was commissioned by Artaxerxes to go to Jerusalem. In Neh. 2:5, Nehemiah asks permission to go and rebuild the city, and for letters to the governors of the provinces asking them to furnish him with proper timber to make the repairs. Thus the phrase of Nehemiah "That I may rebuild it" fits the description issued by Gabriel. But 2:16 indicates that the work had already begun, but for some reason had halted; it further indicates that Nehemiah was chosen by God as a leader of the workmen and, as the one chosen by God to finish the work. There is no room for assumption in the matter. If we choose the commission by Artaxerxes to Nehemiah, we best fit the decree described by Gabriel. When the date is reckoned with, we find no little problem. We will not go into the many historical calendars of that day, but when we recognize that this is a Jewish date and their calendar must be considered, we will arrive at about 453 for the issue of the decree.

D. The work on the house of God had been halted, perhaps by the same people who tried to stop Nehemiah, and Nehemiah went down in the face of danger and repaired the gates and walls. This gave the people faith to finish the work on the temple. If true, then seven weeks or 49 years was allotted to finish the work on the temple, at which time the expiration date would have been 405 B.C. Then would have begun the sixty-two weeks or 434 years, and the period would have expired in AD 30, about the time Christ was baptized. The scripture says, "And after this the Messiah would be cut off and have nothing." At the expiration of the 434 years would be the last and most important week, the one where the Messiah would stop the sacrifice in the middle of that week, or three and one-half years. Christ would be offered on the cross as the last legal sacrifice under the Law of Moses. Heb. 9:26.

E. Observations:
   1. The errorist has willfully ignored the truth of Daniel and has used error to scare unlearned people into a particular belief.
   2. The Church of our Lord in failing to teach the book of Daniel has allowed many of its members to fall into the millennial hog pen. And now the church has waited so long to teach Daniel that, when the truth is presented, one is almost put in the class of false teachers.
   3. Let us remember that Christ himself was classed among the false teachers of his day, and even murdered for his teaching. What is our reputation compared to His life?
   4. There is a pressing need for Daniel to be studied and taught in the church of today. The whole of

the New Testament is a commentary on Daniel, especially the book of Revelation. Compare the visions of John with the sum of the visions of Daniel. Remember that Daniel was not allowed to write some of the visions he saw, but was told by the angel they would be sealed up until the end time of his people. If Revelation does not reveal those matters sealed up until the end time of Israel, where is the book that does?

Verse 26. "Then after the sixty-two weeks the Messiah shall be cut off." The phrase "after the 62 weeks" means that after the first seven weeks expired, the 62 weeks would begin, and after the 62 weeks expired, the Messiah would be cut off; he would die. As stated before, the expiration of this sixty-two week period would be AD 30. We are now concerned with events that should occur in the latter portion of the 69 weeks, and the beginning of the last and final week.

    A. During the latter portion of the 69 weeks, Christ was born, John came as His forerunner, Mal. 4:5-6; Elijah of Malachi was John the Immerser, Matt. 11:11-14. This is the "last days" spoken of in the Old Testament, referring to the period from the coming of Christ in birth, until He came back in the destruction of Jerusalem.

    B. During the expiration of 69 weeks, Christ would come to John to be baptized by him. The coming of the Spirit of God upon Christ at this point would confirm the beginning of the last week. In every case there are notable events that inaugurate a new epoch. And no greater event was present than when God confirmed His Son by sending the Spirit upon Him in the form of a dove and speaking from heaven. And besides this, there was the administration of baptism, a purification which the Jews expected to be practiced in the Last Days in preparation for the coming of the Messiah and His Kingdom (see Ezek. 36:25 and Mal. 3:1-4). These things confirmed that the last week of the seventy weeks had begun.

    C. In the middle of this week, Christ would be tried by the Jews, rejected, and condemned to die on the cross. His sacrificial death put a stop to sacrifice. The fair meaning is that Christ, at the cross, would legally end the Law of Moses where sacrifice was required. By the shedding of His blood, Christ would purchase the kingdom, Acts. 20:28, and by His blood the last sacrifice would be offered. Not only does this confirm the words of Gabriel; it confirms the New Covenant. This is not to say that sacrifice was not offered in the temple at Jerusalem, for it continued there until the temple was destroyed in AD 70. Paul made sacrifice there, Acts ch. 21. Actually, sacrifice was not needed, for the last sacrifice had already been made and the New Covenant established. It shows the longsuffering of God, when He gave the nation of Israel almost forty years after the death of the Son to merge into Christianity before bringing destruction to the temple.

Verse 27. "And He will make a firm Covenant with the many for one week, but in the middle of the week He will put a stop to sacrifice." As has been stated for v. 26, this week began with the baptism of Christ, and continued for three and one-half years in which He taught the New Covenant (the gospel about the Kingdom). At the expiration of three and one-half years, He would put an end to sacrifice by offering Himself as a full payment for man's sin guilt. Only one who was sinless could offer Himself for our redemption. No mere man could offer it. This testifies to the Deity of Christ and to the exclusiveness of the Christian faith as a source for true salvation. No other Name can offer real atonement. Beginning with Adam and Eve (e.g. the skins used to cover their nakedness) and throughout the Old Testament, the sacrifices were symbolic of the Coming One whose sacrificial death would redeem man from condemnation and separation from God's fellowship, and cover their sins.

"And on the wings of abominations will come one who makes desolate even until a complete destruction." Jesus said, "Do not think that I came to bring peace on the earth; I did not come to bring peace, but a sword" (destruction). Therefore, we see the balance of the last week beginning when the Holy Spirit is poured out upon the twelve, and the teaching of Christ goes forth.

A question is asked at this point: What was the main subject of His teaching, since He stated that He came to bring a sword, or destruction? The fair meaning is that all the visions of Daniel would here begin to be fulfilled respecting the end time of his people. We find all the epistles filled with the passing of Israel and the established divine religion of Christ, Christianity, surpassing Judaism as the universal religion.

As we make an overview of Israel from the time they came under the rule of Rome until this period of the last week, we notice that Israel came under the protection, or rule, of Rome when Pompey in 63 B.C. brought this nation under his control. He became the sole ruler of Rome, thus becoming Daniel's first horn.

Daniel's vision concerned the period from the conquest of Israel until the nation was destroyed. This makes Pompey Daniel's first horn and Vespasian the eleventh. Many scholars have tried for many years to make the horns of Daniel and of John fit in perfect order, which makes the book of Revelation a late composition and setting its visions in the future. We have lost sight of the purpose of the visions. They concerned only Daniel's people.

From the time the apostles began to teach, they went first and always to the Jew, relating the abolishment of Judaism in favor of Christianity. On the wings of this testimony by the Holy Spirit the desolation began, a desolation that continued on the wings of abomination until Jerusalem and the temple became a complete destruction. This confirmed the kingdom of Christ in just the same way that the resurrection confirmed Christ as being the Son of God, Rom. 1:4.

Now we move to the destruction itself. Gabriel tells Daniel it will be a complete destruction, Dan. 9:27; Zechariah tells us Christ will return in that destruction and will gather all the nations against Jerusalem for battle, Zech. 14:1-4. Malachi spoke of this as God preparing a day when He would burn the chaff and save the righteous, when they would skip about in the stall as fat calves, Mal. 4:2. Joel spoke of the church age and related the return of Christ to this event, Joel 2:31. Jesus said he would return to reward the wicked with revenge, Mt. 16:27-28, and again in Mt. 23:34-39; 24:29-30; 26:64; Lk. 21:20-32. Matthew 10:23 almost sets the date for His return and this great destruction of Israel.

Daniel sees this event occurring during the period

of the eleventh horn, the time the Ancient of Days would come in judgment, Dan. 7:21,22. The saints would be given into the hands of the horn that caused Daniel so much concern, the eleventh horn. "And they will be given into his hands for a time, times, and a half time."

As already mentioned, some make this time three and one-half centuries, which was the total period of persecution against the church. It is very true the persecution against the church lasted until about the middle of the third century. But, this is not the meaning of the time, times, and a half time, as we see by the following:

A. All the visions pertained to Daniel's people. From the visions themselves we learn that there was a time element involved which began at the conquest of that nation by Pompey in 63 B.C. It began with the first horn who would rule over them, and moved through time until they were destroyed by the eleventh horn, Vespasian.

B. If Daniel 7:25 was rendered as three and one-half years it would not conflict with Rev. 12. Almost everyone admits this refers to the church during the siege against Jerusalem. In v. 14 the church was carried away into the wilderness to be nourished by God for a time, times, and a half time. Now it would be ridiculous to make the point that the church was in the wilderness for 350 years and then made its reappearance. The facts of history dispel this idea. History informs us that after the destruction of Jerusalem, the church became stronger, was more widespread, and even was declared the imperial religion before this period was over.

The church was not shut up for 350 years, but was in the wilderness for three and a half years. So the phrase of Revelation must mean three and one-half years. It seems that both prophets were speaking of the same event. If so, then Daniel also meant three and one-half years.

C. Some interpreters, when discussing New Testament salvation and redemption, will quickly affirm that all the appropriate Old Testament prophecies of redemption, according to Lk. 21:22, were fulfilled when Jerusalem and the temple were destroyed. Yet when dealing with other Old Testament prophecies of the resurrection or judgment or end of the age, they will say that these particular prophecies have not been fulfilled. See the inconsistency?

1. Dan. 7:25. If the time, times, and a half time means three and one-half centuries, or 350 years, the prophecies would extend well beyond the point when Luke said they would all be fulfilled. Why?
2. Notice the prophecy of Joel 2:28-32. Here these same great men will say that verses 28 and 29 refer to the church age, but that verses 30, 31, and 32a belong to the end of the world when Christ shall return to deliver up the kingdom. Then they will return to v. 32b and say it pertains to the escape of the Christians during the siege of Jerusalem.
3. Where is the consistency of such teaching? Luke has just stated that when Jerusalem was destroyed, all that was written shall be fulfilled. Then they say that Luke was speaking only about the destruction of Jerusalem. Sometimes they can get away with such a statement. But Luke said all things written! I submit to you that if certain portions of Daniel and Joel can be moved into the yet future, then there is no limit to the prophesies yet to be fulfilled. Absurd! Who are these people trying to fool! Not God, and not people who believe his Word.

I conclude that Gabriel related to Daniel the full destruction of Israel as a nation and of their religion, and further that all the visions of Daniel would be fulfilled at the end time of that nation, which came at the hands of Vespasian in A.D. 70. Paul states the people were in the tribulation during his writing of 1 Thess. 3:4. John declared in Rev. 1:1-3 that the things written in the Book were at hand, then in the process of being fulfilled. Then he declares in 1:9, "I John your brother in tribulation, and in the kingdom."

Both scripture and history verify a tribulation for the Jewish people beginning AD 66. On the "wings of this tribulation came the one who was to make the final destruction to the nation of Israel. Thus the vision of Daniel finds its fulfillment in this period, Dan. 12:1; Mt. 24:21.

DANIEL CHAPTER 10

Introductory Remarks:

Contrary to the opinions of some authorities, the chapters as they are placed in the book of Daniel are not in chronological order. At first notice we find chapter 10 was written in the third year of Cyrus. Chapter 11 was written in the first year of Darius the Mede, and chapter 12 is not dated, but has strong inference that it is the last of the messages. It is a continuation of chapter 10, where the angel returns to Daniel after having to leave abruptly at the close of chapter 10. Beginning in chapter 12 the angel finishes the message that began in chapter 10.

The following places the vision chapters in proper order.

A. We should read the visions under Belshazzar, chapters 7 and 8,
B. Under the Medo-Persian empire, Gobryas Darius, chapters 6, 11, 9.
C. Under Cyrus king of Persia, chapters 10 and 12.

It is important in the study of Daniel to understand that Gobryas Darius reigned as king over the Babylonian Empire. He reigned some nine years over the Babylonian Empire, while Cyrus reigned over the Persian Empire as king of the lands.

In the first year of the reign of Cyrus, a decree went forth throughout the empire authorizing the Jews to return to their homeland. Ezra 1:1-6. But now, in the third year of Cyrus reign, Daniel was mourning for three weeks. We are not told the occasion for his mourning, however, it could have been that Daniel was distressed over the fact that the majority of his people desired to stay in Babylon with their Chaldean family. Yet another reason could be explained from 10:1. In the third year of Cyrus there could have been great problems arising in the empire as a result of the Jews leaving, there could have been an uprising among the government officials designed to stop the exiles from leaving the country. Whatever the reason, Daniel was in straits.

Now the angel returns, but with more bad news. No

answer is forthcoming respecting Daniel's personal problem. Obviously the angel was instructed to withhold any information which would give answers to Daniel's problem; instead the angel arrives perhaps with a full commentary upon the message given in Dan. 9:24-27. He probably relates to Daniel what will befall his nation at the appointed time. Although not stated, it could be that every detail was told to Daniel, even the reason for God removing the kingdom of God from Israel, and giving it to other nations. The contents of the vision is nowhere revealed. The only portions of the message that we can be sure of is v. 1, a vision of great calamity and sorrow.

In v. 14, the vision and message were directed to the nation of Israel, Daniel's people. This must remain sealed up, since it is not revealed. Daniel is told in 12:4 to seal up the book until the end time (for Israel, not the end of all time). The end time for Israel came in AD 70 when theocratic Israel was destroyed by Rome. There can be no doubt that the things revealed to Daniel respecting his people were later made known by John in the Revelation, which was written in the "end time," and concerns the fall of Israel.

The sealing up, or keeping secret, cannot refer to the book of Daniel being finished. If the phrase meant the book was finished, then it would have been finished in 8:26, and no more would have been recorded.

Verse 1. "And the message was true and one of great conflict, but he understood the message and he had an understanding of the vision." Notice the following:

A. This message and vision given to Daniel was one of great conflict, one as described in Mt. 24; Lk. 21 and the book of Revelation, one of such conflict that Daniel lost his speech, one that brought great sorrow, one in which the angel tells Daniel that he is to seal it up and not reveal it, that it would be revealed at the end time for his people, Dan. 12:4.

B. Could it be that Daniel was so stricken with grief that it rendered him unable to write? We see very clearly that here the second person is involved. Notice the phrase he understood the message and he understood the vision; then in v. 3, we move back to "I Daniel." It is possible at this time in his old age that someone was writing for Daniel, nevertheless, this does not change the import of the chapter.

C. This vision and message that was told Daniel here is nowhere mentioned in this chapter, the only relation to the vision is found in v. 14, where it pertained to Daniel's people, and was yet future, but would have its fulfillment at the end time of his people. This meant that when the Law of Moses was put away in favor of Christianity, the kingdom of Israel would come to its end, the end time for Israel, the end of their world. We know this, for Jesus died at the end of the world, Heb. 9:26, "Whosoever remaineth from all these that I have told thee shall escape, and see my salvation and the end of your world." *Old Testament Apocrypha,* 2 Esdras 6:25.

D. Is it possible to see that under the conditions of Israel present at that time, a message of even further and greater calamities than they had already suffered would have incited them to a quicker rebellion against God? And subsequently have incited God's anger against them sooner than was planned, as shown in Daniel 9:24-27?

If the above observations be true, then Daniel was to reveal only those things at that time that would be profitable to his people. Therefore, those things revealed to him respecting the last days of the Jews would have, if revealed, incited them to more evil and rejection of God. Israel was told by Moses what would befall them in the event they rebelled against God, and this was preached by the prophets, Deut. 28:15-68. But here Daniel is shown when this will take place, and what nation will bring about their end.

But all this was to be sealed up until the end time, then it would be revealed. Jesus began to reveal this to Israel in the book of Matthew, and the apostles likewise revealed much. But John in the Revelation gives a full commentary upon the visions of Daniel.

Notice chapter 5 of Revelation. Here is the book that is to be opened and its contents made known. This is not the book of life; it is opened later at the judgment. This is the book that contains all the calamities that were to befall the nation (the "complete end" or "complete shattering"), and Jesus is the only one found worthy to open that book. Therefore, Jesus began to teach in the nation of Israel, and in all His teaching He warned Israel of that which was about to befall the wicked, those who would reject him as the Christ. Consider the following:

A. In the parable to the Jews respecting the tares, Jesus here quotes almost word for word the prophecy of Mal. 4:1-3, where Malachi speaks of God preparing a day when the chaff would be burned; which refers to the wicked unbelievers of Israel in the last days. Notice the words of Jesus, "As therefore the tares are gathered and burned in the fire, so shall it be in the end of this world," Matt. 13:40. The word "world" is the Greek word AIONOS (from AION), meaning an "age" (duration or period) of time. The plural form of this Greek word is used in Heb. 9:26 where it says Jesus died at "the consummation of the ages." The same word is also used in Mt. 24:3 where the disciples asked what signs would indicate when "the end of the age" was about to occur. W. E. Vine renders the word as follows, "The phrase 'the end of the world' should be rendered 'the end of the age.' AION is an age, a period of time." W. E. Vine, *Dictionary of New Testament Words*, (under "world") p. 233.

   In *Young's Analytical Concordance*, p. 1073, under the Greek word "AION," he says it is a dispensation of time, Mt. 13:39-40, 24:3; Heb. 9:26." The word "world" is translated as an age within all the ages of time, not as the end of time.

   Thayer, "world," aion and plural, "The Jews distinguished the time before the Messiah, and the time after the advent." A past age, or future age, unto the day which is eternity." *Thayer Greek Lexicon*, article "World" p. 19. Other Lexicons consulted confirm the above.

B. Jesus intended, and did a good job, of saying what Malachi had already said, that the wicked would be burned at the end time of Israel; their destruction would be so severe as to say they were destroyed by fire, leaving only ashes. Malachi said there would be no root left unto them. Daniel was shown this in full, but was not allowed at that time to reveal it.

The full revelation was left for New Testament prophets. Peter used the same words as Malachi and Christ. All were speaking to the nation of Israel, and Peter makes it clear the prophets had already spoken of this, 2 Peter 3:1-2.

C. Jesus said that all these things would come upon that generation, Mt. 24:34; 16:28; Lk. 21:32. John said these things must shortly take place, and the time is near, Rev. 1:1,3, and closes his book by saying "The God of the spirit of the prophets sent His angel to show to His bondservant the things which must shortly take place." Rev. 22:6-7, 10, 12, 20, all of which Daniel could not reveal.

Verse 2. "In those days I Daniel had been mourning for three entire weeks." Daniel had set apart this time as an extraordinary fast on behalf of his people, and he was sad and troubled. Daniel does not say why he had set aside this time for fasting and prayer, or why he was so troubled; but the fair interpretation is that he, like Nehemiah, was greatly concerned over the welfare of his people and the rebuilding of Jerusalem.

We find in the record of Ezra that the exiles were not anxious to leave Babylon, and those who did not leave were not totally committed to rebuilding the city of Jerusalem and the temple. Therefore, Daniel could have been grieved over the spiritual condition of his people. But now, the angel comes forth again, not to give Daniel an answer to his prayers, but to further inform him of great distress which is to befall his people in the last days.

Verse 3. "I did not eat any tasty food, no meat, nor wine." It is not to be understood that Daniel ate no food at all, only that he ate no tasty food. At this point we might gain a greater insight into the subject, should we consider chapter 1, where Daniel made up his mind to eat no tasty food, and no wine. Perhaps the statement means that he ate only bread and water. One thing is sure; Daniel here confirms his continued practice of total abstinence of wine and meat.

Contrary to the statement made by Christ about what should be done when fasting Mt. 6:17, Daniel uses no sweet-smelling ointments on himself. Daniel as a governmental official, who could have had the very best, abstained during the period from those things which he ordinarily observed as promoting his personal comfort. Daniel gave himself up to a course of life which would be expressive of deep grief and righteous living, he was overwhelmed with sorrow.

Verse 4. "And on the twenty-fourth day of the first month." At the close of the days of fasting, though he had not set aside this period with any view or expectation that it would follow with such results, Daniel received extraordinary visions and messages. His mind was in a prepared state by this extraordinary season of devotion to receive the communication given. Daniel's mind was on the condition of his people; it was a fitting time to impart to him the extraordinary knowledge of what would occur to his people in future days. But the summary of the vision and messages is not given.

Two great attributes of Daniel are shown here, which should be observed by every Christian. Daniel prepared and conditioned his mind to communicate with God, and to receive His message. Daniel waited upon God with intense and prolonged devotion. He continued to tug at the heart strings of God. It is no wonder that moderns think God is dead! He is very much alive! It is we who are dead, especially when we compare our prayer life to that of Daniel.

Verse 5. "I lifted mine eyes and looked." The way in which Daniel makes the statement would lead us to assume that he was in deep devotion, occupied in deep thought and meditation, perhaps with his eyes closed or fixed on the ground, and then he looked up to see "a certain man dressed in linen, whose waist was girded with a belt of pure gold."

The subsequent disclosures showed this man to be an angel; it is not uncommon for angels to appear on earth as a man, even dressed as royalty. The men who came to Abraham and ate and drink with him were dressed as men of that country, Gen. 18:1-4. Since the purpose behind both these angelic appearances was destroy some wicked cities, it seems possible that the same angel may have appeared in both places, and maybe the same angel who appeared to Daniel on the banks of the Ulai (see Dan. 8:16) and who gave the revelation of the seventy weeks.

Being girded with a waist band of pure gold would

denote one such as was worn by kings and other high officers of the Persian Empire, customary in the East at that time. The angel probably appeared to Daniel as the custom of the day was, and the waist band would denote the angel's high rank.

Verse 6. "And his body was like Beryl." There seems to be much resemblance between this appearance and the one recorded in Rev. 1:13-16. Beryl is a mineral of great hardness, occurring in green and bluish green with six-sided prisms, see the Little & Ives, *Webster Dictionary,* Classical Reference Library, Word Beryl. p. 130.

"And his face as the appearance of lightning." Bright and shining, as John said of the angel in Rev. 1:16, "bright and shining as the sun in its strength." Coming from the presence of the Lord, he would naturally shine with glory. When Moses was in the presence of the Lord on the mountain when he received the law, he had to wear a veil, for his face shone with such brightness the people could not look upon him, Ex. 34:29-35. It is not strange for a being sent from God to shine as the lightning, or as bright as the sun.

Verse 7. "Now I, Daniel alone saw the vision." The others who were with him seemed to hear strange sounds which alarmed them, and it appears they fled from the place. It is not stated as to who the others were.

Verse 8. "So I was left alone and saw this great vision." As has already been stated, no mention is made respecting the events of the vision, only that he received it. Again we have a vision seen by Daniel that is sealed up until the end time. Consider this: if this sealing up until the end time means the end of the present world, then we will have a future prophet who will reveal the contents of Daniel's visions. Absurd! These matters which are not revealed here are found revealed in New Testament books, and just prior to the end time of Israel.

At the end time the visions not explained here would be opened (i.e., Rev. 5) to reveal the curses and plagues that had already been decreed upon this people from their beginnings under Moses. In Deuteronomy 28-33 (esp. Deut. 28:15-68) it talks about the curses that would be poured out upon the final wicked generation of Israel. That idea is in the background of the visions seen here by Daniel. After catching a visionary glimpse of the "complete destruction" that was coming for the Jewish nation off in the future, Daniel was left with no strength. We see a similar condition in John after he had seen some similar visions in the book of Revelation (Rev. 1:17).

Verse 9. "But I heard the sound of his words." What the angel said to Daniel when he appeared to him is not recorded. Daniel says in v. 6 "the voice of his words were like multitudes." It is probable that those who were with Daniel heard these great voices, and because of this were frightened away.

"And as soon as I heard the sound of his words, I fell into a deep sleep on my face, with my face to the ground." That is when Daniel heard the severity of the message, and being so alarmed at the degree of it, he fell prostrate and senseless upon the earth. Perhaps the horror of the things spoken by the angel would have brought sudden fright to Daniel. After all, this pertained to his people.

Verse 10. "Then behold a hand touched me, and set me on my feet." The angel had touched Daniel, restored his strength and reassured him. He was able to stand up, but still very shaken and trembling. The vision of Israel's end time was understandably disturbing for Daniel.

Verse 11. "And he said to me, O Daniel, a man greatly beloved." That is, Daniel was greatly beloved in heaven, and among the angels. "Understand the words I speak to thee." This implies the words would be spoken in a language Daniel could understand.

Verse 12. "Then he said to me, do not be afraid. I have come in response to your words." Daniel had been fasting and praying for his people, and his nation, and thus far in all the messages and visions Daniel had only received sad news. Because of the alarming vision about his people in their latter days, Daniel has been feeble and frightened; he is reassured by the angel.

It is impossible to know the extent of the vision that so upset Daniel, but since this vision looked to the end time for Israel, we can see what later transpired at the end time and see why Daniel was upset. As stated in 10:14, the vision pertained to his people and was yet future. And from 12:1, we can understand that the events seen in the vision looked ahead to the destruction of Israel in AD 70. Jesus gave his dissertation concerning the destruction of Jerusalem and the temple in Matthew 24, and in v. 15

said, "This is that which was spoken of by Daniel the prophet." Therefore, Daniel was speaking in chapter 7 of the end of Israel, and the angel who returned in chapter 9 made it very clear that the city and temple would be destroyed, and even fixed an appointed time.

"In response to your words." The angel came as soon as possible; although the prayer was heard at the beginning, and the angel was dispatched, there were conditions in Persia that delayed the angel from coming directly to Daniel. But the angel came in response to Daniel's prayer.

Verse 13. "But the prince of the kingdom of Persia was withstanding me for twenty-one days." It is revealed here that this angel was a bad angel, a "prince" of the kingdom (of Persia) withstood him. It is also implied that this prince had some guardian care over that kingdom, watching over its interests, and directing its affairs through Cyrus. Satan is the prince of this world, Eph. 2:2, therefore the angels of Satan were directing the mind of Cyrus, not permitting him the decree that would allow Israel safe passage to Palestine. When the angel of the Lord arrived in Persia, the angel of God was challenged. The good angel from God was about to interfere with Satan's plans for the children of Israel, and this angel called upon Gabriel for help.

Perhaps it can best be said that the plans of the kings of Persia at this time did not meet with what God had decreed, and for which Daniel prayed. Thus in Isa. 45:1-3 God makes it clear that He will stir up the mind of Cyrus. No doubt this is the time when God's plan will be put into force, and this was brought about by the prince of Persia withstanding the angel of God, for it was at this point the angel of God called for Gabriel.

Verse 14. "Now I have come to give you understanding of what will happen to your people in the latter days, for the vision pertains to the days yet future." From this statement may we observe the following:

A. It is not to be assumed here that "what will happen in the latter days" pertains to just one event. Rather the events would continue till the end time, when Christ would die on the cross, when the temple would be destroyed, and this people would no longer be God's chosen. Daniel saw the beginning of the end when Antiochus IV began to inflict heavy burdens on the people.

B. "What will happen to your people." Let there be no misunderstanding. Daniel was an exile from Judah, in short, a Jew. The message was for the Jews, not the Gentiles.

The reader is to observe carefully here that these events had their total fulfillment at the destruction of Jerusalem in AD 70, see Lk. 21:22. Jesus said that all Old Testament prophecy (the only prophecy that was written at the time He spoke) would be fulfilled in those "days of vengeance" that would see Jerusalem, the Temple, and Palestine utterly destroyed. Those events are not still future as many today proclaim.

C. "In the latter days." This does not imply, nor can we draw the conclusion, that the statement means the latter days of Christianity, or the end of this present world. Scripture does not speak of an end of Christianity, but rather an end of Judaism. See Isa. 9:6-7 and Eph. 3:21.

From the beginning of this nation, God knew Israel would turn from Him and go after other gods, Deut. 31:29. Thus the "latter days, the last days, in that day, the end time, the end of the world," all indicated a period in time, and not the end of time. Quite a difference. But more especially it named a time when the commonwealth of Israel would pass away, and the temple worship would be abolished in favor of Christianity. This time between the cross, when Jesus legally abolished the law and the destruction of the temple gave the Jews almost forty years to merge into Christianity. These were the last days, the end of the Mosaic dispensation.

All four Gospels contain prophecy that would begin to be fulfilled on the first Pentecost after the death of Christ. He lived and died under the Mosaic Law. The Hebrew writer informs us that Christ was manifested to put away sin, by the sacrifice of Himself! But when? The same writer says at the end of the world—meaning the Jewish world. Heb. 9:26.

Notice also, in the "last days" the church would be established. Perhaps a better phrase would be that the church was born. (Isa. 2:1-3) Within the same period of "last days," Joel records, "In the last days I will pour out my spirit on all flesh, your sons and daughters will prophesy, and your young men shall see visions, and I will grant wonders in the sky above, and signs on the earth beneath, blood and fire, and vapor of smoke, the sun shall be turned into darkness, and the moon into blood." (Joel 2:29-32) Now notice Acts 2:16, "But this is what was spoken of through the prophet Joel, and it shall be in the last days..."

In short, those events that happened after the resurrection of Christ were part of the "last days," the "perverse and crooked generation" that would see the End that had been prophesied not only in Daniel and Joel, but in Deut. 28-33 as well. Now, according to both Joel and Peter, these things would continue until the "Second Coming." The scripture points out many things that would happen before the great and glorious day of the Lord shall come; see the latter portion of v. 20.

Now what does all this mean? It simply means that the Holy Spirit, prophecy, visions, great wonders in the sky, blood and fire, the sun darkened, the moon becoming blood, would continue to be in use until the "coming of the Lord." (See the glossary of symbolic terms.) Yes, it means that the Lord had not yet come, and until then there were sons and daughters who possessed the ability to prophesy, receive visions, and perform miracles.

If the reader is not satisfied that both Joel and Peter say that spiritual gifts will continue "until the Lord comes," then look at 1 Cor. 1:7-8. "So that you are not lacking in any gift, awaiting eagerly the revelation of our Lord Jesus Christ, who shall also confirm you to the end, blameless in the day of our Lord Jesus Christ." In 1 Cor. 1:5, Paul confirms that the Corinthians had the miraculous gifts, since they were enriched in all speech, and in all knowledge. The word "all" means that nothing was lacking. They had "all" the gifts. However, the passage does not promise the continuation of those gifts after the "coming of the Lord." If the "Lord has come," then no one today has powers of the Holy Spirit to heal others, or the miraculous inspired ability to reveal more knowledge, or to miraculously speak in languages that he never learned. However, if Jesus has not returned, then those miraculous gifts of the Holy Spirit must still be active, and God must still be inspiring and endowing prophets today to heal, prophesy, and receive visions.

The prophet Malachi spoke to the Jewish nation, and in Mal. 4:1-5 makes it clear that the calamity was directed to the Hebrew nation "Behold a day is coming" is equal to the "last days"; the expression "last days" does not refer to the annihilation of earth and the end of all time. It meant the end of the old covenantal age of Mosaic Law which was focused upon the Temple and sacrifices. Malachi further said "The day is coming burning like a furnace, and all the arrogant will be burned up; they will be set ablaze." This passage is equal to Matthew chapter 13 respecting the tares. Peter spoke to the same people respecting the same event in 2 Pet. 3. Notice Peter in v. 2 informs the Jewish Christians that the prophets had already informed them of this calamity. Joel and Malachi were two of those prophets. James, when writing to the twelve tribes, Jas. 1:1, told them to be patient, "until the coming of the Lord... Behold the Judge is standing right at the door." This would to be a commentary on Daniel.

Verse 15. "And when he had spoken these words, I turned my face to the ground." Daniel was naturally overcome by the communication which had been made to him. The manner in which the prayer was answered seems to have been different from what he had expected. The angel's revelations respecting the future overcame him, and he lay on the ground, speechless over the future of his people. Lying on the ground was a custom of godly people. 2 Sam. 12:16-20 It was a way to show reverence to God.

Verse 16. "And he touched my lips, and I opened my mouth." The reference here probably is to Gabriel appearing to Daniel in human form, restoring his speech and removing his fright. Now he was able to address the heavenly messenger, and say, "O my Lord." This was a title of respect for an angelic being. Abraham addressed the angels as "my Lord." Gen. 18:1-3.

Verse 17. "How can such a servant of my Lord talk with such as my Lord? There is no strength or speech left in me." Here Daniel acknowledges his humble and lowly state in the presence of an angel, a messenger sent from God. Daniel was utterly overcome and prostrate. The appearance of a mighty angel would be intimidating to anyone. It should be no surprise that Daniel was overcome by the experience.

Verse 18. "This one touched me again and strengthened me." The one mentioned in v. 26 came again and gave strength to him, that he might be able at the end of the revelation to understand its meaning, and be able to receive the full communication without fear.

Verse 19. "Do not be afraid, take courage, and I received my strength, now may my Lord speak." There appears to be nothing in the visitation by the angel to cause alarm, but there were alarming events in the message and vision. But the angel gives Daniel strength, and now Daniel asks that the angel continue with his message "Now let my Lord speak" Daniel was ready to receive the balance of the message, which is not here recorded.

Verses 20-21. "Do you understand why I came to you?" Daniel's answer is not stated. There can be no doubt that Daniel did not fully understand all the message, or how it would be fulfilled.

"But, now I shall return to fight against the prince of Persia." The angel informs Daniel that he must return to fight against the evil prince, so he must leave Daniel quickly, but will return to give the balance of the message, which we shall receive in chapter 12.

This seems to be referring back to what the angel said in verse 13, about the prince of Persia withstanding him for 21 days. But by the interposition of Michael, the affairs of Persia had been arranged so the opposition was in part removed, at least giving time for the angel to come to Daniel and inform him that his prayer had been heard, and the answer was on the way.

But, again trouble has arisen in Persia, and the angel must depart at once to contend with the evil prince of Persia. Obviously there were evil forces in the kingdom of Persia trying to frustrate the plans for the safety of the exiles yet remaining in Persia.

From the tone of the passage, it seems the angel would now return to Persia and after winning victory over the evil angel, would direct the affairs of Persia to protect both the Jews in Jerusalem and those in Persia. After such time, Daniel would receive the balance of this vision and message, which is recorded in chapter 12.

"However, I will tell thee what is inscribed in the writings of truth." The full implication of this statement is set forth in the following observations:

A. "I will tell thee what is inscribed in the writings of truth." Obviously the angel had reference to the written Word of God, the prophets who had gone before, and who had left God's Word inscribed even on stone. Moses had inscribed the fall of Daniel's people, and gave a description of events prior to that fall. Deut. 28:1-68. All the prophets named the spiritual conditions of Israel, pleaded for their return to God, and foretold the consequence of not returning to God.

B. The angel related to Daniel the entire history of Israel's rebellion against God. In addition, the angel related every calamity that was recorded that should befall Israel, before their end came.

C. "That is inscribed in the writings of truth, not only pertaining to those matters recorded by the prophets, but those things which are written in heaven. Revelation chapter 5 begins to expose those truths written in heaven. In short, Daniel was shown, and was told, the complete history of Israel, until the appointed time of their end.

D. Nowhere in the book of Daniel is the vision and message here mentioned recorded, and we have no authority to build where there is no foundation. This was sealed up until the end time, when John in the book of Revelation would unveil those writings of truth recorded in heaven, and to fully explain the matters revealed to Daniel in v. 21.

DANIEL CHAPTER 11

Introductory Remarks.
As noted previously, chapter 11 is not in its proper chronological order. Note the following:
   A. In Dan. 5:31 it is stated that Darius the Mede received the kingdom of Babylon at about the age of 62. There can be no doubt that Gobryas Darius, sometimes called Cyaxares II, lived between Astyages and Cyrus. Therefore, Darius the Mede was the immediate successor of Belshazzar, and reigned over the Babylonian Empire for some nine years, or until his death. Then Cyrus became king of the lands. See Isa. 13:17; Jeremiah 51:1-64; Dan. 5:28. The Babylonian Empire was promised to Darius the Mede so long as he lived, at which time the power of the Medes would blend into the Persian Empire.
   B. No reason need be given for Cyrus having offered the decree for the freedom of the exiles while Darius, as king over the empire, retained the authority to free the Hebrews. However, just as the prophecy respecting the Medes as being God's instrument against Babylon must be fulfilled, there was also the prophecy which said that Cyrus, as king of Persia, in order to fulfill the prophecy of Jeremiah, must give the proclamation for the freedom of the Jews. 2 Chron. 36:22-23. Notice Darius begin to reign over the Empire of Babylon in 538 B.C., while Cyrus began to reign over the Persian Empire also in 538 B.C. Further, where Cyrus the king is mentioned it is stated "Cyrus King of Persia."
   C. Notice in chapter 10 it says, "In the third year of Cyrus king of Persia." By this designation it must mean that Darius is still on the throne in Babylon, for both began to reign the same year. It would not have been uncommon for Daniel to mention either king, since he himself was second in command in the Babylonian Empire, a post which he held during the lifetime of Darius the Mede. In Dan. 10:11 the angel seems to recognize Daniel as a high official in the government of Darius, "O Daniel, man of high esteem." There is no mention of Daniel being

an official for Cyrus. Therefore, I suggest that the "third year of Cyrus" was the "third year of Darius."
D. I further suggest that the "Darius" of Daniel is also the Darius of Haggai and of Zechariah. Notice Haggai 1:1, "In the second year of Darius the king." Notice also v. 2, "The people say, the time has not come, even the time for the house of the Lord to be rebuilt." Notice the phrase in v. 4, "While this house lies desolate." What house? The temple. Notice v. 8, "Go up to the mountains, bring wood and rebuild the temple." Verse 14, "The remnant came and worked on the house of the Lord." We need to examine things carefully here to see whether this Darius is indeed the Persian. See Ezra 1:5, during the first year reign of Cyrus "God stirred up the minds to go up and rebuild the house of the Lord which is in Jerusalem." I suggest that this passage is equal to Hag. 1:14, the message is the same. Now look at Ezra 3:8 and remember this would have been in the second year of Cyrus and the second year of Darius. It seems that Haggai 1:14 is here being fulfilled; "They begin the work on the house of the Lord, again Hag. 1:14 and Ezra 3:8 seems to be pointing to the same event, and at the same time. So does Hag. 2:3 and Ezra 3:12. I further find that when Darius the Persian is mentioned, he is called "Darius King of Persia," not simply Darius the king. The temple began to be rebuilt during Cyrus and Darius the Mede. Ezra 4:5 says that the work was hindered from Cyrus to Darius King of Persia. If Haggai and Zechariah began under Darius the Persian, then Hag. 1:2,4,14 occurred during the second year of Darius, and four years later the temple was finished! Ezra 6:15.

Verse 1. "And in the first year of Darius the Mede, I arose to be an encouragement and protection for him." Because of the language of v. 1, I suggest that this chapter should have followed chapter 8. It appears that the king might have had problems with the exiles, as well as with the general population of Babylon. Daniel rose up to protect the king and to encourage him. Chapter 6 shows that the king had problems in the transition of his government. After Daniel was delivered from the power of the lions he rose up to protect the king. It would appear that ch. 9, also written in the first year of Darius the Mede, was written under more tranquil conditions. Daniel says of Darius in 9:1 that Darius was made king over the Chaldean Empire. That is to say Darius the Mede received the Chaldean Empire as his share of war treasure, in order that prophecy might be fulfilled. Accordingly, Daniel enjoyed success during the reigns of both Darius and Cyrus the Persian, that is, after the death of Darius the Mede when the Empire blended into the Persian Empire.

Verse 2. "And now I will tell you the truth. Behold, three more kings are going to arise in Persia, then a fourth will gain far more riches, he will arouse the whole empire against the realm of Greece." In the beginning of this chapter, there is no mention of this message being a vision, or message from the angel. However, v. 14 informs us that these things must come to pass in order that the vision be fulfilled. It would appear that Daniel writes in such style as to show the angel as being the first person. "I will tell you (Daniel) the truth." Daniel states on different occasions that he was astounded with the visions, and had no one to explain it to him. It appears that the angel in chapter 11 is giving the interpretation to Daniel.

Assuming this is the message of an angel, we find he informs Daniel that three more kings will arise in Persia. Cyrus was the first, then after the next three, a fourth would arise, and he will arouse the Persian Empire against Greece in war. Here is another place where only the kings, or rulers, are shown which will consummate a certain event, only four kings are mentioned. The same is shown with the 10 horns of Dan. 7, and then in the same way another horn arises, thus making eleven horns. In Dan. 7, as well as in 11:2, only the kings are mentioned which will consummate a certain event in the history of the world. This is not the only two places where such patterns are shown. Daniel 8:8 is another case where only four horns are mentioned. Like the other two cases, these four horns after Alexander's death would receive the Grecian Empire; they would consummate a certain event in the history of the world. There were other kings who followed the four, just as there were other kings who followed the four mentioned in the Persian Empire, and just as there were others in the Roman Empire. Notice:

A. "Three kings will arise in Persia." There would be three kings in Persia, excluding Cyrus, which he mentions as outstanding, and then the fourth is mentioned who will arouse the empire against Greece. The angel giving the message evidently designs it to touch on the great and leading events respecting the Persian Empire, and so far as they would constitute prominent points in world history.

B. The three kings here referred to were Cambyses, Smerdis, and Darius Hystaspes.

C. The fourth king was Xerxes.
1. Xerxes was far richer than them all.
2. Cyrus, who was to come to the throne in 536, had collected vast amounts of wealth by the conquest of Lydia, and the subjugation of its rich king, Croesus.
3. Cambyses increased the wealth he inherited from Darius the Mede by his victories in the south and by his plundering the temples wherever he went.
4. The wealth was further increased by the conquests of Darius Hystaspes and his heavy taxes on the people.
5. All this vast wealth was inherited by Xerxes.

D. By Xerxes "strength and by his riches" he would stir up all the realm of Greece, that is, he would make war with Greece. Greece had not come under the subjugation of Persia yet, and Xerxes was eager to conquer the small nation of Greece. Will Durant, *The Life of Greece,* p. 538ff.
1. There were several kings after Xerxes, but these are not mentioned because the real ground for the invasion against Greece was laid by Xerxes. The next great conflict would arise when Alexander the Great would invade Persia.
2. Xerxes by his great wealth was able to collect and equip one of the largest armies ever assembled.
3. Xerxes spent four years preparing for the invasion of Greece.
4. The army was gathered out of all parts of Xerxes' empire.
5. The historian Herodotus estimates that the army in all could not have been less than five million men. Herodotus, book 3, Persian Kings.

6. Xerxes was unsuccessful in his war against Greece, and was defeated.

7. From this event with Xerxes, we move to the history of Alexander the Great in v. 3.

Verses 3-4. "And a mighty king will arise, and he will rule with a great authority and do as he pleases." Alexander the Great rose to power at the untimely death of his father Philip of Macedon. Alexander had been schooled well, not only in education, but in war. His father had trained him well to inherit the empire of Macedon, and perhaps not enough credit has been given to Philip of Macedon for the preparation of his son Alexander.

With a small army, Alexander begins his conquest, and with success the army grew. It was God's time for the fall of Persia, and no one could stay God's instrument. Soon Persia fell to Alexander. Then Alexander moves to bring all the empire under his subjugation. When this was accomplished he "stood up and ruled."

A. When Alexander was in the height and glory, with full authority and power, his kingdom was broken by his untimely death in Babylon.

B. The fair meaning is that the empire would not gradually diminish and decay, but his sudden death would effect the rendering of the kingdom into four parts.

C. Alexander's kingdom was "divided to the four winds of heaven" and did not pass to his own posterity.

1. Alexander's wife and son were killed, his half brother also met his death; all who would lay claim to the throne left by Alexander were killed.

2. The four leading generals, *Cassander*, *Lysimachus*, *Seleucus*, and *Ptolemy Soter* were responsible for the death of all the posterity of Alexander.

D. No one of Alexander's successors ruled "according to his dominion which he ruled." Meaning there was no ruler among his successors who ever obtained as wide a dominion as Alexander the Great. *Outline of History*, Vol. 2, by H. G. Wells, pp. 375-410.

E. The above has explained v. 4; v. 5 begins the divided kingdom of Greece, and will look at that division and the four rulers.

Verse 5. "And the king of the south shall be strong."

A. The angel who gave Daniel the message had previously spoken of the general history of Alexander and his empire. The angel now leaves that period and confines his predictions to the two more powerful kings of the divided empire, the king of the north and the king of the south.

B. In dividing the kingdom of Alexander, Cassander received Macedonia, Lysimachus received part of Asia Minor and Thrace, Seleucus received Syria the larger part of the kingdom, Ptolemy Soter received Egypt. The kingdom to the south was south of Palestine, and the kingdom to the north was north of Palestine.

C. The events of these kingdoms would particularly affect the Jewish people. When the Northern Kingdom would make war against the southern kingdom, they would pass through Israel, and Israel would also suffer.

D. "The king of the south" is Ptolemy, king of Egypt. The Egyptian part of the empire was in the hands of the Ptolemies until Egypt was subdued by Rome.

E. The angel further declared, "And one of his princes who shall be strong above him." This was one of the princes from Alexander; one of his generals would receive a greater empire, and would rise to a greater power than Ptolemy of Egypt. This prince would have a more extended empire. The reference here is to Seleucus I Nicator. In the division of the empire he obtained Syria, Babylon, Media, Susiana, Armenia, a part of Cappadocia and Cilicia. His kingdom stretched from the Hellespont to the Indus. He reigned from 312 to 280 B.C.

Verse 6. "In the end of years they shall join themselves together." In the end of the years means in the future of these two kingdoms. In short, the events would not occur in the lives of these two kings, but many years later. It would be their heirs that would bring the two kingdoms together.

The statement of the angel, "they shall join themselves together" means that an alliance would be made, or an attempt would be made to unite the two kingdoms. This unity would be affected by a marriage. "For the king's daughter of the south shall come to the king of the north to make an arrangement."

The compact referred to here was the one formed by the marriage between Bernice, the daughter of Ptolemy Philadelphus, king of Egypt, and Antiochus Theos, king of Syria. Ptolemy made this arrangement in order to stop the war with Syria in which he was engaged. One condition of this alliance was that Antiochus would divorce his former wife, Laodicea. Another condition was that the children of the former should be excluded from succession to the throne. Ptolemy hoped that the kingdom of Syria might become ultimately attached to Egypt.

The angel then declared concerning the agreement, "But she shall not retain the power of the arm." Bernice would not hold her power; her father Ptolemy Philadelphus died two years after this marriage was consummated. Antiochus then restored his former wife Laodicea. Then Laodicea murdered Antiochus. The officers of the court of Syria planned the death of Bernice and her children, but she fled with them to Daphne, and there was put to death.

The angel declared, "Neither shall he stand," meaning that the king of the south would not prosper in his ambitious purpose to bring Syria, by the marriage alliance, under his control. Instead, he died.

The angel's statement, "But she shall be given up," means that Bernice would be given up to death. The statement, "And he that begot her," seems to say that he who sired her (Ptolemy) would also be given up to death, and her offspring would be put to death. *The Life of Greece*, by Will Durant, pp. 572-599.

Verse 7. And the angel stated, "Out of a branch of her roots shall come one who shall stand up in his estate, and which will come with an army, and shall enter into the fortress of the king of the north, and shall deal against them, and shall prevail." This means that one of Bernice's family would rise up to avenge her. And out of Bernice's roots, her brother Ptolemy Euergetes hastened with a great force out of Egypt to rescue and defend her. While Ptolemy Euergetes failed to rescue his sister, he, in connection with an army that came from Asia Minor for the same purpose, set out to avenge her death. Ptolemy made himself master, not only of Syria and Cilicia, but passed over the Euphrates, and brought all under subjection to him as far as the river Tigris.

Verse 8. "And he will take their gods and metal images back to Egypt." Jerome states that Ptolemy took with him back to Egypt forty thousand talents of silver and a vast number of precious vessels of gold, 2,400 images, among them many Egyptian idols. Many of the idols were those which Cambyses took into Persia when he had conquered Egypt. Ptolemy restored the idols to their temples. Because of this service he rendered to his country he was called Euergetes, the Benefactor. Ptolemy Euergetes survived Seleucus for about four years. *The Life of Greece,* by Will Durant, pp. 572-599.

Verse 9. This verse seems to give a summary of what has been said of Ptolemy invading Syria.

Verse 10. "But his sons will be stirred up." This has reference to the sons of the king of the north, or of Syria. Seleucus Callinichus was killed by a fall from his horse. His two sons, Seleucus Cerannus and Antiochus the Great, continued the war until the death of the former, then it was continued by Antiochus alone. Antiochus the Great succeeded to the kingdom when he was only fifteen years of age.

"And shall assemble a multitude of great forces, and one shall certainly come and overflow, and pass through, then shall return, and be stirred up, even to his fortress."

Only one of the sons, Antiochus the Great, actually engaged in war, he "passed through" the land, not the land of Egypt, but Syria. We recall that Ptolemy had before brought all Syria under his rule, now Antiochus was marching with his army to regain all Syria.

"Then shall he return and be stirred up" means he would be aroused or stirred up after his defeat, and would on the second expedition enter into the strongholds of the land. This was literally true. Ptolemy marched into Syria with an army of 75,000 footmen, 5,000 horses, and 73 elephants. Antiochus met him with 62,000 footmen, 6,000 horses, and 102 elephants, and defeated.

Antiochus the following year rallied his forces of Syria, took Gaza, and subdued the whole country of Syria including Palestine. *Syllabus, Inter-Testament Period*, Rex Turner, Sr., pp. 93-94. Unpublished class material.

Verse 11. The angel further declared, "The king of the south shall be moved with anger and shall come forth and fight with him, even the king of the north." The reference here is to Ptolemy Philopater who succeeded Ptolemy Euergetes in Egypt. Ptolemy Philopater was exasperated at the conduct of Antiochus the Great. He assembled an army and marched to Raphia, where he fought a battle with Antiochus the Great.

The angel further stated "He (Ptolemy) shall set forth a great multitude. The "multitude" of Antiochus "shall be given into the hand of" (Ptolemy)." The multitude may refer to the fact that the inhabitants of Syria and Palestine would hasten to submit themselves to Ptolemy of Egypt. They had long been under the government of Egypt, and preferred that to the government of Antiochus the Great.

Verse 12. "When the multitude is carried away, his heart will be lifted up." Ptolemy would glory in the many ten thousands he had cast down. "But he was not strengthened by it." Ptolemy gave himself up to the enjoyment of pleasure and weakened his position with his own people. His people had expected much more of him and became dissatisfied with his conduct. They broke out into rebellion, and this set the stage for another war between the king of the north and the king of the south.

Verse 13. And the angel declared, 'The king of the north shall return." Fourteen years later Antiochus the Great came again into the regions of Syria and Palestine to recover lost territory. Antiochus came with a great army, the same forces with which he had invaded the East with success.

Verse 14. "Many stood up against the king of the south." The angel tells Daniel what would be done during these times by his people to fulfill the vision. "The robbers of thy people shall exalt themselves." A portion of the Jews would take advantage of the weakness of the youthful monarch of Egypt to make conspiracies in his own kingdom, in an attempt to throw off his authority. These were called the robbers of the people. Josephus records that the Jews went over to Antiochus the Great, *Josephus Antiquities of the Jews,* bk. 12 ch. 3 v. 3, p. 251.

The Jews, while carrying out the terms of the vision, "would fail." The angel said they would not accomplish their objective.

Verse 15-16. The king of the north, according to the angel, "Shall establish himself in all the provinces," and shall stand in the glorious land. The glorious land was Palestine. The arms of the south were not able to withstand Antiochus the Great. He was entirely successful in establishing his rule over Syria and Palestine. Josephus records that the land of the Jews was sorely harassed while Antiochus the Great was at war with Ptolemy Philopater of Egypt. Palestine was centered between the kingdoms of the south and north. Each time a battle was fought the troops passed through Palestine, and left it open for attack at any time by either.

It is to be remembered that, as long as the Jewish nation obeyed God, he did not allow this to happen, but during those years when the nation fell away from God, he turned his face against them. Deut. 31:16-17.

We Christians have been told by many that the Old Testament is meaningless. This is not true. Paul stated that these things were written that we might read and understand just how God will turn away when people fall away from Him. Rom. 15:4; 1 Cor. 10:1-12. God's pattern for physical judgments would continue until Christ came back to deliver up the kingdom to the Father. Then God would render due and just punishment to those He loves, Rev. 3:19, that they may return to Him.

Verse 17. "And he will set his face to come with the power of his whole kingdom."

Antiochus the Great then set his face to bring all Egypt into subjection. He became involved in war with the Romans and was hindered. In this emergency, and to avoid the possibility of Egypt joining with the Romans, he gave his daughter Cleopatra "the daughter of women" in marriage to an Egyptian prince, Ptolemy Epiphanes, to accomplish his ends. The marriage was to take place as soon as the parties were of suitable age. Syria and Palestine were to be given as Cleopatra's dowry. The contract was made in 197 B.C. The marriage was consummated in 193 B.C.

Antiochus the Great instilled in his daughter's mind evil principles that she might betray her husband, and through her help obtain possession of Egypt.

But the angel had stated, "She shall not stand on his side." That is, she would not stand on her fathers side.

Verse 18. "Then he will turn his face to the coastlands and capture many." Antiochus took many of the isles of the Mediterranean constituting a part of Greece, accomplished during his war with the Romans. He supposed that the marriage of his daughter and the Egyptian prince would guard him from army interference from the Egyptians.

The angel further stated that "A prince for his own behalf shall cause the reproach offered by him to cease." This refers to Lucius Cornelius Scipio Asiaticus.

A. In the war against Antiochus the Great, Scipio succeeded in retrieving the honor of the Roman name. The disgrace that Antiochus the Great had given the Romans was now turned back on himself.
   1. Antiochus the Great experienced successive defeats, and he experienced a final and complete overthrow in the battle of Magnesium in 190 BC at the hands of the Roman commander Scipio.
   2. Antiochus was forced to quickly withdraw his forces from all the cities on the Hellespont. In his hasty flight, he was forced to abandon much of his military equipment and supplies, leaving him very weak.
B. Antiochus the Great sued for peace, the terms were:
   1. He would surrender all his possessions west of Taurus.
   2. He would defray the expenses of the war.
   3. He would keep no elephants (elephants were used as tanks are used in modern war).
   4. He would keep no more than twelve ships.
C. To insure the performance of those terms, the Romans required Antiochus the Great to deliver twelve hostages, including his son Antiochus Epiphanes. This residence of Antiochus in Rome would later have significant impact upon the Jews.

Verse 19. "He will stumble, and fall and be found no more." Antiochus the Great turned his face back to his own land, where he died; his rule would be found no more.

Verse 20. "Then in his place one will arise." This refers to Seleucus Philopater, the eldest son of Antiochus the Great, who took the throne after his father's death. He reigned eleven years, during which time he heavily taxed the people. He later was poisoned by Heliodorus who sought to raise himself to the position of king.

Antiochus Epiphanes, then in Athens on his return from Rome, applied to Eumenes, king of Pergamus, and to his brother Attalris, and they deprived Heliodorus of his authority.

Verse 21. "And in his place a despicable person will arise, and seize the kingdom by intrigue." As was mentioned above, Antiochus Epiphanes gained the throne by intrigue. By this course of action Antiochus Epiphanes ruled from 175 to 163 B.C. The Jews gave him the nickname of Epimanes, the madman.

He was born in Athens and had served as chief magistrate of the city whose every culture was the epitome of everything Greek. He had spent twelve years as a hostage in Rome where he learned to respect the new power which was to conquer the world. With a sense of mission he determined to civilize or hellenize the domain over which he ruled. The preceding facts are from the following sources: *History of Nations*, Vol. 2, pp. 511-520, and *The Life of Greece*, pp. 457 469.

Verses 22-45. These verses are grouped together, since they all relate to the same king, Antiochus Epiphanes (Antiochus IV). They deal with his plunder of Jerusalem and the destruction of the city itself, as well as the wars between the government of Antiochus IV and the remnant of faithful Jews, the Maccabees.

The following historical sketches parallel the events in vv. 22-45:

   A. Many of the Jews advocated a greater conformity to the Hellenistic manners and customs. Strange as it may seem, history is today repeating itself! Look at the modern Christians who more and more seem to be conforming to the customs of the world! One look, on the Lord's day, at the public beaches of the world will confirm this!
   B. In the early days of Antiochus IV, Jerusalem was ruled by the high priest, Onias III, a descendant of Simon the just and a strict Orthodox Jew.
   C. The Jews who looked favorably on Greek culture opposed Onias and espoused the cause of his brother Jason. To Antiochus IV, the high priesthood was a political office, but to the pious Jew it was of divine

origin. When Jason promised a larger tribute to Antiochus than Onias III was paying, Antiochus appointed him high priest in the place of Onias III. Jason encouraged the Hellenists who had sought his election. A gymnasium was built in Jerusalem; the Jews played games in the nude along with the Gentiles. (Again, it seems like something one would see on the beaches today).

D. Josephus states the following, "The sons of Tobias took the part of Menelaus, but the greater part of the people assisted Jason, and by that means Menelaus and the sons of Tobias were distressed, and retired to Antiochus, and informed him they desired to leave the laws of their country, and the Jewish way of living, and to follow the king's law, and the Grecian way of living. Wherefore they desired his permission to build them a gymnasium at Jerusalem. And when he had given them leave, they also hid the circumcision of their genitals, that even when they were naked they would appear as Greeks." *Josephus Antiquities of the Jews,* bk. 12 ch. 5 v. 3. p. 257.

E. Later the Hasidim party was infuriated when Antiochus IV appointed Menelaus as High Priest, and there developed a resistance movement. The pious Jews (the Hasidim) resisted Antiochus' unlawful attempts to control the Temple and the Priesthood, and defended the Biblically prescribed rules for those institutions.

F. In keeping with Daniel's prophecy concerning Antiochus IV (Dan. 11:21-27, this Antiochus made war against Egypt, v. 25. In the course of his reign he invaded the land of Egypt four times with various degrees of success. His third invasion of Egypt was on the pretense of supporting the claims of Ptolemy against the usurpation of his brother Ptolemy Physcon, whom the Egyptian people preferred to rule instead.

G. Daniel 11:27 says, "And both these kings' hearts shall do mischief." Both Antiochus and Ptolemy each had their own agenda. Antiochus IV invaded the country under pretense of aiding Ptolemy and establishing him in the government, and for the same reason, under pretense of protecting him, he had Ptolemy held under guard. Ptolemy, though a captive, was treated as a king; this was a matter of policy. Ptolemy while dining with Antiochus entered into engagements and agreements which he never intended to keep, v. 27. Neither could trust the other.

1. Antiochus IV, on his return from Egypt, paused to bring desolation in Jerusalem. "His heart was against the Holy Scriptures," Dan. 11:28.
2. Antiochus IV made another campaign into Egypt, Dan. 11:29 and he came very close to completely subduing the empire of the Ptolemies.
3. Antiochus was deterred from the coveted victory by the Romans. Rome was not ready to annex Syria and Egypt, but Rome nevertheless was not willing to permit Antiochus to strengthen himself by annexing Egypt. Antiochus had long ago learned to respect Rome. In a famous scene outside the city of Alexandria, the Roman envoy demanded that Antiochus, before he stirred from a circle drawn around him, make up his mind to evacuate Egypt or fight Rome. Antiochus chose to evacuate Egypt.
4. About this time Rome began to emerge as a world power, and from this point continued their conquest.

H. With dreams of grandeur suddenly dissipated, Antiochus IV, sorely grieved at heart (Dan. 11:30), turned back in bitterness. "He had indignation against the Holy Covenant," v. 30. In his march back through Palestine, he detached from his army 22,000 men under the command of Apollonius and sent them to Jerusalem to destroy it. *Josephus* "Antiquities of the Jews", bk. 12 ch. 5 v. 4, p. 257.

1. Pretending peace, he got possession of the opponents of the high priest, Menelaus. On a Sabbath he slew large numbers of the Jews. He plundered the temple and left it bare, he forbade the Jews to offer daily sacrifices, and then pillaged the whole city; the walls were destroyed, v. 31.
2. A citadel was built in the lower part of the city, fortified with high walls, where dwelt the impious Jews, and the wicked part of the Jewish mul-

titude. An altar was built upon God's altar, offering idol worship. Antiochus IV sacrificed a sow on the altar, and compelled the Jews to cease and forsake the worship to their God.

3. Antiochus required the Jews to build temples and to raise idol altars in every city, and to worship by offering swine upon them every day.

4. Antiochus prohibited the Jews from circumcising their sons, and he caused to be strangled the sons who were circumcised, and further caused the dead child to be hung around the mothers neck and worn for days, as punishment for disobeying Antiochus.

5. An elderly Athenian philosopher was sent to Jerusalem to supervise the enforcement of the order, where all books of the Jewish law and the books of the prophets were burned with fire, *Old Testament Apocrypha, 1* Macc. 1:56.

6. The Athenian identified the God of Israel with Jupiter and ordered a bearded image of the pagan deity, perhaps the likeness of Antiochus, to be set upon the temple altar.

    a. This was an "abomination that maketh desolate," Dan. 11:31. Of course, this was not the final "abominable sacrilege" that Jesus referred to in connection with the downfall of Jerusalem in AD 70.

    b. Greek soldiers and their officers performed licentious heathen rituals in the temple court.

    c. The drunken orgy associated with the worship of Bacchus was made compulsory.

    d. Truly Antiochus IV was the "vile person" of Dan. 11:21, the madman against the Jews, who boasted that the religion of Jehovah had ceased.

Verse 32. "And by smooth words he will turn to godlessness those who act wickedly toward the covenant, but the people who know their God will display strength and take action." This verse does not change the course of Antiochus, but does bring about actions of the Maccabees, the righteous lot of Israel.

Mattathias led a revolt against the cruelties and persecutions of Antiochus IV. Maccabaeus Mattathias was a modest, God-fearing man. He was a priest, and he came to be known by the title of "Maccabaeus." He lived in a small town, five miles from Jerusalem.

Certain officers of Antiochus came transversing the country, enforcing an edict for all Jews to sacrifice to the gods. The officers called upon Mattathias, as a man of influence, to set an example of obedience for the others to follow. Mattathias was ready for death, but not for apostasy. An apostate Jew stepped forward, anxious for favor, to be the first to sacrifice to pagan gods. With a single blow Mattathias laid the apostate dead. *Old Testament Apocrypha,* 1 Macc. 2:24

A. The die was cast, Mattathias' five sons gathered around, the villagers responded, the guards were put to flight, the war for country and creed had begun.
B. Mattathias had five sons:
   1. John, surnamed Gaddi, called the "Holy."
   2. Simon, surnamed Thassi, called the "Guide."
   3. Judas, surnamed Maccabaeus, also "the Guide."
   4. Eleazar, surnamed Avaran, "The Beast Sticker."
   5. Jonathan, surnamed Apphus, "The Cunning."
C. These sons were loyal to each other, they were free from selfish ambition, and they were single in devotion to a cause. Each came to the front in his own time, one by one they each came to the front, but not in order of age. Maccabaeus Mattathias soon become old and sank under the years of hardships, but to the end he was faithful. He recommended on his deathbed that Judas assume the supreme command of the forces that would go against Antiochus IV. Judas was "In his acts like a lion, and like a lions' whelp roaring for his prey." 1 Macc. 3:4. "He received unto him such as were ready to perish." *Old Testament Apocrypha,* 1 Macc. 3:9. From the fugitives of the hills, he formed an infantry whose steady discipline (inspired by religion) broke, at odds of ten to one, the troops of a mighty king. This people who knew God would receive a little help, v. 34.

Verse 35. "And some of those who have insight will fall, in order to refine, purge, and make them pure, until the end time. Because the end time is yet to come." We have seen already how those who loved God planned actions against the evil forces of Antiochus IV. But here again, in the history of the Jews, they are under severe stress because they have, as a nation, forsaken God, the one who gave this nation to them.

Again, we see that this period of desolation is not their end. That is, it is not the end of Judaism, or the final destruction of Jerusalem and the temple. It sets forth very clearly that even the severe trials under Antiochus were not "the end." The prophesied end is yet future, at an appointed time. God planned that Rome should bring the final destruction to Israel, not Antiochus IV.

Verse 36. "And the king shall do according to his will." The king shall be absolute and supreme, with supreme power. Although there was a small Jewish revolt, this in no way seemed to worry Antiochus.

"He shall prosper till the indignation is accomplished." This refers still to the appointed time when this indignation should come to its final end. The Lord seemed to be angry against his people, and suffered this heathen king to pour out his wrath upon them. Meanwhile, "Judas the hammer" was making war against the armies of Antiochus.

Verse 37. " Neither shall he regard the gods of his fathers." Antiochus would not be bound or restrained by the religion of his own land, or by any of the laws of religion. Antiochus would worship any god he pleased, or none as he pleased.

Verse 38. "But instead he will honor a god of fortresses." The fair meaning seems to be that Antiochus would honor a god, as it were, on his own throne, or in his own temple. Pride had lifted the heart of Antiochus so high he would not be associated with the people in the worship of idol gods, but instead worshiped his own throne.

"Shall he honor" (pay respect to). This would be his own god. He would show no respect for the gods of his fathers, nor to any of the idols the people worshiped, but he would "honor the god of forces."

The reference is to strongly fortified places, to those places which had been made strong for purposes of defense. In his wars, Antiochus came into possession of strong places, Jerusalem, Sidon, Tyre, fortified cities which he subdued.

Verse 40. "And at the end time." This end time must consummate the events under consideration here. This "end time" is clearly defined as occurring during the time of this king. The "end time" spoken of in chapters 7, 8, 10, 12 describes the time by using the fourth beast and the eleven horns. Thus, it is used as a period in time, and not the end of time.

"At the time of the end." We are to notice here that vs. 40-45 seems to sum up what should occur in what is here called appropriately "the time of the end," the period when the predicted termination of this series of important events should arrive. "Yet he will come to his end and no one will help him," v. 45.

Antiochus took leave from Syria and visited Egypt— and never returned. There was no one to help him in Egypt.

The war with the forces of Antiochus continues, but, Lysias the governor of Syria, in the absence of Antiochus, attacked the forces of Judas Maccabaeus. Judas defeated the Syrians at Emmaus, *Old Testament Apocrypha*, 1 Macc. 4.

Additional sources used to confirm the fulfillment of chapter 11:

A. *The Apocrypha of Old Testament, First, Second, Third and Fourth Maccabees.*
B. Josephus, *Wars of the Jews.*
C. *Guizot's Ancient History*, 1844 edition, pp. 131-158.
D. F. F. Bruce, *Israel and the Nations.* Grand Rapids, Michigan: Wm. B. Eerdmans Publishing Co., 1963.

DANIEL CHAPTER 12

Introductory Remarks:

We are here concerned with the destiny of the Jews in the period of the Last Days. In preceding chapters I have shown that this was a period in time, and not the end of time!

Admittedly, this period began when Christ died on the cross and legally abolished the Law of Moses. God granted the nation of Israel forty years to be "grafted back into" His true spiritual nation (cf. Rom. 11:17-24) before destroying the temple, along with the city of Jerusalem.

The destruction of the Jewish temple ended the period of "the last days." If this is not true, then we have Luke to blame, for he said, "These be the days of vengeance that all things written may be fulfilled. Lk. 21:22. There are objections to this.

A. Some Bible scholars teach that the time, times, and a half time of Dan. 7:25 is 350 years, so the prophecy was not fulfilled until 350 AD. But this time can also be rendered as three and one-half years, and this rendering fulfills the prophecy just before the destruction of Jerusalem, which agrees with both Luke and history of the time.
   1. Notice the inconsistency of these same scholars. When dealing with other subjects, they affirm that the Old Testament was fulfilled at the destruction of Jerusalem. But then:
   2. When teaching the book of Joel, everything has been fulfilled, until they come upon Joel 2:28-32. Notice how this is chopped up. They affirm that vs. 28-29 have been fulfilled, then turn about and say that vs. 30-32 have not been fulfilled. They then apply this to the end of time! But notice: In Acts 2:16, Luke said, "But this is what was spoken of by the prophet Joel, and he makes no exception for vs. 28-32. Again, Lk. 21:22 states that all things written would be fulfilled at the destruction of Jerusalem. And notice further:
   3. These scholars affirm that Joel 2:32 looks to the end of the world, when everything will be de-

stroyed, but Joel says, "For on Mount Zion in Jerusalem there will be those who escape." So these scholars have people at the end of the world escaping God's wrath and destruction! Absurd.

4. I submit to you that Joel was fulfilled, just as Luke wrote in Acts 2:16-21 where he stated that the things happening then was the fulfillment. I further believe that inconsistency is the twin brother to assumption, and assumption is error.

B. In chapter 12, there are some things here that parallel chapter 10 so closely that chapter 12 seems to be a continuation of chapter 10. The words are by the same angel and during the same period of time. Dan. 12:6 says, "One said to the man clothed in linen who stood upon the river." Now notice 10:5, "A man clothed in linen" standing on the river.

1. Both angels were standing on the river, and both dressed in white linen.

2. Again, notice Dan. 10:21. The man clothed in linen is about to tell Daniel what is written in the Book of God respecting his people in the last days. Then the Angel breaks the thought and moves to the protection Michael the prince will give to his people in that day, Dan. 12:1.

3. In chapter 10 nothing more is said respecting the visions of that chapter, and of the messages received concerning his people.

4. But, when we move to chapter 12, we see the sum of the visions and message given to Daniel, and it all concerns his people in the day when God will bring about the abolishment of their national religion, because of their transgressions, and to favor Christianity.

5. The angel states respecting the period of desolation: "And there will be a time of distress such as has never occurred since there were a nation." The angel says this period which is to come upon the Jews is even worse than that period when Assyria and Babylon came against Israel, and Jesus confirms this in his discourse of Matt. 24:21. Therefore, Daniel saw, and was told in full detail, the complete distress of the Jews in the "last days," but was told not to write it, for it is to be sealed

up until the "end time." This is not uncommon for a prophet to see things and be told not to expose it. John was also told to seal up, or "do not write" a part of his vision in Rev. 10:4. The things that Daniel could not write were to be revealed at a later time, at the "end time" of Israel.

Verse 1. "And at that time." That time refers to the day of the Lord, when He shall take vengeance on those who rejected the Son of God. Those wicked Jews, whom Jesus called the tares, would be gathered out of the kingdom and burned in the furnace of fire. Malachi 4:1-3; Mt. 13:39-49; Mt. 23:36-39.

A. That day, when the greatest desolation known to Rome would occur. Mt. 24:21; Lk. 21:20-32

B. That day, when the armies of Rome will encompass the city of Jerusalem for the final destruction. Lk. 21:20-32

C. That day, when the Lord shall return in spiritual and physical judgment upon the wickedness of the world, and especially to Jerusalem. Zech. 14:1-4 and Mt. 16:27-28; when He shall abolish the national religion of Israel. Mt. 24:30,31

D. That day, when the wicked would be judged in fire. 2 Pet. 3:3-7. See the *Gospel Advocate Commentary, Peter, John, Jude,* by Guy N. Woods, on 2 Pet. 3:7.

E. That day, when the son of perdition shall stand against the holy ones, after the restrainer was taken out of the way. But that son of perdition would be consumed with the spirit of Christ's mouth. 2 Thess. 2:7,8

F. That day, when Michael shall stand up for the righteous of Daniel's people, and will provide them a way of escape, Dan. 12:1; Joel 2:32. Josephus speaks of this escape, 5:9:1 and 5:10:1. Micah 2:12-13

G. That day, when the court sat, and the books were opened, Dan. 7:9-10, and all found written in the book of life were rescued, while those not found in the book of life were destroyed.
   1. May we not say that this judgment scene of Dan. 7:9-10 is the same judgment scene of Rev. 20:4?
   2. May we not say also that these judgment scenes

are the ones Jesus referred to in his discourse of
Mt. 16:27,28?
H. "At that time" identifies the period of time of which
I speak, and that which shall befall the nation of
Israel in the "last days." Dan. 10:14

Notice Michael will stand up to protect his people,
the people of God, those who remain faithful. Such expressions do not mean afflictions will not befall the child
of God, but it does indicate that God will make a way for
His children to escape.

Note how God cared for the righteous of Jerusalem
when Nebuchadnezzar came against the city. God said,
"Go through the city and place a mark in the foreheads of
those who mourn the unrighteous acts of the wicked,"
Ezek. 9:1-8. Just prior to the final destruction of Jerusalem in AD 70 this same method of marking was used, in
order that the righteous escape, Rev. 7:1-14.

Verse 2. "And many of them that sleep in the dust
of the earth shall awake, some to everlasting life, and some
to shame and everlasting contempt."
A. "Many of them" is used in the scriptures to denote a
multitude. However, it is undeniable that the word
is sometimes used to denote a whole, "constituted of
many." In Rom. 5:15-16,19, it clearly represents the
whole, or all.
B. The "many" here may be those who would come forth
at the appointed time in a general resurrection.
1. Here it seems to be applied to the Israelites who
at the end of their world (the last days) would arise
in the resurrection taught by the prophets of Israel, Hosea. 6:2-3.
2. Revelation chapter 7 mentions those tribes of Israel, and then mentions those of all nations who
had come through the tribulation.
C. This resurrection occurs in connection with the great
tribulation (Dan. 12:1; cf. Matt. 24:29-31), the complete shattering of the nation of Israel (Dan. 12:7;
Lk. 21:20-24), and the end of the age (Dan. 12:13;
Matt. 24:3). A careful comparison of Dan. 12 with
the Olivet Discourse in Mt. 24 and Lk. 21 will notice
a tight connection between the resurrection mentioned in Dan. 12 and the gathering of the elect in

Matt. 24:31. Daniel is talking about a "complete shattering" of the Jewish nation at the "end of the age" when there would be a great tribulation upon the Jews. Matt. 24 and its parallels talk about the same thing, which was fulfilled in AD 70.

D. This is not the resurrection mentioned in Matthew 27:52, which was "the first resurrection." (Rev. 20:4) Dan. 12:2 refers to the resurrection of the "rest of the dead" (Rev. 20:5) who would be raised out of Hades "at the time of the end" (Dan. 12:4,8,9,13) when "the power of the holy people" would be completely shattered. (Dan. 12:7)

E. The evidence points to a resurrection that would occur when Israel would be in its time of great tribulation (AD 66-70). See Dan. 12:1.

"And some to shame, and everlasting contempt." The word "contempt" in Hebrew means a casting away. Abhorrence to be stinking, to reject, as Dan. 12:2, to be destroyed from the face of God. *Young's Analytical Concordance*, "contempt" p. 200.

At this time, there would be those who received recompense of fury from God, and who were cast into everlasting punishment, such as Malachi describes in 4:1-3, such as Jesus warned of in Mt. 13:39-49 respecting the tares, and to which Peter directs his letter of 2 Pet. 3:7.

Verse 3. "And they that be wise." This is the general language of the scriptures used to denote the righteous, or those who serve God. True religion is wisdom, and sin is folly, and those who live for God and for heaven are truly wise. They have chosen the path of true wisdom—the one in which man should walk.

"Shall shine as brightness of the firmament." This refers to those in the "last days" who would accept Christianity, who would by their lives be the image of Christ, and who would shine forth among men as stars of the heaven. To these Jesus said, "Let your light so shine among men, that they will see your good works and glorify God in heaven, Mt. 5:16.

"And they that turn many to righteousness." The fair meaning is that those who chose Christianity would be instrumental in converting men to Christ and the New Covenant. The life that men live before the world are often more effective than many sermons. This is what was meant by Christ when he asked the Jews to live such lives before the Gentiles, that such would convert them.

Verse 4. "But thou, O Daniel, shut up the words, even till the time of the end." The angel's statement combined with Daniel's restraint in writing about the visions and messages, imply that much was said and seen that is not recorded. It was to be sealed up in the Book of God until the end time. Only parts of the vision were recorded, and other parts remained sealed up, "until the end time." The end time would be the time of the end of Israel, the end of the Mosaic age. Then the things not written by Daniel would be revealed through another prophet. We find a book being opened in Revelation chapter 5 where the events parallel those revealed by Daniel. Could it be that John in the Revelation, at the close of Israel, saw and foretold those events that the angel commanded Daniel to seal up? After a careful research of Daniel and John, both foretelling the destruction of Israel and the temple, I fully affirm that the Revelation is that book of events that would be revealed at the "end time."

Notice the following evidence:
    A. This seems to parallel the seven curses of Deut. 28 (cf. Lev. 26).
    B. It is similar to the seven woes Jesus pronounced on the Jews in Mt. 23.
    C. It also parallels the seven plagues of the seven angels in Rev. 7, while Rev. 7 parallels the woes of Mt. 23.
    D. There can be little doubt that the matters Daniel was prohibited from revealing would be revealed at "the end time."
        1. There are those who contend that the phrase "seal up" meant that the book was finished. If so, then where is the revealing of the visions that pertained to Israel?
        2. These people have not noticed Rev. 10:4 where the same phrase is used, "Seal up the things that the seven peals of thunder have spoken, and do not write them." Now, if in Daniel the phrase means the book is ended, and the angel will have nothing more to say, then by the same standard, it means the same here. But, there are 12 more

chapters in the revelation, so it does not mean that the book is ended. It very simply implies that there are certain things which are not to be revealed at that time. That's what it means in Revelation, and that's what it means in Daniel.

"Many shall run to and fro," and, "As when they persecute you in this city, flee ye into another, for verily I say to you, ye shall not have gone over the cities of Israel until the Son of Man be come," Mt. 10:23.

1. Both scriptures look to those who will pass up and down in the world with the gospel of Christ.
2. They refer to a time when this would be characteristic of the age when the church was first born, to those years when the apostles went into all the world to preach the gospel, and train others who would do the same afterwards.

"And knowledge will be increased." The angel means that by men going forth into all the world to preach the gospel, knowledge would increase. This would be one of the characteristics of this age, and this would be the means by which the gospel would be spread into all the world. Notice a comparison is made here to the Law of Moses.

Verse 5. "Then I Daniel looked, and behold there stood two others." It seems that the attention of Daniel had been fixed on the angel who was giving instructions to him, but now his attention is directed to others, the one who stood on this side of the river Tigris (the same river in Ch 10), and the one who stood on the opposite side. The names of these angels are not mentioned. Their significance is in the vision itself.

Verse 6. "And one said to the man clothed in linen." It would appear that these angels were present during the vision, but unseen by Daniel. They had listened with interest to the communication given Daniel concerning his people and their future. And now one addressed the angel who had been given the ability to disclose the future to Daniel. It appears that not all angels are subject to the same information "The man clothed in linen" seems to be the man in 10:5, the angel being upon the river would denote that divine control was over the whole earth.

"How long shall it be to the end of these wonders?" Here the one angel must have understood the beginning point of the desolation; he asks the question, "How long shall it be to the end." The angel here was concerned with the period in which the desolation would occur, and just how long could the people endure. Tell me how long this will last. Tell me how long must the people suffer, before it ends.

Verse 7. "And I heard the man clothed in linen say, it shall be for a time, times, and a half time. This is the same phrase as given Daniel in 7:25, and in that verse I mentioned that the phrase meant the actual period of tribulation for Israel. Here it refers to the period of that same tribulation. From history we learn that this period began in February AD 67 and lasted until Jerusalem was destroyed by Titus in AD 70 (the period of the siege).

There is not the least inference here that any of the message belonged to the nation of the Gentiles, or to the period of church persecution. The period must mean three and one-half years, and would bring about the end for the nation of Israel. Here is another place where the interpretation of 350 years just won't fit. We would have the angels concerned about the Gentile nations, and the angel who said "your people" to Daniel would have meant Gentiles as well—or meant that Daniel was Gentile! Nonsense.

If this chapter is speaking of the last days of the Jewish commonwealth, then John saw in his vision the same period when the temple was to be destroyed. (Rev. 11:1-2) Also, the church was to be carried away into the wilderness for the same period of time, forty and two months, "or time, times, and a half time." (Rev. 12:6-12)

It is evident that the one angel understood when the desolation would begin, therefore, the angel giving the answer did not relate the beginning period, but informed the angel of the time involved in the complete destruction of Israel (the siege period).

Dan. 9:26-27 is also speaking of the same period, "And in the middle of the week." The week had reference to the seven-year period; "in the middle of the week" was one-half of that week, or, three and one-half years, or forty-two months, or time, times, and a half time.

If Dan. 7:25 meant 350 years, then by the same rule Dan. 9:27 would mean 350 years. This position would have its fulfillment long after the destruction of Jerusalem, and Luke said, "When you see Jerusalem compassed about with armies, know that her desolation is near... For these be the days of vengeance that all things written may be fulfilled." (Lk. 21:20-22)

"When he has accomplished to scatter the holy people, all these things shall be finished." The "he" mentioned here refers to the eleventh horn, or eleventh ruler of Rome. When he had finished the destruction of Jerusalem, and had killed 1,100,000 Jews in Jerusalem, and had taken 20,000 captive to be scattered over the Roman Empire as slaves, then all these things shall be finished." Not 350 years later!

Verse 8. "And I heard, but I understood not." That is, Daniel did not fully understand the language used by the angel, "time, times, and half time." He said, "O my Lord." This is language used by an inferior when respectfully addressing one of superior rank, and is here used in respect for the angel.

"What shall be the end of these things?" In asking the question, Daniel shows anxiety and a desire to know when the termination of the events would be. Perhaps the enigmatical expression used by the angel caused Daniel to place greater emphasis on the question "What shall be the end of these things?"

Verse 9. "And he said, go thy way, Daniel, for the word is closed up and sealed until the time of the end." Daniel is told to "go his way" and ask no more questions, make no more inquiries, nothing more will be said or revealed until the end time.

This statement makes it very clear that at the end time for Daniel's people, more will be said concerning their end, their desolation. Jesus began to reveal the end time for the Jews as soon as he began to teach, followed by all the apostles. But the phrase "seal it up until the end time" has caused many diverse opinions to arise as to the sealing of the book. Consider the following:

    A. Many contend that all that is implied here is that Daniel is to finish the book, the twelve chapters, and he is to write no more, for all the revelations have ended. Thus it is implied that the mention of "sealing up the book" simply means, "stop writing."

    B. This conjecture has been adopted without due respect to the entire phrase, and has been used to justify certain deviant positions!

1. Either the twelve chapters of Daniel were to be sealed up and not be revealed until the end time for Israel, or there were other revelations that Daniel was not allowed to understand, or was unable to explain at that time, which would be revealed or explained later at the time of the "complete end" when the holy people would be "completely shattered."
2. We know that Daniel did not seal up the twelve chapters, or cause them to be unknown to his people. This portion of the visions were known. *Old Testament Apocrypha*, 1 Macc. 2:59-60.

C. But turn again and look at the text. The angel intended that portions of the visions should not be made known to the people at that time, not until a later date, and thus his statement "Seal it up until the end time" means what it says, at the end of the dispensation all that Daniel had seen would be revealed. The Book of God would be opened, "unsealed." I submit to you that these things were revealed at the end time, beginning with Christ, and ending with John the apostle in the book of Revelation.

Verse 10. "Many shall be purified." This has reference to a divine system of religion that would be introduced before the end time, wherein many would have the remission of sins. This arrangement, which God would introduce, would allow many of the human race to be cleansed from sin through the blood of Christ. How Daniel would apply this we cannot know, but it was of immense importance to Israelites (as well as the whole human family), before the consummation of their nation.

"And made white." White denotes innocence or purity, and so the application is made to the righteous, who washed "their robes in the blood of the lamb." The meaning here is that many of the earth would be made holy before the end would come, and many of the Jews did accept Christ; we can see the fulfillment of this at Jerusalem on Pentecost when the church was born. As we look into the letters of the apostles we see that over a vast empire Jews became Christians. There were many righteous Jews in Rome as a result of the dispersion, they accepted Christ, and became as the angel describes them, "made white." But as a nation they rejected Him.

"And tried." Tried as in a furnace, as Daniel's friends were. Those who accepted Christ would also be tried; they would be subjected to severe persecutions by their own people, and other forms of suffering. However, this would test the faith of the saints, as well as the nature of the new religion.

"In that day there shall be a house opened to the house of David." Zech. 13:1. Zechariah states that many trials will come upon the saints, and that He will try them and those who are tried and are refined will call upon His name, and He will hear them, Zech. 13:8-9.

The seven letters written to the seven churches of Asia Minor were setting forth the same idea as depicted here. Warning, exhortation, a period of trials, Rev. 2:1-3:22. The balance of the book contains a full description of those events which would try the saints and destroy the wicked.

"But the wicked shall do wickedly." Notwithstanding the fact that they have been warned of the impending judgments to come upon them, and would be called to share in the saving blood of Christ, still they would reject Christ and continue to do wickedly.

When Jerusalem was being destroyed, the Jewish historian states, "Now if anyone consider these things, God takes care of mankind, but when men perish it is by their own miseries which they bring upon themselves, madly and voluntarily. The Jews had it written in their sacred Oracles, that the temple and city should be taken." *Josephus* "War of the Jews", bk. 6 ch. 5 v. 4, p. 582.

"And none of the wicked shall understand." The true import here is that none of the wicked would understand the New Covenant, they would have no desire to understand. Their depravity of heart would prevent it. Their desire to lead a wicked life would cloud the mind, pervert their moral judgment, and make them unable to appreciate the government of Christ, Isa. 9:6.

Paul said, "But the natural man receiveth not the things of the Spirit of God: for they are foolishness unto him, neither can he know them, because they are spiritually discerned." 1 Cor. 2:14. To comprehend religion, a man needs a pure heart, under the influence of God's Spirit. Only such a one can appreciate the death of Christ on the cross, the blood shed for the sins of the world.

"But the wise shall understand." The wise are those who love God and have been washed in the blood of "the Lamb." The pure in heart will understand the will of God. In Daniel chapter 1 Daniel prepares himself, even as a young boy, to receive God's messages to him. John said, "If any man is willing to do His will, he shall know of the teaching." John. 7:17. Without a pure heart man cannot understand the full import of God's will to man.

Verse 11. "And from the time that the continual burnt-offering shall be taken away, and the abomination that maketh desolate set up, there shall be a thousand two hundred and ninety days." (ASV)

The prophecy pertains to that time Jesus spoke of in Mt. 24:15 regarding the destruction of Jerusalem by the Romans in AD 70. *Old Testament Apocrypha,* 1 Macc. 1:41-62, an abomination of desolation is spoken of. Yet, it does not totally fit Daniel's prophecy here. See Daniel 12:7.

"There shall be a thousand two hundred and ninety days." A physical number as used here would represent the days of siege by the Roman armies against Jerusalem. This does not correspond with the "time, times, and a half time" of Dan. 12:7. Here we must take into account the Jewish sacred calendar. There is less than a half-month difference.

Verse 12. Daniel 12:12 "How blessed is he who keeps waiting and attains to the 1,335 days." The time, times, and a half time (3-1/2 years) of Daniel 7:25, the 1,260 days and 42 months of Revelation 11:2, and the 1,260 days of Revelation 11:3 have given Bible scholars no little problem. I offer another way to understand this text.

A. First we must understand that chapter 12 deals with the war between Rome and Israel. Having been in combat on the front lines before, I can certainly understand certain privileges given to an army who conquers a city and drives the enemy back. This war was no different. Verse 7 is proof of a war, plus the time given for this war to be won – time, times, and a half time (3-1/2 years) – Feb 10, 67 AD to Sept. 10, 70 AD. Now we must diligently answer the reason why two different dates are attached to the 1,260 days of Daniel 12:7. Notice the following:

1. When the US Army Third Division moved through North Korea, and we fought to win a city, the war

policy was first to secure the city, round up the prisoners, then the troops were given time to loot and take the spoils of war. Sometimes this would take a week, sometimes two or three weeks. Keep in mind Jerusalem was a very large city, so it might have taken thirty days for the Roman troops to gather up the captives into one location for processing, and take the spoils of war.

2. The text first mentioned 1,260 days. The war began and ended within that period. Then if we add 30 days for gathering all the people together and taking the spoils of war, we come to 1,290 days. We must remember that Josephus informs us that Rome took the spoils of war, even to the extreme of cutting open the stomachs of the Jews to obtain the gold that they might have swallowed.

B. I believe it might be helpful at this point to look at Hebrews 9:28, the only passage in the New Testament which speaks of the "second appearing." Notice that Christ is not to appear the second time to bear sin, but rather to appear to those who were eagerly awaiting him. Notice again what it says in Dan. 12:12, "How blessed is he who keeps waiting and attains to the 1,335 days." Is there a connection between these two texts? Are the "waiting" ones in Daniel 12 the same group in Heb. 9:28 who were "eagerly awaiting" his return?

1. After a city is conquered, the prisoners are processed. After being questioned, it is decided what to do with each of them. Rome did not want to feed the prisoners they had taken. They sold as many of the Jews for slaves as possible. The Lord revealed to Moses just what would happen to those people in their Last Days. Deut. 28:48-68 tells the whole story even down to the details of exiling or scattering them to other nations. (Verse 64)

2. Just when they were down to the last group of Jews to process, it suddenly happens – Jesus appears personally, to lead those who "kept waiting" out of Jerusalem, without being seen by anyone. Quite a shock to the Roman army. Yet it was planned this way by God. See Micah 2:12-13. It is done.

3. Therefore, another 45 days is taken in processing and selling the people as slaves. If we add this 45 days to the 1,290, it totals 1,335, the fulfillment of Dan. 12:12. Dan. 12:7 says, "As soon as they finish shattering the power of the holy people, all these events will be completed. Notice the phrase, "Finish Shattering." It took Rome 75 days after they conquered the city to process the people and gather the spoils of war. On the 75th day, Jesus "appeared the second time" and led the remnant out without being seen.

Verse 13. "But as for you, go your way to the end, then you will enter into rest and rise again for your allotted portion at the end of the ages" (dispensation).

The full import of this chapter is the end time of the Jewish nation, foretold by all the prophets. We have already noticed that the end time would not come for many years until after many world events and many years.

There would be scenes of revolution, commotion, and turmoil. Momentous changes would occur before the full consummation of this prophecy would be completed. As 12:7 states, the power of the holy people would be shattered before the end time for Israel would occur. In v. 13 Daniel is to "enter his rest." He would die, and he would rest in the dust as is shown in 12:2, but he will rise again. That is, he would be resurrected at the end of the dispensation along with those of v. 2, and of Hosea 6:1-2. He would have his allotted portion, which could well be to sit on thrones judging Israel, Mt. 19:26.

This judgment was allotted to the apostles. However, John was yet living at the time of this judgment against Israel. Daniel could have been the 12th. So, Daniel is to come forth at the "end time."

We should notice that this resurrection began when Jesus Christ became the first fruit of the resurrection. 1 Cor. 15:14-23, and every man in his own order according to Hosea 6:2; Dan. 12:2; Mt. 27:52-53.

Like the subject of the kingdom, there are objections to the subject of resurrection. For the purpose of deeper study, and perhaps better unity, I submit the following questions. First I will present questions on the resurrection, then questions respecting the kingdom, and this will conclude the book of Daniel.

A. If "death," which God promised to Adam and Eve, really meant separation from God in a spiritual way, and could only be removed by the death of Christ, Rom. 5:12-18, how is it that we teach "death" (separation) has not been abolished?

B. How is it that we discount "death" (separation) as being fulfilled in Christ? 2 Tim. 1:10.

C. If the sentence of this "death" was not abolished by Christ, why was Christ predicted after the fall of man, and why was His death necessary?

D. Why did Isaiah in Isa. 26:14 depict the wicked as dead, and say their departed spirits would not rise? (See also Ps. 9:17; 34:16; 49:14; 49:19-20; 50:22) And why did Isaiah say that the spirits of the righteous would rise, that the earth would give birth to their spirits? And why did Jesus say the Old Testament would be fulfilled in Him? (Luke. 24:44; 22:37) Luke 21:20-22 also says that when armies surrounded Jerusalem, and people begin to leave the city, that these would be "days of vengeance" in order that all things which were written may be fulfilled.

E. Why did Hosea foretell that there would be a resurrection on the third day, the day Christ arose, if indeed there were no spirits being resurrected on that day except our Lord? Matthew recorded that there were those who came out of the graves, Mt. 27:52,53. Admittedly, this passage does not say whether those who arose went back into the graves or to heaven. However, Isa. 26:14 says that "the dead," or wicked, would not arise at all. Can it be said that these were wicked? Or could it be said that these spiritual bodies are yet floating around in space? What is the scriptural implication?

F. If there was no resurrection at all, or not until the end of time, then why did Paul say that "God gives us the victory through our Lord Jesus Christ"? 1 Cor. 15:57. Accordingly, the subject of 54-57 was the "death" passed upon all ancient people until the cross. Here and in 2 Tim. 1:10, we do not see Christians suffering bondage in the grave, but rather, as Paul also taught in 2 Cor. 5:1-5, we receive a spiritual body (provided that person is righteous) at the time when the spirit leaves the physical body. Or do we wait for Christ to return in order to abolish the sentence of death?

G. Who are the Sons of God? Who has been redeemed? What do Rom. 8:19-23 and Eph. 3:14-15 really mean? "For this reason, I bow my knees before the Father, from whom every family in heaven and on earth derives its name." If there has been no resurrection, then there is no family in heaven, is that correct? When was the day of redemption as in Eph. 4:30?

H. What does Paul really mean in 2 Tim. 2:18? Did Philetus and Hymenaeus have any knowledge of a resurrection in order to say it was past? Could it be that they concluded that since the ancients were resurrected with Christ, the Christian would also suffer bondage until God decided to raise them?

Perhaps Paul had the answer in 1 Cor. 15:23, "For as in Adam all die, so also in Christ all shall be made alive. But each in his own order, Christ the first fruits, after that those who are Christ's at His Coming." Does this say that there are two periods of resurrection? One when Christ arose, and another when He appeared the second time? Is it wrong and sinful to be consistent? Do we not say that Christ now has His kingdom, and that He is now sitting on His own throne, and that He is now our king? Well if we do, we disagree with Matthew 25:31-33 which informs us that His kingdom, His reigning on His throne, and being our King was predicated upon His "Second Coming." Is it sinful to believe that which the scripture teaches? Or should we continue to teach tradition rather than truth?

Closing Statement.

I believe that mankind acknowledges his belief based upon his level of knowledge and understanding. Therefore, mankind is required to continue to study, in order to increase his knowledge. As he learns, he is also required to accept the truth and be willing to change his position on religious matters. The leaders of the Restoration Movement never laid claim to having arrived at a perfect understanding of all truth, so why should we stop where they left off? Instead, we should pick up where they left off and build higher and better. Like the reformers always said, "reformed and always reforming."

BIBLIOGRAPHY OF WORKS CONSULTED

Bibles

The *New American Standard Version* was used throughout Daniel, unless otherwise noted.

New American Standard, Foundation Press Publications, The Lockman Foundation, 1973.

King James Version, Collins Clear Type Press, Glasgow, England. 1958.

Books

Apocrypha of the Old Testament, American Bible Society, New York, N.Y.

Benjamin, Benjamin. *Itinerary of Tudela*, "Travels in the Middle Ages", Nightingale Resources 1983.

Beach, C. B. *Students Reference Works Cyclopedia*, New York, N.Y. F. E. Compton & Co. 1910 Ed.

Barnes, Harry Elmer. *Illustrated World History*, New York, N.Y. Wm. H. Wise & Co. 1939.

Bruce, F. F. *Israel and the Nations*. Grand Rapids, Michigan: Wm. B. Eerdmans Publishing Co., 1963.

Durant, Will. *Caesar and Christ,* New York, N.Y. Simon & Shuster, 1966 Ed.

Durant, Will. *The Life of Greece,* New York, N.Y. Simon & Shuster, 1966 Ed.

Ellis, J. & Adam Ward. *History of Nations,* New York, N.Y. P. F. Collier & Sons.

Encyclopedia Britannica, Cambridge England, University Press 1911.

Guizot, M. *Ancient History,* New York, N.Y. D. Appleton Co. 1844 Ed.

Josephus. *Complete Works*, "Antiquities of the Jews", "War of the Jews", "Against Apion", Trans. by William Whiston. Grand Rapids, Michigan: Kregel Publications, 1960.

Little & Ives. *Webster Dictionary & Reference Library,* New York, N.Y., J. J. Little & Ives. 1867.

Man and His History, World History and Western Civilization, Doubleday & Co., Inc. Catholic Textbook Division, Garden City, N.Y.

McNall, Edward & Barnes. *Western Civilization,* New York, N.Y. W. W. Norton & Co.

Milligan, Robert. *New Testament Commentary on Hebrews,* Nashville, Tenn. Gospel Advocate, 1962.

Oman, C. W. C. *History of Nations,* Vol. 2, New York, N.Y. P. F. Collier & Sons.

Orr, James. *International Standard Bible Encyclopedia,* 5 vols. Grand Rapids, Mich.: Wm. B. Eerdmans Pub. Co., 1939.

Pfeiffer, Charles. *Wycliffe Historical Geography,* Chicago, Illinois: Moody Press, 1974.

Rolfe, J. C. *Suetonius,* Vol. 2, The Loeb Classical Library, Cambridge, Mass., Harvard University Press. Reprinted 1970.

Schwartzkop. *Outline of The Life of Christ,* Cambridge, Mass., Loeb Classical Library. 1943.

Streatfield, G. S. *The Self Interpretation of Jesus Christ,* Vol. 1, New York, N.Y. Jennings & Graham. 1905.

Turner, Rex A. *Sound Doctrine,* "Periodical", Nashville, Tenn., Gospel Advocate. 1980. Paper Nov. p. 13.

Thayer, Joseph H. *Greek Lexicon,* Article "World", Peabody, Mass., Zondervan

Wells, H. G. *The Outline of History,* Vol. 2, New York, N.Y. P. F. Collier & Sons Co. 1922.

Whitcomb, Dr. John C. *Darius the Mede,* Grand Rapids, Mich., Baker House.

Winston, John C. *Fox's Book of Martyrs,* Grand Rapids, Mich., Zondervan Publishing House.

Woods, Guy, N. *Commentary on Peter John Jude,* Nashville, Tenn., Gospel Advocate Co. 1960.

Vine, W. E. "Article World", *Vine's Dictionary of the New Testament Words,* Old Tappan, N.J. 1940.

Young, Robert. *Analytical, Concordance to the Bible,* Grand Rapids, Mich., Wm. B. Eerdmans Publishing Co.

RESULTS
of Fulfilled Prophecy
By Jessie E. Mills, Jr., Ph.D.

"...researched and written over almost fifty years by a man of impeccable character and self-sacrificing dedication. ...countless insights into difficult texts you won't find anywhere else. Dr. Mills was already teaching "fulfilled prophecy" as early as 1952. He did not learn until the 1970's that others held similar views known as 'preterist.'"

Edward E. Stevens
International Preterist Association

208 pages. pb
ISBN # 0-9621311-8-0

$14.00
postpaid

Some Topics Covered:

- The Second Coming
- The Resurrection and 1 Cor. 15
- The Judgment Scene (Rev. 20)
- Second Peter Three & the New Heavens and Earth
- The End of the "Age" (not "world")
- Survey of Daniel 7 and 12
- Significance of Matthew 10:23

How to Order:

- Order on our website: **www.preterist.ORG**
- Email order info to: **preterist1@aol.com**
- Call Toll-Free **1-888-257-7023** (orders only)
- Fill out and mail this form to IPA (address bottom left)
- VISA, Discover, and MasterCard accepted

International Preterist Association, Inc.

122 Seaward Ave • Bradford, PA 16701 USA

This book and over 100 other fine
Preterist resources are available from:

International Preterist Association

Ask For A Free Information Packet

The FREE information packet includes:
- "What Is the Preterist View?" article
- Book List and Order Form (over 100 books and other resources available)
- Tape List (audio and video)
- Information about other new or featured resources and upcoming events of interest

How to Contact IPA:
- Call Toll-Free to order **1-888-257-7023** (USA only)
- Email: preterist1@aol.com
- Browse Our Web Site: www.preterist.ORG
  - Read, copy and print articles stored there
  - Buy Books & Tapes (VISA, M/C, Discover accepted)
  - Ask Questions
  - Contact Other Preterists Online
- Traditional Mail (see IPA postal address below)

122 Seaward Avenue • Bradford, PA 16701-1515 USA
(814) 368-6578 (for all other calls)